Library of Arabic Linguistics

The reasons behind the establishment of this Series on Arabic linguistics are manifold.

First: Arabic linguistics is developing into an increasingly interesting and important subject within the broad field of modern linguistic studies. The subject is now fully recognised in the Universities of the Arabic speaking world and in international linguistic circles, as a subject of great theoretical and descriptive interest and importance.

Second: Arabic linguistics is reaching a mature stage in its development benefiting both from early Arabic linguistic scholarship and modern techniques of general linguistics and related disciplines.

Third: The scope of this discipline is wide and varied, covering diverse areas such as Arabic phonetics, phonology and grammar, Arabic psycholinguistics, Arabic dialectology, Arabic lexicography and lexicology, Arabic sociolinguistics, the teaching and learning of Arabic as a first, second, or foreign language, communications, semiotics, terminology, translation, machine translation, Arabic computational linguistics, history of Arabic linguistics, etc.

Viewed against this background, Arabic linguists may be defined as: the scientific investigation and study of the Arabic language in all its aspects. This embraces the descriptive, comparative and historical aspects of the language. It also concerns itself with the classical form as well as the Modern and contemporary standard forms and their dialects. Moreover, it attempts to study the language in the appropriate regional, social and cultural settings.

It is hoped that the Series will devote itself to all issues of Arabic linguistics in all its manifestations on both the theoretical and applied levels. The results of these studies will also be of use in the field of linguistics in general, as well as related subjects.

Although a number of works have appeared independently or within series, yet there is no platform designed specifically for this subject. This Series is being started to fill this gap in the linguistic field. It will be devoted to Monographs written in either English or Arabic, or both, for the benefit of wider circles of readership.

All these reasons justify the establishment of a new forum which is devoted to all areas of Arabic linguistic studies. It is also hoped that this Series will be of interest not only to students and researchers in Arabic linguistics but also to students and scholars of other disciplines who are looking for information of theoretical, practical or pragmatic interest.

The Series Editor

North east
Arabian dialects

Library of Arabic Linguistics

Series editor
Muhammad Hasan Bakalla
University of Riyadh, Kingdom of Saudi Arabia

Advisory editorial board
Peter F. Abboud *University of Texas at Austin*
M. H. Abdulaziz *University of Nairobi*
Yousif El-Khalifa Abu Bakr *University of Khartoum*
Salih J. Altoma *Indiana University*
Arne Ambros *University of Vienna*
El Said M. Badawi *American University in Cairo*
Michael G. Carter *University of Sydney*
Ahmad al-Dhubaib *University of Riyadh*
Martin Forstner *Johannes Gutenberg University at Mainz*
Bruce Ingham *University of London*
Otto Jastrow *University of Erlangen-Nurnberg*
Raja T. Nasr *University College of Beirut*
C. H. M. Versteegh *Catholic University at Nijmegen*
Boguslaw R. Zagorski *University of Warsaw*

Bruce Ingham
University of London

North east Arabian dialects

Monograph No. 3

Kegan Paul International
London and Boston
1982

First published in 1982
by Kegan Paul International
39 Store Street,
London WC1E 7DD, and
9 Park Street,
Boston, Mass. 02108, USA
Printed in Great Britain by
The Thetford Press Ltd,
Thetford, Norfolk

Library of Congress Cataloging in Publication Data

Ingham, Bruce.
North east Arabian dialects.
(Library of Arabic linguistics; monograph no. 3)
Bibliography: p.
Includes index.
1. Arabic language—Dialects—Arabia.
2. Arabic language—Dialects—Iraq.
I. Title. II. Series.
PJ6841.15   492'.77'09538   81-20871

ISBN-0-7103-0018-2   AACR2

To Musa'id ibn Saif al-Saif

Editor's note

Arabic dialectology is an important branch of Arabic linguistics. The interest in Arabic dialects is not a new phenomenon, in fact it goes back to the early stages of Arabic studies. This interest, though limited in scope and confined to certain geographical regions, did not concentrate on the dialects per se. It, however, served as a means of definition and clarification of Classical Arabic as described by the early Arab and Muslim grammarians. Many statements on dialectal variations covering many linguistic levels of the Arabic language were reported in works dealing not only with Arabic grammar and philology but also with the sciences of *Tajwid* and rhetoric, in addition to biographical dictionaries among others. For instance, traditional discussion of vocalic variations such as *imala* and consonantal changes covers some important areas of Arabic phonology. Variations in the morphological syntactic and semantic properties of Arabic were discussed by early Arab and Muslim grammarians and philologists or linguists. Therefore there is a rich mine of information in early Arab works which may be considered one of the main sources in Arabic dialectology.

The modern interest in Arabic dialectology started seriously around the middle of the 19th century, partly as a result of the general tendency to study modern societies anthropologically as well as linguistically. Since then scores of Arabic dialects have been investigated. The Arabian Peninsula received the least attention amongst the dialects studied.

Again very little has been written on North East Arabian dialects. The present volume attempts to fill this gap in Arabic dialectology. It is the result of several years' field work in the region under investigation. Geographically speaking, the area covered includes the East Arabian region of al-Hasa and Kuwait, the northern parts of the Kingdom of Saudi Arabia, southern Iraq and Arabistan or Khuzistan. The present work, as is made clear here, is not a full description of any one dialect studied. It rather pinpoints the differences between the dialects of the region.

There are two characteristics upon which this work is based. Firstly it is an areal linguistic study in which the distributions of the dialectal features is made and shown on the linguistic maps provided. Looked at from another angle, this study provides an excellent typological analysis of the dialects in the region under discussion.

Secondly this work is based, in part, on sociolinguistic principles, particularly those developed by W. Labov and J. J. Gumperz among others. In this regard the book attempts to stress the relationship between dialect geography and extra-linguistic (sociolinguistic) parameters, such as communication structure, geographical location and occupational groups. In addition this study relates language change to ethnic movement, an idea which has been followed by some sociolinguists such as P. Trudgill.

Although the book admits that there is no such thing as a North East Arabian dialect group, the reader will soon discover the close relationships between the dialects under discussion. The book also illustrates the close affinity of the Arabistan (Khuzistan) dialects to the southern Iraqi dialects, and the other North East Arabian dialects, therefore the term introduced here is correct. The first five chapters of the book spell out the linguistic affinities and their distribution within the regions concerned. Chapter 6 includes the texts with translation and annotation.

In Chapters 2 and 5 the author follows the traditions of the European dialect geographers, in particular the German neogrammarians, in tracing the geographical spread of dialect features and relating them to general diffusion tendencies and historical population movements. An interesting parallel arises in the work of the American dialectologist Marvin Herzog, writing in 1965. Although the author does not follow Herzog's typological dichotomy between "communicable" and "non-communicable" innovations, nevertheless the overall approach is summed up well by Herzog in "The Yiddish Language in Northern Poland", IJAL xxxi, pt III, No. 2 (April 1965), p. 5:

> "The spread of highly communicable innovations can then be analyzed as reflecting the channels of communication in a sedentary society, while the spread of relatively non-communicable innovations becomes a clear sign of migration of populations. The goal of dialect classification is abandoned and the geographic cross-section of a language comes to be scrutinized as a reflection of the determinates of linguistic structure, communication facilities and outside sources of stimulation."

As a methodological approach this is in accord with a recent tendency in Arabic dialect studies following earlier more historically orientated methods. The work of Ibrahim Samarrai (1968) on the Iraqi dialects, of J. Cadora (1979) on the Syro-Lebanese dialects and the unpublished thesis of el-Hazmi on the dialects of the Hijaz (1975) all follow this trend. One very clear characteristic of this approach is that it is areal but non-political. This is stated very clearly by Cadora (1979:17) "The inclusion . . . shows clearly that lexical items do not necessarily change at political boundaries . . . Therefore no classification can be considered valid or adequate if its groupings are correlated primarily with political entities."

In Chapters 3 and 4 the author treats a subject which linguists may feel will warrant a more detailed study in order to reach definite conclusions; namely the question of linguistic conservatism versus linguistic levelling and the correlation of these two opposite tendencies with the extra linguistic conditions of geographical and social isolationism versus cosmopolitanism. The author attempts to illustrate a scale of complexity particularly with regard to the grammatically relevant verbal measure system. The Polish linguist A. Czapiewicz, writing in 1975, proposed a similar typological scale but based his description on a cyclical view of morphological development going from complex to simple and then through amalgamation back to the more complex type. It may be that such a cyclical process underlies the tendencies outlined by Ingham which on the short-term scale seem to be unidirectional. Both Ingham's unidirectional and Czapiewicz's cyclical hypotheses may be confirmed or refuted by later researchers.

The author is an authority on the dialects of the region under review. He was born in 1942 and obtained his BA in Arabic at the School of Oriental and African Studies, University of London, in 1964. He was awarded his PhD in Linguistics in 1974 from the same school. He has been a lecturer in the Linguistics Department at the School of Oriental and African Studies since 1967 and has supervised many students working for their MPhil and PhD degrees. He is fluent in both Arabic and Persian as well as being conversant with several European languages. Dr. Ingham has travelled widely in the Middle East and carried out research on Arabic dialects in Iran, Iraq, Kuwait, Saudi Arabia and Afghanistan.

He has published several papers and reviews covering not only Arabic dialects but also child language and speech audiometry with emphasis on Arabic. One of his latest articles is entitled "Languages of the Persian Gulf" which appears in "The Persian Gulf States, a General Survey" edited by Alvin J. Cottrell et al. which is published by Johns Hopkins University Press, 1980.

M. H. Bakalla
University of Riyadh
1 October 1981

Contents

PREFACE xi

ACKNOWLEDGEMENTS xiii

TRANSCRIPTION AND TRANSLITERATION SYSTEMS xv

INTRODUCTION 1
Collection of the Data 3
Availability of Data on the Dialects of the Area 4

1 THE AREA: NAJD AND THE OUTSIDE WORLD 6
Emigration from Najd to Mesopotamia and the Gulf 11
The Causes of Emigration 13
The Jabal Shammar 15
Southern Mesopotamia 17
Summary of the Communication Structure of the Area 22

2 THE NATURE OF DIALECT CONTRASTS 26
The Multivalency of Dialect Features 31

3 REDUCTIONAL CHANGES IN THE DIALECTS OF MESOPOTAMIA AND THE GULF 33
General 33
The Verb Transitivity System 39
Geographical Distribution of the Transitivity Systems 45
The Noun Indefinite Marker 53
The Treatment of Final Clusters 56
Summary 61

4 NON-REDUCTIONAL CHANGES IN THE NORTH NAJDI DIALECTS 63
The Analogical Basis of the North Najdi Features 74

5 GENERAL ISOGLOSS DISTRIBUTION OF THE AREA 77
Features Separating S. Mesopotamia from Arabia 79
Features Separating Northern and Southern Areas 87
Features Separating the Central Area from the Outer Fringe 95

6 TEXTS WITH TRANSLATION, BACKGROUND NOTES AND INFORMATION ON SOURCES 102

Najdi:
1 ʻAjmān: The Story of Thāmir ibn Suʻaidān 103
2 Muṭair: 107
a The Story of Turki ibn Ḥumaid
b Extract from the Bani Hilāl Epic
3 Ḥarb: A Conversational Monologue Relating to Modern-day Life Among the Ḥarb of Hijaz 112
4 ʻAniza: A Conversation Between Two Students at Kuwait University 116
5 ʻAwāzim: A Conversation with the Poet Sālim al-Dawwāy 120
6 Shammar: The Story of the Shilgān Raid 131
7 Rufaiʻ: Poems and Sentences about Nomad Life 136
8 Shammar (Masʻūd): Qasīda from the Bani Hilāl Epic 139
9 Ahl al-Shimāl: The Story of Ibn Jashʻam and Ibn ʻAraiʻir 142

Mesopotamian:
10 Kawâwila (Gypsies): Extract from the Bani Hilāl Epic 147
11 ʻAmāra: The Story of Mughdād 162
12 Kūt Sayyid ʻAnāya: Life in Kūt Sayyid ʻAnāya 167
13 Gachsārān: A Conversation with an Old Sayyid 170
14 Bani Ṭuruf: An Account of the Tribes, Dialects and Occupations of the Region of Ḥuwaiza 173
15 Kaʻb: The History of the Kaʻb in Khuzistan 178
16 Mihirzi: Palm Cultivation on the Kārūn 185

BIBLIOGRAPHY 190

INDEX 196

GLOSSARY OF TECHNICAL TERMS 203

Maps and tables

Maps

1 NORTHERN AND EASTERN ARABIA 6

2 SOUTHERN IRAQ AND KHUZISTAN 18

3 APPROXIMATE DISTRIBUTION OF */y/* AND */ž/* 36

4 RECORDED DISTRIBUTION OF NORTH NAJDI FEATURES 64

5 ESTIMATED DISTRIBUTION OF THE MAIN ISOGLOSSES characterizing North Najdi, Central Najdi and Southern dialect types before recent population movements since the 17th century; and PRESENT DISTRIBUTION OF THE MAIN ISOGLOSSES characterizing North Najdi, Central Najdi and Southern dialect types, showing direction of population movements 78

TABLES

I INTERNAL VOWEL MORPHOLOGY OF THE VERB AND POPULATION GROUPS 52

II DISTRIBUTION OF NORTH NAJDI FEATURES 71

Preface

Linguistic studies of dialects or groups of dialects can be either mainly theory-orientated or mainly data-orientated. In the theory-orientated type the data is used to test the theory and a study of this kind aims to advance some part of the theory by applying it to new data. In the data-orientated type, on the other hand, the aim is to give an account of the data at hand making use of the techniques evolved by descriptive linguistics. In this approach the theory, or more strictly the "metalanguage" as such is not of primary interest; nevertheless consistency of approach and terminology must be observed, although this is more a matter of presentation and readability than a theoretical tenet.

The theoretical branch of dialectology has seen a number of "models" which reflect the advances of the theory in general linguistics as a whole. The "historical" model was an off-shoot of 19th century studies in historical linguistics and used the data from the German dialects to test the sound-laws of the Neogrammarians. With the beginning of the structural phase various synchronic models were proposed which aimed to characterize the mutual relationship of cognate dialects or, in Weinreich's words, "to characterize partially differing systems." Early structural models were Smith and Trager's "Overall Pattern Analysis" (1951) and Weinreich's "Diasystem Construct" (1954). Since the 1960s various researchers have applied the techniques of generative grammar to dialect description with considerable achievement. In all of these models the basic procedure was to construct an underlying framework "a deep structure" and then to state rules by which the actual dialects "the surface structure" is derived. In all of these techniques the recoverability requirement is foremost and the researcher seeks to separate predictable dialect correspondences from random dialect correspondences. In the transformational approach random correspondences constitute differences of input, predictable correspondences differences of rule.

Following the transformational phase the sociolinguists, led by Labov, have changed the focus of interest from rule governed phenomena to the ragged edges of the linguistic system, those areas where a speaker hovers between one system and another and where factors of age, occupation, class or group identity may be seen to have an active effect on the speech of the individual.

The present study is data-orientated in so far as it is not primarily involved with questions of linguistic theory but seeks to present a descriptive analysis of a body of data. The approach is basically geographical and seeks to relate dialect geography to extra-linguistic factors of geographical location, communication structure and occupational group over a wide area. It does however tend to confirm some of the observations of other writers such as Trudgill on the effect of ethnic mobilization on language change and to that extent adopts a rather determinist stance.

In inspiration it owes a lot to the work of Labov (1972) and also Gumperz (1962) although the rather different nature of the data may obscure this relationship in parts. In the use of the concept of the linguistic "system" it owes much to Halliday's and Palmer's work on the verb in English in particular, and in general reflects the writer's upbringing within a Firthian environment. The linguistic description falls into three parts. Chapter 3 examines the relationship of linguistic reduction or levelling to population mobility and conversely the relationship of linguistic conservatism to geographical isolation. Chapter 4 examines certain non-reductional innovations which have developed within the North Najd area and relates these to geographical isolation and occupational group solidarity. Chapter 5 examines the general isogloss structure of the area apart from the particular features examined in Chapters 3 and 4 and shows how they relate to the geography of the area and to the history of folk migrations in the area.

In essence this book is the result of an interest in methods of linguistic description on the one hand and an interest in traditional Arab life and customs on the other. As such I hope it will be of interest both to the general linguist and to researchers in the ethnography of the Arabian Peninsula and the Gulf.

Acknowledgements

My initial thanks must go to the various institutions which have assisted in the research which forms the basis of this book. The School of Oriental and African Studies, London, financed wholly or in part visits to the Middle East in 1969, 1971, 1974, 1977 and 1978. The University of Riyadh also gave valuable financial help towards my visit to Saudi Arabia in 1978. The Universities of Jundi Shahpur (Ahwaz), Basra and Kuwait and also the Kuwait Radio and Television services have also been of valuable assistance.

My thanks are also due to Charlotte Coudrille who produced the final typescript and contributed valuable editorial advice; also to Elain Holly who produced the maps at the School of Oriental and African Studies.

Mentors who at various stages have contributed useful guidance, advice and discussion include Professor J. Carnochan and Professor T.M. Johnstone of the School of Oriental and African Studies, Sir John Glubb, Dr. Muhammad Bākalla and Dr. Theodore Prochazka of Riyadh University, Alan Rush of Kuwait and Dr. K. MacLachlan and Dr. D. Bivar of the School of Oriental and African Studies.

The many friends and informants in the Middle East to whom this book owes something would be far too numerous to mention. All of them I remember by name and some of them are mentioned at various places in this book. Some of them are no longer alive but they will always be alive to me in memory. Here I mention only a few. In Saudi Arabia I owe a great debt of thanks to the late Muḥammad ibn Aḥmad al-Sudairi and to Musā'id ibn Saif al-Saif; also thanks go to 'Ajimi ibn Suwaiṭ, Muḥammad ibn Sa'dūn al-Suwaiṭ, 'Abdallah ibn Baikhān, 'Abdallah Duhaithim, 'Uraifij ibn Zaid al-Shilāźi and 'Abdallah al-Tamīmi. In Kuwait to Sayyār Rāḍhi al-'Anizi, Mamdūḥ Rāḍhi al-'Anizi, 'Āyiḍh Ṭu'ma al-Ḍhafīri, Murshid al-Badhdhāl, Sālim al-Dawwāy, Ṣāliḥ Manṣūr al-'Alayyān and Ṭalāl Sa'īd. In Iraq to 'Ābir ibn Fahd ibn Sharshāb, Ḥusain al-'Agāb al-Ṣarāyifi and Abu Shahāb. In Khuzistan to the late Ṭahrān Ka'bi and Ḥāj 'Abd al-'Azīz

Fāḏhili, to Hasan 'Arab and to Maḥmūd and Sālim Fāḏhili, also to Ḥajji Fāliḥ and Shaikh Muḥi of Shādigān.

Last but not least my thanks go to Shokooh and her family who introducted me to the Middle East.

Transcription and transliteration systems

The system of transliteration used for Arabic names is, with some exceptions, a transliteration of the classical equivalent of the form, using the system normally used for Arabic. Thus *mṭēr* is rendered Muṭair, *sdēr* Sudair, etc. In the above, the correspondence of written *ai* with spoken *ē* and the elision of unstressed short vowels is fairly well known. This allows the use of the more familiar forms of names, e.g. Kuwait rather than *kwēt*. This system is held to wherever it does not lead to a too-wide divergence between spoken and written form. However, where there is a difference of syllabication, vowelling or stress, the spoken form is reflected, i.e. 'Aniza not 'Anaza, Gḥaṭān not Qaḥṭān. Indeed, in the case of forms like Sba'a, Ṣmida, etc. it is difficult to know what the corresponding literary form should be. Certain sound shifts have occurred with regard to the letters ض , ظ , ك , and ق and these are also reflected in the transliteration, i.e. Ḍhafīr not Ḍafīr, Shilāźi not Shilāqi. In some cases also the more strictly accurate form is eschewed in favour of the one which is more familiar or which looks less unusual in the Roman script, i.e. 'Ajmān, not 'Ujmān; 'Arai'ir, not 'Rai'ir.

Glottal stop, as a phoneme, has disappeared in the core vocabulary of these dialects. In initial position it occurs as a feature of initial vocalic position, i.e. *amal* for *ʾamal* "hope". In medial position it has been replaced by ' in many forms, i.e. *sa'al* for *saʾal* "he asked" or has been elided as in *yijjill* for *yuʾajjil* "he postpones", *maddiba* for *maʾdiba* "correction, chastisement". It is only transcribed in the rare occasions where it occurs medially in words, i.e. *masʾūl* "responsible". Glottal constriction also occurs at the junction of one vowel with another across word-boundary [*ana wʾant*] "you and I", transcribed *ana w ant*. The alternative form without glottal constriction [*ana want*] would be transcribed *ana want*.

The subscript /./ is used to mark pharyngealization in *ḷ* and *ṛ* which are not distinguished in the Arabic script. Pharyngealization can also occur with the bilabial, velar and uvular consonants, but this is not marked as it can be referred to the occurrence of one of the consonants *ṭ*, *ṣ*, *ḏ̣*. With /ḷ/ it is minimally distinctive in a number of forms, i.e. *aḷḷa* "God", *alla* "yes". Similarly with *ṛ* it occurs in cases where it cannot be referred to any other consonant, i.e. *ṛāy* "opinion", *ṛadd* "he returned". In these cases it is marked. Special symbols used in Arabic transcription are:

CONSONANTS

ṯ voiceless interdental fricative

ḏ voiced interdental fricative

š voiceless palato-alveolar fricative

j voiced palato-alveolar affricate
or palatal plosive (in Najd)

x voiceless uvular fricative

ġ voiced uvular fricative

q voiced or voiceless uvular plosive

ḥ voiceless pharyngeal fricative

' voiced pharyngeal continuant

' glottal stop (rarely used)

ṭ voiceless alveolar plosive, pharyngealized

ṣ voiceless alveolar fricative, pharyngealized

ḏ̣ voiced interdental fricative, pharyngealized

The following sounds also occur which represent sound changes from the Classical system:

ž voiced palato-alveolar fricative ('Amāra area)

č voiceless palato-alveolar affricate

ź voiced alveolar affricate palatalized

ć voiceless alveolar affricate palatalized

ḱ voiceless palatalized velar plosive
(Ḥarb dialect, see Text 3)

ǵ voiced palatalized velar plosive
(Ḥarb dialect, see Text 3)

VOWELS

ā long open vowel, central to front in most environments [*a:*] or [ʌ:], back in pharyngealized environments [ɑ:] i.e. [*z*ʌ*:d*] *zād* "provisions", [*ṣ*ɑ*:r*] *ṣār* "he became"

ī high front spread vowel *šīl* "take!"

ū high back rounded vowel *kūd* "except"

ē mid front spread vowel *hēl* "cardoman"

ei *glide from the above to fully close *zeit* "oil" (Najdi)

ie *glide from high front spread to central [ɩɛ] or [ɩə] *ziet* "oil" (Mesopotamian)

ō mid back rounded vowel *mōt* "death"

ou glide from the above to fully close *mout* "death" (Najdi)

The type /*ou*/ occurs in the Najdi dialects where certain non-guttural plosives or fricatives follow, i.e. *mout* "death", *xouf* "fear", *zoud* "increase", *ṯoub* "dress", *ṣoub* "towards". In the outer dialects /*ō*/ is general for all environments, i.e. *mōt*, *xōf*, *zōd*, *ṯōb*, *ṣōb*.

a half open vowel ranging from [ɛ] through [ʌ] to [ɑ] depending on consonantal environment, i.e. [*s*ɛ*bb*] "he reviled", [*š*ɛ*bb*] "he lit", [*k*ʌ*bb*] "he let go", [*ṭ*ɑ*bb*] "he entered". In Mesopotamia the realisation [ɛ] is more widespread than in Najd in some environments; compare Iraqi [*s*ɛ*bb*] [*li:f*ɛ], Najdi [*s*ʌ*bb*] [*li:f*ʌ].

i In all these dialects, in non final position, the vowel
& sounds covered by these symbols can be regarded as reali-
u zations of one phoneme /I/. These range through [i], [ɩ], [ə], [ɤ], [ʊ], [u].

Preceding *w* [u] occurs, emphatics produce [ɤ], [ʊ] when in conjunction with a bilabial. Apicals, palato-alveolars and palatals produce [i] or [ɩ], the rest [ə] : [*xluww*] "emptiness", [ẓɤḷḷ] "remain", [*b*ʊ*ṣal*] "onion", [*š*ɩ*l*ɩ*b*] "rice", [*liyy*ɛ] "to me", [*x*ə*rza*] "bead" [*s*ə*r*ʌ] "queue".

In final position the symbols *i* and *u* represent the short tense vowels [*i*] and [*u*]. Sometimes also with a gliding quality [ɩy] and [ʊw] as in [*xa:ḷ*ɩ*y*], *xāḷi* "my uncle", [*gaḷṭ*ʊ*w*], *gaḷṭu* "come in!" (m.pl.).

*For details of the distribution of these vowels, see Chapter 5, p.79-81.

In the Shammari text certain phonetic details are included which would not be recoverable from a more generalized transcription. These are the labio velar glide after /ḅ/ and /ṃ/ in some environments, i.e. *lugṃwitin* "a mouthful", *ṃwiḥzam* "belt", and the vocalic transition /ᵊ/ between certain consonants, i.e. *faxᵊḏu* "his thigh", *miṯᵊlu* "like him".

STRESS

Word stress is not marked except in order to illustrate certain dialectal differences. In the main all dialects agree as regards stress in accordance with the following rule:

1 Stress falls on the long syllable(1) nearest the end of the word, counting final CvCC, Cv:C and Cv: and non-final CVC, CVCC, CV: and CV:C as long; *xalī́j, kitā́b, kitā́bna, kitábt, kitábna, kitábti, kitā́baha, kitábtaha, mádrasa, šā́laha.*

2 If no long syllable occurs, stress falls on the initial syllable: *wálad, dáxaḷ, kítab, šílib, wlídi, wlídak, ktíbaw.*

Differences between the Central Najdi and the outer dialects occur in connection with the following two cases:(2)

a In forms of the type *inkisar, yinkisir*, the Najdi type shows initial stress in accordance with rule 1 above: *ínkisar, yínkisir*. The other dialects show *inkísar, yinkísir*.

b In nominal forms of the type mentioned under 2 above, where the definite article precedes, the Najdi type shows stress on the article: *álwalad, álmuṭar, áluxu, álubu.* The Mesopotamian type shows stress on the initial syllable of the stem: *ilwálad, ilmúṭar, ilúxu, ilúbu.*

1 Note that the feminine ending *-eih* of the Shammari dialects (see Ch.4) does not count as a long syllable and is equivalent to the *-ah* or *-at* of other dialects, i.e. short. The slight lengthening of the vowel is purely a function of pausal position, thus *sinjā́reih* or *sinjā́rah* "Sinjāra".

2 See also p.60.

North east Arabian dialects

Introduction

The title of this book could be misleading. There is in fact no North East Arabian group of dialects and the designation North East Arabian is used here territorially rather than genetically indicating that the dialects are found in the north-eastern corner of the Arabian peninsula and the areas of southern Iraq and Persia adjoining it. Linguistically these dialects fall into two main groups, an Arabian and a Mesopotamian one. The Arabian dialects examined here include those of the Gulf Coast in the area of Kuwait and al-Hasa, the northern parts of Saudi Arabia and the dialects of the bedouins of the western borderlands of Iraq. Mesopotamian dialects examined are those of the river lands of southern Iraq and Khuzistan in southern Persia. In a general way they share certain characteristics and can be classed as North Arabian(1) in contrast to (i) the South Arabian type of Yaman, Hadhramawt, Oman and the Shi'a dialects of Eastern Arabia and (ii) the West Arabian group comprising those of Hijaz, Syria, Jordan, Palestine, Lebanon and Egypt.

However they are treated here together for a different reason. The area of north-eastern Arabia and the river valleys of Iraq and Khuzistan have from the beginning of the Christian era been subject to immigration from the central Arabian peninsula. Further, considerable trade contact has always been maintained throughout the area facilitated by the existence of nomadic tribes linking them across national boundaries. The dialects studied therefore cover a continuous geographical area crossing national boundaries, but group around certain foci of population which form the core political areas of the states of Iraq, Saudi Arabia and Kuwait with Khuzistan forming an Arab enclave within the state of Iran. The procedure is therefore that we have chosen a geographical area in which we know that patterns of human interaction exist and then proceeded to study the linguistic geography of

1 See also JOHNSTONE (1967b)p.1-18.

the area and attempted to relate it to what we know of its communication structure. Certain general principles of dialect geography can be well illustrated from the data obtained. One is the correlation of linguistic conservatism and non-reductional change with geographical and political isolation and of reductional change and linguistic "simplification" in areas of international contact where new social structures are being evolved. It also emerges that in areas of continuous population, classification into distinct sub-dialects is impossible and the whole participates in a linguistic continuum. Among the nomadic tribes on the other hand, it is possible to distinguish separate dialects for given tribal groups not necessarily related to their present geographical location.

As regards the linguistic procedure, I do not here attempt a full linguistic description of any one dialect, but concentrate on the differences between them, and the geographical distribution and demographic relevance of these differences. The procedure is therefore to pick on certain variables relevant to the whole area and to plot their realisation. These are in the main phonological and morphological, but lexical items of high frequency of occurence are also treated.

Considerable use is made of the traditional oral literature of the area which consists of tales of tribal battles and raids of the recent past and older semi-mythical stories dating back to the early centuries of the Islamic era. Also included is poetical material consisting of gaṣīdas or "odes" or fragments of these. The Arabic gaṣīda of the area consists of rhymed couplets and is often of a highly standardised structure. The imagery, vocabulary and epithetical usage are also highly standardised so that, as a poetical type, it is highly mobile and poems originating in the southern region of Saudi Arabia are understood and appreciated by the bedouin of the Syrian desert and vice-versa. Local dialect features are, however, usually apparent in individual poems either as an inherent part of the poem and expressive of its origin or unconsciously introduced by the reciter. Therefore although it is true that as a literary vehicle this type of poetry is inter-tribal and inter-dialectal, one can in no way say that the language used is an interdialectal Koiné. The origin of a poem or its reciter is always discernible to a certain degree. Collections of these poems are available both as volumes published in the Arab world and included in the works of orientalists in the earlier part of this century. However as far as I know most of the gaṣīdas presented here are published for the first time in the West. They may also be interesting in that they cover a fairly wide geographical and linguistic area, whereas earlier collections such as Montagne's Shammari texts and Musil's Ruwala texts were usually from one tribe only.

Collection of the data

The collection of the data on which this study is based was begun in 1969 on a visit to Khuzistan in southern Persia. The main aim at the time was to collect data for a phonological study of the Arabic dialects of the area. Gradually however the comparison of dialect type to social and regional group became interesting especially as, to the speakers themselves, this was of primary importance. In order to obtain further comparative data I visited Basra and Zubair in southern Iraq in 1971. By this time it was becoming clear that the dialects of Khuzistan were rather like the tip of the iceberg and that many facts relevant to them were probably to be found in the Arabian peninsula, their original geographical homeland. Khuzistan in fact represents the final eastern outpost of continuous Arab population, although there are pockets of Arabic speech in northern Afghanistan and Central Asia. In 1973 I visited the marshlands of the Haur al-Ḥammār in southern Iraq and also the area of Nāṣiriyya on the Euphrates. In 1977 I was able to make recordings of the speech of nomadic groups in Kuwait and in the area around Nāṣiriyya. Finally in Saudi Arabia in 1978, based in Wadi Turmus in the northern Qaṣīm, I collected data on the dialects of neighbouring nomadic and sedentary groups and also visited the Jabal Shammar and Ḥafar al-Bātin on the borders of Iraq and Kuwait.

At this point perhaps it is wise to make a point about the general orientation of the study. As a member of a highly industrialised western society, I was attracted towards the aspects of life in the Middle East which were materially different from our own. Therefore the study concentrates on the dialectology of the traditional society of the area, based in the rural areas, rather than the technological society of the towns. It is therefore not a sociolinguistic study of the type typified by the classic studies of Labov, Trudgill and others which describe the dynamic factors of change alive in the great urban centres and the relevance of personal speech variation to these factors. This is not to say that these processes are absent there, and indeed the growth of urban or national standard dialects is noticeable in Iraq, Kuwait and Saudi Arabia although not so much in Khuzistan, since there the standard language is Persian. In the past, though not so much in the last decade, the influence of the dialects of Egypt and the Syrian area has been quite strong within the educational system and news media tending towards the evolution of a type of international educated dialect. Recently a trend in the opposite direction has taken place in the Gulf countries and there has been a revival of interest in local culture; but nevertheless a tendency towards the formation of urban regional standards is noticeable. It is therefore true that the urban dialectology of the area is not unlike the situation familiar to us from the writings of the sociolinguists. In the present study however this is disregarded since it seemed that even within the field of the relatively static rural dialectology there was interesting work to be done both in the field of the "discovery" of undescribed dialects and in the description of dialect geography. I say "relatively static" since the historical perspective is one of considerable dynamism, while the dialects are treated here as though not subject to change at the rate of the urban dialects.

Availability of data on the dialects of the area

A fairly clear picture of most of the main dialect types of the area can be obtained from the work of earlier linguists. The standard dialects of Iraq and the Gulf are covered by the studies of Blanc (1964), Erwin (1963) and Johnstone (1967). A rural dialect of the Hilla area is also described by Meissner and Weissbach and the dialect of the Baḥārna of eastern Arabia and Bahrain by al-Tājir. The dialects of some areas of central Arabia are covered to a greater or lesser extent: Johnstone (1967a) discusses phonological problems in the dialect of 'Anaiza; Socin gives texts and poetry in a mixture of central Arabian dialects which can be used with circumspection; 'Abboud gives a comprehensive description of the dialect of Hail and Badawi's intonational study of the dialect of Riyadh gives useful, if scanty, phonological and morphological data. The dialects of the bedouin of the area are also surprisingly quite well covered in varying degrees of comprehensiveness. The work of Landberg (1919) and Wetzstein (1868) provide useful data on an 'Anizi dialect of the Syrian desert. Musil's ethnographic work on the Ruwala supplies many interesting quotations and poems in their dialect, which can be used in conjunction with some knowledge of the dialects of the area. Montagne gives some very useful texts and poems in the dialect of the Jarba Shammar of the Jazīra. Of great importance is Cantineau's "Études sur quelques parlers de nomades arabes d'Orient" which gives material from a number of smaller tribes of the Syrian desert and also from 'Anizi and Shammari groups. Most recently Blanc (1970) has given a detailed comparative description of the dialect of the Negev bedouins. For the central Arabian bedouin groups, Hess gives very useful and nicely transcribed data from the dialect of the 'Utaiba; al-Ḥāzmi gives an account of the dialect of the Ḥarb over a wide geographical area from Hijaz to Central Najd, being probably the only one of its kind from the inner Arabian peninsula, and Johnstone (1961 and 1964) gives extremely interesting texts and comparative remarks on a dialect which is mainly 'Ajmi but with Dawāsir influences. In addition, in his "Eastern Arabian

Dialect Studies", he provides a text from the Bani Hājir dialect. Much useful comparative data was also made available to me by Theodore Prochazka on the dialects of the Ruwala, South Western Arabia, the Central Najd region and al-Hasa. Much of this is to appear in his forthcoming "Saudi Arabian Dialects" and "The Shi'i Dialects of Bahrain".

Dialects for which generally accessible data in any great detail is not available except in the writings of the author, here or elsewhere, are the speech of the sedentary population of Khuzistan and Iraq(1) south of Najaf, the dialect of the Euphrates bedouin and the Budūr shepherds of the Nāṣiriyya region, and the Kawāwila or gypsies of the area. For the Arabian type, the dialect of Sudair and of the Ḍhafīr, Muṭair and 'Awāzim tribes are, I think, dealt with here for the first time in any great detail.

1 An unpublished manuscript on the dialect of Ahwaz by D.L. R. Lorimer exists in the library of SOAS London; also Edzard gives a list of vocabulary which he designates as of Mi'dān origin; however the greater part of it is general to much of southern Iraq.

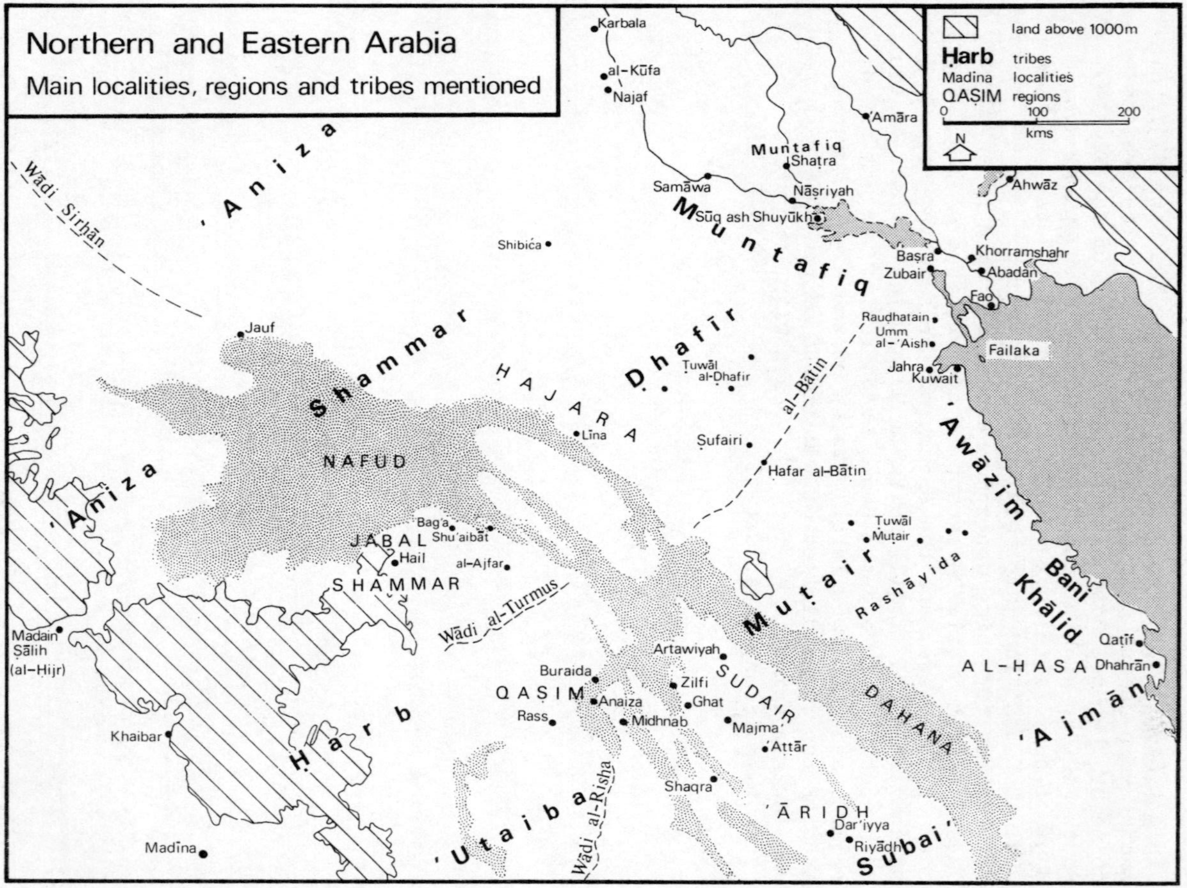

MAP 1. NORTHERN AND EASTERN ARABIA

1 The area: Najd and the outside world

The study concentrates on an area of northern Arabia where interaction takes place between three main centres: the settlements of Central Najd, the settled area of Mesopotamia, and the Gulf coast, in particular Kuwait. The history of the area has been described by many writers and the rise and fall of Emirates in the area is, according to one theory, dependent on the balance of power between these centres.(1) However for our purposes there are two main themes which throw light on the dialect geography of the area. These are the constant process of immigration from Central Arabia to these outer areas and the existence of permanent centres of civilisation in these areas, each of which has had periods of growth and decline and changes of dynasty and affiliation but nevertheless remained. A further factor which is less well-documented is that it seems that there is also a process of emigration from southern Mesopotamia to the Gulf settlements.(2)

Between these centres is a thinly populated area of steppe and sand desert where permanent agriculture is impossible except at scattered wells. These do not constitute an agricultural region but exist as islands of settlement within a nomadic environment. This region supports a population of nomadic camel and sheep herders who form an important link between the three centres. At one time it was supposed that the nomads formed a quite separate and somewhat lawless community. However more recently it has become obvious that the nomads and settled people form two halves of a distinct economic community.(3) In the area of north-east Arabia each centre has its own particular nomadic tribes. These

1 MUSIL (1928b), p.303.
2 See LORIMER (1908), articles on Bahrain and Kuwait.
3 MUSIL (1928b), p.302, 316-19; also "Encyclopedia of Islam", Badw, p.881, 885.

may be ethnically and sometimes also politically distinct from the centre to which they are attached, but they are nevertheless economically quite closely tied either to Kuwait, Mesopotamia or Najd.

To understand the nature of this connection we must look at the yearly life cycle of the nomads. This has been described in great detail by earlier writers at a time when western technology had not intervened to cause quite striking changes in their mode of life. However these changes have only been in operation fully over the last thirty years or so and the present overall dialect geography of the area relates to the original situation rather than the present modified one. The changes in fact affect mainly the type of flocks used, the main means of transport and the area over which grazing is possible while the basic nature of the life-cycle is to a large extent unchanged.(1) It divides mainly into a grazing period and a non-grazing period. In winter and spring when the weather is cool, rain causes grass and various saline plants to grow in the desert. The rain falls sporadically here and there and collects in hollows and depressions known as *riyāḍh, faiḍhāt* or *khuffiyyāt*. This enables the nomads to graze over a large area moving from place to place as grazing is found.

1 In my statements about nomadic life in the area I am heavily indebted to earlier writers particularly DICKSON (1949), (1956), MUSIL (1928a,b), GLUBB (1960). These writers describe the life of the nomad population and their relations with the settled areas. In addition to this the author visited nomad encampments and summer wells in southern Iraq, Kuwait and Saudi Arabia and was able to check the observations of earlier writers. These visits cover the following areas: summer camps of the Ḥumaid, Rufai', Āl bu Ṣāliḥ and Budūr north of Nāṣiriyya in southern Iraq in 1977; families of Muṭair, Bani Khālid and Shammar at Rauḍhatain and Umm al-'Aish north of Kuwait town also in 1977. In the spring of 1978, thanks to the hospitality of Prince Muḥammad ibn Aḥmad al-Sudairi, I stayed for three weeks in the area of Wādi Turmus in Qaṣīm in Saudi Arabia. There I was able to visit numbers of families of Ḥarb, Muṭair and Shammar camped in the Wādi Turmus area and on the edge of the Nafūd. At the same time I visited Shu'aibāt, a summer well of the Sinjāra Shammar, north of Hail on the southern edge of the Nafūd, and the settlement of Ṣufairi near Ḥafar al-Bāṭin which is the centre of the Ḍhafīr tribe in Saudi Arabia and the home of their leader 'Ajimi ibn Suwaiṭ.

The nomads have a remarkable knowledge of topography and the flow direction of the various valleys and depressions of the area and are able to make accurate guesses from the sight of distant rainfall or lightning as to where grazing will be found. The tribal system of the nomads is based on the need to defend a large grazing area within which they can support large herds. The tribe will have a grazing area or *dīrah* within which they control grazing and may in good years also allow neighbouring tribes to graze. In the area between central Najd Mesopotamia and Kuwait the *dīrahs* of a number of large tribes converge. Although these *dīrahs* do of course change with the changing pattern of power in the area and with the changing alliances of the nomads, they have as far as we know remained fairly stable over the last two hundred years or so, although tradition tells of different configurations in earlier times.(1)

In the late spring and summer grazing grows short in the desert and the nomads come in to converge on certain permanent wells and along the rivers of Mesopotamia. At this time of year they are in close contact with the settled population and also with other nomadic tribes. The main watering places to be considered here are:

1 The Euphrates including the Haur al-Ḥammār region and the various channels and subsidiary rivers such as the Gharrāf.
2 The Jabal Shammar region. An area centred on the mountains of Aja and Salma in northern Najd. It is bordered on the north and east by the great Nafūd and within its perimeter a number of important permanent wells and settlements are situated.
3 A number of smaller wells scattered between Jabal Shammar and the Gulf Coast including Jahra to the north of Kuwait and Ḥafar al-Bāṭin southwest of Kuwait. Also between Jabal Shammar and Mesopotamia the centres of Zubair and Khamīsiyya.(2)

In the case of area 2 and to a large extent also area 3 the wells are owned by the nomads and maintained by hired men or else the settlers and the nomads are members of one tribe. In the case of area 1, some of the nomads are in

1 Toponmy also is indicative of the earlier location of the tribes. This is referred to in some detail by PHILBY (1922), p.108,249,288 as regards the earlier location of the 'Aniza in central Najd. DOUGHTY (1964) also gives indications of older tribal areas on his map appendixed to Volume I.
2 Other unpopulated wells are also important, such as the Ṭuwāl al-Ḍhafīr wells between Iraq and Najd and the Ṭuwāl al-Muṭair wells towards Kuwait.

contact with ethnically quite distinct populations and have to enter into treaty relationships with them. It is however equally true for all three cases that we see here the relationship between settled and nomadic people and also at another level the relationship between the interior of Arabia and the outer regions.

Although the nomads produce much of their own goods such as woven tent furniture and traditionally also have amongst them as clients certain craftsmen or *ṣannā'*, who produce saddles and other hardware, they must visit the towns to buy clothing, kitchen utensils, arms, certain foodstuffs and, more importantly perhaps, coffee, tea, sugar and tobacco which form the centre of their social life and are the main manifestations of hospitality. In the area we are considering this takes place mainly in the early autumn just before the annual migration. Also during the summer tribes whose wells are near the Euphrates will come in for shopping occasionally although at this time travelling is more difficult. These shopping excursions, known as *musābilah*(1), are made with the consent of the leaders of the settled areas and are of economic benefit to both the settled and nomad populations. The degree of contact and the actual relationship of nomad groups to the settled areas may differ but in all cases the result is that of a basically Najdi/Arabian population in terms of dialect, religious affiliation and culture coming into regular contact with the populations of the settled areas of Mesopotamia and the Gulf, who are in closer contact with the outside world and to some extent live a far easier life.

At the time of the Shammar rule of Northern Arabia centred on Ḥail under the Ibn Rashīd dynasty this link was strengthened by the existence of a colony of traders from Najaf on the Euphrates who were allowed to settle in Hail and organised regular caravans of goods to be brought to Hail.(2) The general picture is therefore one of the economic dependence of Northern Najd on Mesopotamia in particular and also on Kuwait. As expressed by a Shammari informant: *kānaw innajd killaham 'āyšin min al'arāg*, "All the people of Najd used to live on the produce of Iraq." The Najdi expression: *annajd tuwallid wa lā taġda*, "Najd gives birth but does not nourish" also reflects this situation.

1 See DICKSON (1949), p.49.
2 These are mentioned by various writers: MUSIL (1928b), p.241,253; DOUGHTY (1924), p.656-7. The yearly caravan was known as the *ḥadra* or "going down", i.e. to the Euphrates. This term is still used by bedouins who summer along the Euphrates for the yearly migration; see Text 7.

EMIGRATION FROM NAJD TO MESOPOTAMIA AND THE GULF

We know from historical records and from the oral tradition that there has been from throughout the historical period a process of emigration from Najd out to the settled lands. This has been of two types: the movement of nomadic groups on the one hand and the more sporadic movement of individuals or families from the settled areas of Najd on the other. For our purposes it seems that the larger movements of nomadic groups are the most important and have had the greatest effect on dialect geography, since in most cases the nomads have moved in as élite groups and taken over as rulers of the settled areas.

Particularly in southern Mesopotamia this has resulted in what has been referred to as "nomadization" meaning that the nomadic section has had a profound effect on the culture of the original settled inhabitants. It has been remarked by earlier writers that in an area where the Caliphate of Baghdad and the Shahs of Persia were well within historical memory, the local oral literature disregards them completely and the main themes are those of nomadic life. Tales of the Bani Hilāl, the 12th century nomad invaders of North Africa, and of more recent heroes such as Sulṭān ibn Ḥumaid and Kan'ān al-Ṭayyār are the universal folk literature of the area.

In material culture, too, the style of dress and household furniture even among such a tightly-knit and isolated group as the Mi'dān or marsh-dwellers of southern Mesopotamia are basically those of central Najd as transmitted by the nomads.

This process has, it seems, in most cases been a gradual one. Tribes whose main wells were in the Najd but grazed in winter up to the borders of the settled lands and visited them for provisions and trade may have gradually found it easier to camp in summer in those very settled areas. Changes of political structure of the area may influence them in this and may indeed cause them to move back again if times change.

During the last two centuries three large tribes of Najdi origin have transferred their summer quarters to the Euphrates. The 'Amārāt branch of 'Aniza, a group coming originally from western Najd, now camp from Najaf northwards. The Tūmān branch of Shammar camp from Najaf to Samāwa and the Ḍhafīr, a tribe of mixed origin, partly Shammar and partly of diverse other elements, camped near Nāṣiriyya and south to Zubair.(1)

1 See MUSIL (1928a), p.130,210, (1928b), p.31-33, 166-84; LORIMER (1908) II A p.411-42, 83-88, II B p.1749-52; and GLUBB (1960), passim, for these tribal areas. Lorimer and Musil differ on the extent of the distribution of the

All three of these however retained their purely Najdi type of dialect and distinctive culture.

Within the last century during the early years of the Saudi regime and later with changes of regime in Iraq, various further movements of these tribes have taken place. In the earlier years when times were troubled in Najd large sections of the Shammar took refuge in Iraq, but have since returned.(1) The Ḍhafīr who were originally an Iraq tribe in terms of their main grazing grounds and summer quarters(2) are now split between Iraq, Saudi Arabia and Kuwait, and have their main centre at Ṣufairi near al-Ḥafar in Saudi Arabia while sections of them still summer in Iraq.

Towards the Gulf the same process also takes place. In the Kuwait area the tribes of longest standing would seem to be the 'Awāzim and Rashāyida whose dialect is in many ways very close to that of the settled population.(3) Later arrivals such as the Muṭair speak a dialect closer to that of central Najd. It is not certain when they arrived on the Gulf, but local tradition regards them as being more recent arrivals than the 'Awāzim and Rashāyida. A western branch of the tribe exists in western Najd which is said to be their original home.(4) While on the subject of tribal groups and population movement, it must be admitted that we cannot be sure that a tribal group such as Muṭair constitutes a homo-

Shammar in southern Iraq. I am here following MUSIL (1928b) p.32, as regards the Shammar, who states that the Tūmān branch extend from Shibića to Iraq, as this was confirmed by my own Shammar informants. 'AZZĀWI (1956) puts the date of the arrival of the Ḍhafīr in Iraq as 1805 following friction with the Āl-Sa'ūd; vol.I, p.295.

1 My information on recent movements of the Shammar is from 'Abdallah Baikhān of the Shilgān branch of the Sinjāra.

2 GLUBB (1960), passim.

3 See p.96f.below. According to their own tradition the 'Awāzim originate in western Najd in the area between Abān Aḥmar, Abān Aswad and Marrān within the present 'Utaiba dīra, al-'UBAYYID (1970), p.29.

4 See DOUGHTY (1964); his map gives the localities of Ḥarrat Bani 'Abdallah, S'feyna, Swergiah and El-Fereya as belonging to the "Meteyr". Also vol.II (1924), p.366-67, he refers to their original home "Meteyr are of old Ahl Gibly (southerners) and their home is in the great Harra which lies between the Harameyn... They are now in part Ahl es-Shemāl (northerners) for every summer these nomads journey upward to pasture their cattle in the northern wilderness; their borders are reckoned nearly to Kuwait and Basra." For the northeastward expansion of the tribes see for the Murra COLE (1975) p.106; for the Dawāsir and 'Utaiba PHILBY (1922) II p.203-4; for the 'Ajmān ibid 297 and also DICKSON (1949) p.284.

genous group of people distinct from surrounding groups and moving as a unit through geographical space and historical time. Nomadic alliances and genealogies are remarkably fluid(1) and even the oral tradition records the absorption of foreign elements into tribes. However from our point of view this is irrelevant, since whatever the ethnic make-up of the population, it seems to be the case that the dialects do move across the geographical landscape in a way which reflects the movements of the main groups in terms of prestige, whether or not the internal make-up of these groups may be constantly changing.

THE CAUSES OF EMIGRATION

Different views have been advanced as to the causes of the existence of large-scale nomadism in Arabia. Since it seems to be the case that most Arabian nomad groups eventually settle on the soil in the outer countries, the question arises as to what causes them to adopt nomadic life in the first place. One view is that progressive dessication of the Arabian peninsula over the last millenia has led settled people to forsake stable agricultural pursuits for the nomadic life. Arab tradition traces the beginning of many large Arab tribes in the breaking of the Maarib dam in Yemen. Other authorities rather see the desert as the place where strong tribal groups can survive, and where weaker groups who could not protect their herds and grazing areas were forced away to take up the settled life.(2) Whatever the case, it does seem to be incontrovertible that there is a gradual movement northward of nomadic groups through Arabia and out into the steppe land of the Syrian desert, where they come

1 BARTH (1961) discusses in detail the different ethnic and political loyalties of tribal groups in southern Persia and formation of new social groups by splitting of old ones and the aggregation of diverse units. See particularly p.50-54, 130-33. The same process can be supposed to have happened for Arab tribes of the area. Although no detailed accounts exist, nevertheless local tradition recalls their aggregational process for the Ḍhafīr and Muṭair tribes, both of which are said to include elements of different tribal stocks. The name Ḍhafīr is expressive of this, meaning "plaited, bound together".

2 See MUSIL (1928b) for a discussion of these two theories, of which he favours the latter; Appendix p.311-13,316-19. Also MONTAGNE (1935) p.38-9; "Encyclopedia of Islam", Badw, p.881-5.

into contact with the settled lands. The reasons for this seem to have been analogous to the reasons for emigration from Europe to the New World. Within Arabia competition for grazing land was fierce. If a tribe was strong and could hold on, it did. However some found it easier to move northwards towards the Syrian desert, where land was more spacious and grazing was better.(1) Another incentive also must have been easier access to the products of the settled lands, plus the fact that the more temperate climate gave better opportunities for grazing and in general conditions are better. The relative prosperity of the northern nomads is reflected in the size of herds and tents and greater stature of the people.(2) One flaw in this theory is that we have to presume that groups who have been forced out of one area are then strong enough to displace other groups already in control of another more desirable area. It may be that the background of these tribes in the harsher environment of Arabia gave them an advantage over those already accustomed to the better conditions of the Syrian desert. Whatever the case, the important point from the linguistic point of view is the existence of a continuous process of nomadic population movement northwards through Arabia to the Syrian

1 This seems to be the case for the 'Aniza of the Syrian desert who were displaced within Arabia as regards access to the better grazing areas by the Dawāsir; see PHILBY (1922) II p.108. This view of the causes for the northward movement of the 'Aniza was also repeated to me by informants in Saudi Arabia. However inter-tribal rivalry still plays a great part in the interpretation of such historical events, and these accounts, although fascinating for the investigator, cannot always be relied upon as historically accurate. DOUGHTY (1924) p.400 mentions droughts in the 19th century as the cause. AL-'UBAYYID (1971) p.32 gives the succession of nomad power in central Arabia as: Bani Lām up till the 10th century AH, then 'Aniza in the 11th, who were ousted by Muṭair in the 12th and forced northwards. Muṭair in turn were followed by Qaḥṭān and then by 'Utaiba, who gained ascendancy over both Muṭair and Qaḥṭān.

2 See also DOUGHTY (1964) p.316,385,389; (1924) p.400, for comments on the relative prosperity of the northern and southern 'Aniza. It would seem that the middle area around Khaibar is a poor area for nomad life. He also mentions (1924) p.367, 461-2, 511, that the land between Qaṣīm and the Mecca country is regarded by the nomads as good pasture country. This is now occupied by the 'Utaiba.

bādiya area. This same process can be seen to happen in eastern Arabia where tribes from the southern Najd area on the borders of the Rub' al-Khāli have gradually transferred their centres of influence northeastwards towards the Gulf. In particular here the 'Ajmān and Āl-Murra tribes from the area of Najrān are now basically al-Hasa tribes. Cole in his fascinating study of the Āl-Murra tribe attributes this to the existence of more favourable grazing lands in the northeast corner of Arabia and a desire to be nearer to the coast settlements.(1)

THE JABAL SHAMMAR

The above remarks concerning the reasons for emigration from central Arabia to Mesopotamia and the Gulf must be taken to refer to the areas south of the Jabal Shammar area. The Jabal Shammar seems to form a natural enclave as regards dialect geography and to have had a somewhat separate evolution from the rest of the area. Situated as it is within easy travelling distance of southern Mesopotamia and the Gulf, with a good supply of wells and cultivable land and easy access to the good summer grazing of the Nafūd and the steppe land to the north of it, it seems to have maintained a very stable population over a long period.

1 COLE (1975) p.106. The only example I have found of the opposite movement is the movement southward of the Qaḥṭān in the 19th century from central Najd as a result of pressure from the north by the 'Utaiba. However this is more a matter of contraction back towards a centre of influence from a temporarily expanded area. See Text 2, Story 1, for oral tradition on this point. DOUGHTY (1924) Ch.XV gives an account of a similar war between the Qaḥṭān and the Muṭair where the Qaḥṭān are pushed back towards the south. For movements of other tribes within Arabia in a generally eastward and northward direction, see PHILBY (1922) II p.13, 203-4, 297, referring to the eastward movements of 'Utaiba, Qaḥṭān, 'Ajmān and Dawāsir. Also DOUGHTY (1924) p.354-56 for movement of Bani Khālid and 'Ajmān from Hasa to Kuwait, of the Subai' from al'Āriḍ to Qaṣīm. The important houses of Āl-Sudair and Āl-Saif, both of Sudair, are respectively from the Dawāsir and Subai' in the southwest in the areas of the Wādi Dawāsir and Wādi Subai'.

The distinctiveness of the Shammar in dialect and other cultural aspects has been noticed by a number of writers.(1) One particular feature is the greater cohesion of nomadic and sedentary sections of the various sub-tribes, which distinguishes them somewhat from other tribes.(2) The wells and villages to which the nomadic Shammar return in summer are in most cases occupied by their fellow tribesmen and little social distinction is made between them. This makes the Jabal Shammar and its desert hinterland a natural economic or ecological area of some permanence. The Shammar traditionally regard the town of Hail as impregnable because of its ring of mountains and this may have something to do with the stability of Shammar occupation of the area.

Movements of other groups northward such as the 'Aniza and the non-Shammari sections of the Ḍhafīr(4) and the Muṭair have passed to the west and east of the area.(5) This will be important in explaining the relationship of the Shammari type of dialect to those of surrounding groups.

In this connection we cannot do better than to quote Hogarth(6) on the basic difference between the social structure of northern and central Najd:

> "This (the difference) resides in the fact that its main constituent now settled and part of fellāḥ life has not lost the spirit of the Badawin population from which it sprang. To take the ruling family for instance; the

1 LORIMER (1908) II B p.1749. CANTINEAU (1937) II p.234.
2 Another example of this is the Dawāsir of southern Najd as described by PHILBY (1922) p.203-204.
3 MONTAGNE (1935), p.39.
4 PHILBY (1955), p.26-7, 28, 47, 70, 108, 112, seems to trace the Ḍhafīr (Ṣamada i.e. Ṣmida) through Sudair and Sibila to Ṣafwān and the Iraq borders.
5 The only explicit reference to this I have found is in LAWRENCE (1935), Ch.1, p.36. However the permanence of the tribal names associated with the area do seem to imply the absence of invasions.
6 HOGARTH (1904), p.166-7. See also DOUGHTY (1924) p.443, for a similar comparison between north and south: "But Zâmil (the governor of Buraida) did not ride in company with his nomad friends (el-Meteyr); the bedouins say the townspeople are utterly deceitful ... It is only Ibn Rashîd riding among the rajajîl and villagers who may foray in assurance with his subject Beduw."

chiefs of the house of Rashīd are not as the chiefs of the house of Sa'ūd in Riyad, rulers of settled communities with which they are at one, and surrounding tribes of Bedawins, distinct from themselves; but they are chiefs, in the first instance, of a great dominant Bedawin tribe, and in the second of the settlements which serve that tribe for markets and rallying points... Instead of dominant oases surrounded by diverse distinct tribes of Bedawins, who must be reckoned with as a potentially antagonistic, and for geographical reasons a very influential element, and can be but indifferently controlled, as is the case of southern Nejd, we find the northern oases subject to one tribe, whose members have the closest relations and community of interest with the settled members."

SOUTHERN MESOPOTAMIA

The area of southern Mesopotamia dealt with here covers the southern sections of the rivers Tigris, Euphrates and Kārūn and their confluence, the Shaṭṭ al-'Arab, which runs into the northern end of the Gulf. The northern limits of the area within Iran are fairly easily set at the end of the Khuzistan plain which forms the end of the continuous Arab population as defined both linguistically and ethnically. Arabs are found sporadically to the north of this line also, but it does seem to form a fairly observable linguistic and ethnic boundary.(1) The linguistic boundary between Arabic and Iranic dialects crosses the Iran-Iraq border on a northwest-southeast axis, following roughly the border between mountain and plain. In Iraq to the north of this boundary are found the Kurdish population who speak an Iranic dialect and form a continuous ethnic area into eastern Turkey, western Iran and the southern Caucasus. Within Iraq this area, as distinguished by linguistic and cultural features, is centred around Basra, 'Amāra and Nāṣirriyya, extending north to Kūt on the Tigris, and gradually blending into a central area around Baghdad, Musayyab, Ba'qūba and Ḥilla. The whole of southern Iraq up to about Baghdad in fact forms a large general dialect area as distinguished from the areas to the north.(2) However we are concerned here with a more limited area centred on the lower reaches of the rivers and more strictly connected with the Gulf and the area of northern Najd defined above. Some reference will however be made to the central area where comparison is helpful.

1 The so-called "'Arab" tribes of Fārs such as the Khamseh are in the main Turkish speaking, CHRISTIAN (1918) p.5.
2 For this division see in particular BLANC (1964) p.7.

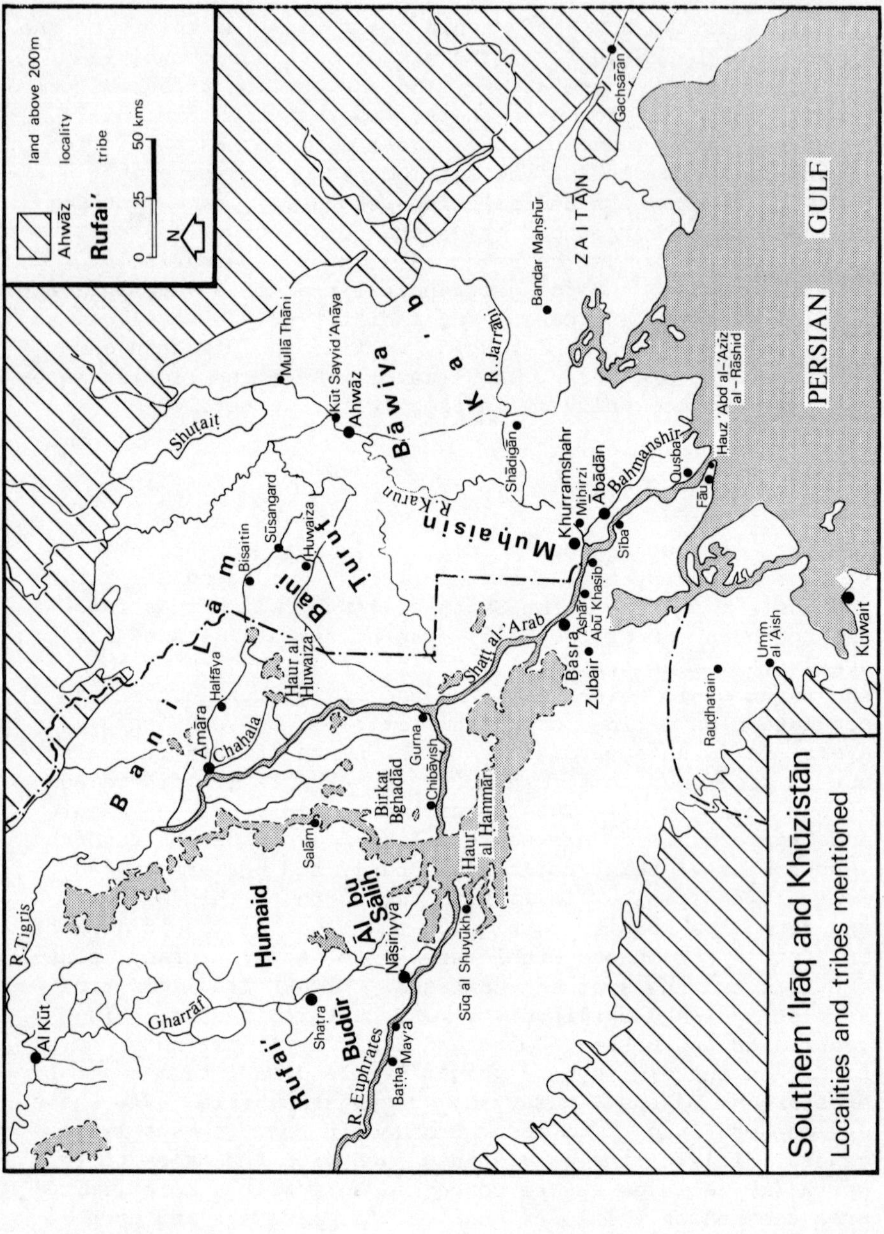

MAP 2. SOUTHERN IRAQ AND KHUZISTAN

The area can be divided into three regions, from the point of view of land use, which are relevant to its linguistic and ethnic structure:

1 The core of the area, that part of it least open to outside influence and from which it seems linguistic influences emanate, is the highly irrigated areas along the banks of the main rivers. This includes both banks of the Shaṭṭ al-'Arab, the Khaur Bahmashīr, the banks of the Jarrāḥi around Shādigān, and some parts of the Euphrates south of Nāṣiriyya, and perhaps also parts of the Tigris below 'Uzair.(1) This is an area of intensive palm cultivation spreading out in a continuous band along the rivers of a thickness of about two miles either side in some cases. The land is divided into *ḥauz* (pl. *aḥwāz*) or irrigation units, which is to a large extent the basis of the social structure. A *ḥauz* is the area between two *anhār* or irrigation channels. Within the palm area other crops are easily grown, such as grapes, vegetables, etc. and fishing is also carried on in a small way. The population of the palm groves are of diverse tribal origin in many cases, especially along the Shaṭṭ al-'Arab. Non-Arab elements, mostly Persian, are also present to a large degree in various stages of assimilation to the predominant Arab elements. At certain times the area has been united on a tribal basis. From the 17th century to the late 19th century the Ka'b ruled the area, while subsequent to that a tribal confederation called the Muḥaisin, based at Khorramshahr, superseded them. Both of these were based economically on their control of this rich agricultural region and also on their maritime strength in the Gulf. Even today the local dhow trade of the north of the Gulf is basically in the hands of the Khuzistan Arabs who bring cargoes of dates and other agricultural products, even animal fodder, down to Kuwait and return with luxury goods. In Kuwait also the dhow builders are mostly emigrated Khuzistanis. This central region, being based as it is on an internal river network of communication, has quite strong links with the Gulf area, in particular Kuwait, Bahrain and al-Hasa. The nature of this relationship and some complications which it poses for our model are dealt with later in Chapter 3, p.23 and p.51.

1 See also INGHAM (1976) p.76-7. Localities visited in southern Iraq and not mentioned specifically elsewhere were the following: on the Shaṭṭ al-'Arab: Sība, Abu al-Khaṣīb, Fao and Ḥauz 'Abd al-'Azīz al-Rāshid; near Naṣiriyya: Shaṭra, Sūq al-Gharrāf, al-Ṭumār, Khafāya, Māy'a, al-Fuhūd, and Chibāyish; also Najaf, Karbala, Kūt and Zubair. Mi'dān settlements were visited near Birkat Bghadād, an Āl bu Ṣāliḥ camp north of al-Fuhūd and a village of the Āl Azīrij near Salām south of 'Amāra. Āl bu Muḥammad informants from Ḥalfāya were also interviewed.

2 A second sub-region is formed by the marshlands of the Haur al-Ḥammār and Haur al-Ḥuwaiza. This is an area of marshlands and lakes interconnected by narrow channels. The population, the Mi'dān or marsh-dwellers, are semi-nomadic living in reed huts. They live by animal husbandry, keeping sheep, cattle and water-buffalo (*duwāb*) and by the production of reed matting for sale to the main towns of the area. The term Mi'dān is used here as applied to them by outsiders and includes all populations living in reed dwellings. Within the area, however, the term Mi'dān applies strictly only to the groups who keep buffalo. From the point of view of the main dialect features, in fact, there is little difference between Mi'dān and other marsh-dwellers.

3 A third sub-region is the Bādiya or open country between the rivers. Although here also irrigation channels are found, non-irrigated cultivation of arable crops is also possible. Animal husbandry of sheep, cattle and to some extent also camels is also important. The population here includes sedentary and nomadic groups. In some cases tribes include nomadic and sedentary sections. Although breaking into two parts, a western bādiya in Iraq and an eastern one in Khuzistan, the bādiya forms a continuous belt of land communication across the easily fordable rivers going north of the Haur al-Ḥuwaiza. The bādiya blends into the northern part of the Haur al-Ḥammār and here semi-Mi'dān tribes like the Āl bu Ṣāliḥ and Āl-'Īsa exist, who are divided between marshland and bādiya activities. It is also open to influence from the bādiya west of the Euphrates of which it forms a continuation and there are nomadic groups who spend the summer in the bādiya east of the Euphrates and the winter out in the bādiya to the west. It seems that this zone is one of gradual infiltration from the desert to the west. The transition from Najd-based bedouin visiting the Euphrates towns for supplies, to bedouin spending the summer months along the western bank of the Euphrates, then leads to sections of the tribe crossing the Euphrates to camp in the Ḥamād in summer. In the region of Nāṣirriya some sections of the Ḍhafīr(1) and the tribes of the Ḥumaid and Rufai'(2) spend the summer north of Nāṣiriyya. Nowadays the nomads bring their flocks across the Nāṣiriyya bridge by night when it is open to livestock. Before the construction of the bridge they used fords, as they still do at other points on the Euphrates. The Ḥumaid as a tribe consists of a nomadic section who still follow this pattern and settled sections living around Sūq al-Gharrāf.

1 OPPENHEIM (1939) p.57, referring to the Jawāsim section.
2 These two and other members of the Jash'am were west of the Euphrates in the 18th century. See Text 9; also OPPENHEIM (1952) 1-2, p.408-13.

A similar fringe Shammari group is mentioned by Glubb.(1) These are the Kwida, a small sub-tribe of seven or eight tents of camel-breeding bedouin west of the Euphrates near Samāwa. This Shi'ite group have probably been in Iraq for three or four centuries in his estimation.

Also important in this link between Mesopotamia and Najd is the existence of specifically Iraqi shepherd nomads known as *shāwiya* (also *shawāya* and more usually *shūyān* in Najd).(2) These shepherd tribes are completely Iraqi in culture(3) and Shi'a by religious persuasion, like the rest of southern Iraq and Khuzistan. These, of which the most important in the area are the Budūr and Zayyād, also comprise sedentary sections along the Euphrates, the Budūr being around Nāṣiriyya and Baṭḥa, the Zayyād near Samāwa. Sheep and camels graze on different pasture. While both can eat grass, camels also eat the tough saline plants of the desert (*ḥamḍh*). Further, camels move over larger distances at an easy speed and can subsist for long periods without water. They are therefore not in direct competition for grazing. The shepherd tribes also use donkeys as their main means of transportation; they were therefore in the days of free raiding at the mercy of the faster-moving camel-mounted bedouin. Therefore in the winter grazing months when the shepherds came out into the desert they would enter into a client relationship with the more powerful bedouin.(4) In the past the Budūr and Ḍhafīr formed a particularly strong alliance crossing ethnic, occupational and religious boundaries and raiding in all directions.(5) A further occupational distinction can be made between strictly Euphrates-based bedouin such as the Ḥumaid and Rufai' and others such as some clans of the Ḍhafīr, less intimately connected with the settled lands. The Ḥumaid and Rufai', also the Ṣmida section of Ḍhafīr, breed the *jūdi* (pl. *jwāda*), camels of Iraq which are immune to the ticks and insects which breed along the rivers in early summer. This enables them to come in to the river banks early in summer as soon as grazing grows scarce in the desert. The Buṭūn section of Ḍhafīr, on the other hand,

1 GLUBB (1978), p.108.
2 They are also referred to in Najd and Kuwait as *hakar* or *hukra*.
3 See also MUSIL (1928a), p.45. He mentions that the bedouin regard the *shawāya* as *'ruḥm al-dīra*, "relatives of the settled land".
4 For details of the grazing routes and relationship of shepherds and bedouin in the area see GLUBB (1960) passim but particularly p.32-4; also DICKSON (1949) p.546. MUSIL (1927), p.107, states that among the Zayyād at the end of the year each tent would give a sheep with all its young to the protecting sheikh.
5 See BELL (1940) p.36, 39, 40, 43-4.

breed the Najd camel and are forced to stay in the desert longer until the danger of disease to their flocks is lessened. (1) Correspondingly, the Euphrates bedouin are Shi'a like the rest of southern Iraq, while the Ḍhafīr are Sunni.

SUMMARY OF COMMUNICATION STRUCTURE OF THE AREA

The study of the distribution of linguistic variables in conjunction with the geographical and demographic structure of the area outlined above enables us to describe the dialect geography in terms of three zones of communication around certain cultural centres and of interaction between them. The nature of the interaction is as far as we can see that of the spread of linguistic features by the immigration of groups using them and their subsequent adoption by the surrounding population.

The term "zone of communication" is used here to denote an area within which the internal lines of communication are stronger than between the area and the outside. The three zones are:

1 Najd. Comprising Jabal Shammar, Qaṣīm and Najd proper (2) an area in which a concentration of wells, wādis and basins exists which form a comparatively continuous agricultural region and where important towns have grown up based on this agricultural economy.

2 The Coastal Region. The towns of the Gulf and the region of al-Hasa, which contains the important towns of Qaṭīf, Dammām, Hofūf and Ḍhahrān. The last three are now important primarily as oil industry centres; however they were originally important as part of the Gulf trading area and because of their agricultural prosperity.

3 Southern Iraq and Khuzistan. The river network of the Tigris, Euphrates and Kārūn and their confluence, the Shaṭṭ al-'Arab, also the Jarrāḥi canal. This area contains the important ports of Khorramshahr, Basra and the later developed agricultural centres of Ahwaz, Nāṣiriyya and 'Amāra, also the important oil industry centre of 'Abbādān.

The nature of the linguistic interaction between these three areas is to be seen in the light of a sea and a land network. The sea network is traditionally based on the community of interests in fishing, trade and particularly the pearl industry (although this is now almost completely

1 J.B. Glubb in a private conversation, but see also GLUBB (1960) p.227.

2 I.e. the districts of Sudair, 'Āriḍh and Washm. As a general term it denotes the central region of the Arabian Peninsula within the desert ring of the Nafūd and Rub' al-Khāli. See also PALGRAVE (1965) I, p.336-7 for the use of the term Najd.

extinct). A strong connection exists between the coast settlements and those of the Shaṭṭ al-'Arab and Khuzistan, and even the Persian side of the Gulf. This is seen in a certain racial, religious and architectural uniformity. The land connection is dependent mostly on the existence of nomadic populations living in the steppe-lands between the three areas and particularly on the following factors:

1 The necessity of the nomads to camp on wells for four months of the summer at which time their living area will contract inwards towards one of the three main zones.

2 The necessity for them to visit the settled areas in order to buy supplies. The coastal region and southern Iraq being in closer contact with the outside world are naturally preferable to Central Najd for this purpose.

3 The tendency either because of population pressure inside the Najd or general expansionist tendency for Najd tribes to move their main grazing areas and summer encampments from Najd up to the Euphrates and the Gulf Coast.

The basic division of communication zones as indicated by the linguistic and human geography of the area is into a Mesopotamian and an Arabian area, with the Gulf Coast forming a sub-division of the Arabian(1) one. One factor difficult to fit into this model is that there are sections of the population of Kuwait who had traditionally very little contact with the interior of Arabia at all, and it is therefore difficult to see why their dialect should retain a basically Arabian character. These people, the Baḥārna(2) (pl. of Baḥrāni) "seafarers" were seafaring by culture,

1 The term Arabian is used here to indicate the north central and eastern areas discussed here, i.e. Jabal Shammar, Qaṣīm, al-'Āriḍh and the eastern region. No implication is made that Arabia as a whole is distinguishable linguistically in any easily definable way from Mesopotamia as a whole. These larger areas fit into a major dialect continuum which it is not so easy to separate along these lines. However in the area we are discussing a fairly discernible polarization into these two types can be traced.

2 For the use of this term see LORIMER (1908) Baḥrāni. In dress and general appearance these coastal population are strikingly different from those of the interior of Najd or Iraq. The Arab of Iraq and Najd wear the head-cloth (*ghutra*, *shmāgh* or *chaffiyya*) with head-rope (*'agāl*) in the traditional Arab way. The coastal population wear a thin white head-cloth without head-rope in the form of a turban, or sometimes as a scarf over the shoulder. This turban style was always the mark of the Ka'b of Khuzistan (WILSON (1911), p.117). I have never seen the *'agāl* worn in Khuzistan except by holy men although it appears in

Shi'a by religious persuasion and in terms of communication nearer to the populations of the Shaṭṭ al-'Arab than to those of the interior. In dress and other cultural externals also they resemble them closely, while their dialect shows no such affinity.

One explanation for this may be that in the Gulf settlements over the last two hundred years or so the ruling groups have been of Najdi origin; the Āl Ṣubāḥ of Kuwait, Āl-Thāni of Qaṭar and Āl-Khalīfa of Bahrain all arrived within the last two centuries. It is possible that the more racially mixed Baḥārna, the earlier inhabitants of the coastline, have been influenced by these prestige groups and their dialect has become increasingly of the Najdi type, particularly in Kuwait.

The history of the Gulf region is important in this connection. In the 9th century the Qarāmiṭa dynasty controlled the whole area of al-Hasa, the Kuwait region and southern Iraq. The Ottomans also at the height of their power united the region on two occasions as part of their empire for more than a century. These historical indications and the ethnological factors mentioned earlier would seem to support the conjecture that in earlier times there was a greater degree of uniformity between the Shaṭṭ al-'Arab area and the coastal

photographs in the 50s as worn by the Ka'b tribesmen in general. Lately also during the period of revolution in Iran the Khuzistan Arabs took to wearing the *'agāl* as symbolic of Arab identity emphasising claims to autonomy within Iran. Dress is important as a tribal and general ethnic "diacritic" in this area. In Iraq non-coastal Arabs refer to themselves as *jamā'at il'ugul* (people of the *'agāl*) referring disparagingly to the coastal people as *ahl iṭṭa'ṭi'ōh* (people of the *ṭa'ṭi'ōh* - a type of coastal amphibian frog) implying that this was eaten by them. Coastal groups also refer to those of the interior as *badu* "bedouins" or Arab "nomads" in a similarly disparaging way. To the people of Najd and the tribes of bādiya of Iraq racial purity is important and they will often refer to the coastal population as "non-Arabs". The term Baḥārna in some ways implies this. To the coastal groups this is unimportant. They are cosmopolitan in their attitude,depending for much of their livelihood on contact with the outside world. For a discussion of various views on the origin of the Baḥārna, see al-TĀJIR (1979), p.31, 49. For our purposes the question of actual racial origin or ancestry is unimportant in this connection and we would only point to certain cultural contrasts.

region(1) as regards dialect.

It is important also to stress here that the relevance of these ethnic factors is different in Iraq and the Peninsula. Along the coast the division into Baḥārna and *badu* or *ahl innajd* correlates with the Shi'a-Sunni division, while in Iraq the whole population is Shi'a and the difference is rather between a completely sedentary somewhat de-tribalised society and a traditional, tribally organised society, with some connection with the nomadic way of life.(2) These occupational factors are of course also relevant to the coastal region.

1 See also JOHNSTONE (1967b) on pre-'Anazi elements in the dialects of the Gulf, p.90-2. The discussion here is mainly with reference to Kuwait. In Bahrain and al-Hasa a specific Baḥrāni dialect exists cognate with the 'Omani dialect. See PROCHAZKA (1981).

2 For further discussion of this division see also FIELD (1949) I, 2, p.251-52, who divides southern Iraq into non-tribal, semi-tribal and tribal regions, the non-tribal region being the lower Shaṭṭ al-'Arab region. In the relevant passage she states that "Although the majority of rural settled Arabs have a regular tribal organization such as the 'Abūda or Bani Asad, there are many thousands who belong to so mixed a community that tribal ties have become entirely or almost entirely extinct. Such conditions are found in the highly civilized areas and among the population of the date-gardens on the banks of the Shaṭṭ al-'Arab downstream from Basra."

2 The nature of dialect contrasts

A problem which has vexed dialectologists from the earliest days of the subject is that of the impossibility of making clear-cut divisions between dialect areas, especially in regions with an uninterrupted geographical spread of population. The German neogrammarians of the 19th century noticed that in such areas one speech variety blends imperceptibly into the next through intermediary varieties so that rather than discrete entities we are confronted with a continuum which is only dividable into clearly demarcated regions if we choose very simple criteria for differentiation. As an example of this we may take the important isogloss which divides areas with /*j*/ from areas with /*y*/ as a reflex of OA *j** in such forms as /*rayyāl, rajjāl*/ "man". The pronunciation /*rayyāl*/ is regarded in Iraq as "southern" as contrasted with /*rajjāl*/ which is the pronunciation of the central area and north. Disregarding for the moment the pronunciation /*ražžāl*/ which is characteristic of parts of the southern marshlands, this gives a fairly clear division into a /*j*/ area north of Baṭ̤ha on the Euphrates and Kūt on the Tigris, and a /*y*/ area south of it. This is an important "characteristic" isogloss since the pronunciation /*rayyāl*/ is widely recognised as a "southern" characteristic and it would be tempting to take this line as the demarcating one between "southern" and "non-southern" types in Iraq. However when we examine other isoglosses which are equally regarded as dividing "southern" and "non-southern" types, we find that they do not correspond to this. For instance the suffix /*-an*/ characteristic of first person singular verbal forms, such as /*arīdan*/ "I want" /*arūḥan*/ "I go", is used as far north as Najaf on the Euphrates, while the occurrence of the suffix /*-man*/ "who" or "which" post-verbally in such forms as /*šifit-man*/ "who or which did see", /*šāf-man*/ "who or which did he see" is used as far north as Ḥilla on the Euphrates. Thus we are faced with the decision as to whether to regard as "southern" only the core dialects which have all three characteristics or to include all dialects up to the outer ring at Ḥilla. Furthermore there are other contrasts which cannot be strictly called "isoglosses" since their geographical distribution is more fragmented, which cut across these boundaries entirely, dividing "nomadic" from "sedentary" speech types.(1) Therefore, if we persist in trying to divide "southern" from "non-southern" types we are forced to consider a "core" area of "southern" speech with a band of "border dialects", while disregarding the fact that nomadic "southern" and nomadic "non-southern" are united by some features which separate them from their non-nomadic counterparts.

The above type of situation is typical of areas with a high population density and has led some dialectologists in the past to despair of the possibility of dividing a speech area into discrete dialect areas. Others, on the other hand, have maintained that a sufficient conglomeration of dialect characteristics is a good enough justification for talking about a "dialect area" even though the isoglosses may not follow each other exactly. However, in view of the emphasis on exactness and scientific demonstrability which has become the hallmark of modern linguistic studies, one is forced in the end to accept the view that the search for discrete geographically defined dialects is probably a fruitless one in the majority of linguistic landscapes. Only when one speech community is cut off from the next by some impassable geographical barrier are distinct and geographically definable dialects likely to exist in close proximity.(2) The more usually found situation is for different speech varieties to blend into one another without definable cut-off points.

However since native speakers themselves have no difficulty in the majority of cases in making statements about the regional and social identity of particular speech varieties, one feels that the linguist should be able to incorporate these statements into the main body of his discipline. The most striking advances in this direction have been made in the branch of sociolinguistics, where particular contrasts or "speech variables" are analysed in terms of their social distribution and significance both from the point of view of the speaker and the local hearer. In this type of approach one is not bound to make definite statements about the geographical distribution of the variables, but rather

1 These are referred to in Chapter 3 "Reductional Changes".
2 In our area good examples of this occur. The island of Failika off the coast of Kuwait has a dialect easily distinguishable from standard Kuwaiti. Similarly the dialect of al-Zubair southwest of Basra in an area of non-settled steppe is geographically clearly separated from the dialects of the Mesopotamian river network.

concentrates on discovering their social significance. Recent studies of this type have often pointed to a situation of confrontation between two or more social groups with which this contrast correlates. A classic study of this type is Labov's early work on diphthong variation in the speech of the island of Martha's Vineyard in Massachusetts.(1) Here he showed how the contrast between open and close vowel types was socially significant in the confrontation between the native islanders, the "Vineyarders" and the mainlanders or "Yankees" on whom the Vineyarders were gradually becoming economically dependent. One advantage of this approach is that since one is freed of the necessity of drawing a definite boundary between dialects, one is not forced to regard so many features as "exceptions" to the main rule which is itself only a rule because it is in the majority. Since one is interested in a situation of confrontation between two poles, just as it is natural to find that populations between the two poles may be indeterminate or historically fluctuating in their political affiliation, so it is natural to find that their speech shows features common to both poles. Following Labov we also recognise the possibility that certain contrasts may be non-distinctive(2) from the point of view of the speakers although noticeable to the linguist.

If we keep in mind the fact that we are now concentrating on the relevance of individual linguistic contrasts and not looking for exact geographical borders between discrete geographical dialects, we can now go back to early dialectologists' difficulties with the definition of the dialect. The German dialectologists of the 19th century found that, although isoglosses did not follow each other exactly, nevertheless there was a pattern to their occurrence. They found that it was possible to distinguish "core" areas which had all the features of a particular type and in which no conflicting isoglosses occurred, and "transitional" areas between these "cores" in which isoglosses crossed one another. The "core" areas were situated around cultural and political centres while "transitional" areas occurred at the borders between these. Thus although this meant one could not exactly speak of "dialects" one could with more justification speak of "dialect areas", since the geographical configura-

1 LABOV (1972).
2 See LABOV's (1966) reference to the lower degree of sensitivity of speakers to variation in initial *th-* than to variation in the vowels *eh* and *oh* in New York speech. p.85-113; p.91-93 especially.

ation plainly reflected the spread of particular linguistic features out from centres of influence into the intervening areas. Therefore we are justified in talking of dialect features of a particular area i.e. "northern" features or "southern" features. We can also with reasonable justification talk, for instance, of "core" northern dialects and "core" southern dialects. Transitional dialects in such a configuration would not be classified as of either type primarily, but described purely as transitional types.

In our area of interest this type of approach gives a highly satisfactory picture of the dialect distribution. This is because the population distribution, as mentioned before, is one of certain highly populated zones of sedentary population separated by large intervening areas roamed by nomadic tribes who, although extremely few in number, cover immense geographical areas with great mobility. This means that it is easy to talk of "core" dialect areas centred on the main populated zones with transitional types at their borders. The dialects of the nomads in turn can be related, within a historical perspective of two to three hundred years, to the population zones from which they originate. Typologically also we can distinguish between the isogloss structure of the sedentary speech area and that of the nomads. As mentioned above, in areas of continuous settlement such as the river valleys of Mesopotamia or bands of relatively closely situated wells and settlements such as the central Najd area or the Gulf coast, different dialect types blend into one another without definite boundaries. This linguistic configuration is parallel to the communication structure of such areas, where people are in touch with neighbouring groups in a continuous way across the landscape. With the nomads, on the other hand, group identity and cohesiveness are much stronger and tribal units cover a larger geographical area although the numbers are probably less.(1) For this reason actual tribal dialects are more easily discernible although geographical and ethnic proximity between tribes is also reflected in dialect similarities. If we examine the area of southern Mesopotamia we find that the main factors correlating with dialect identity are geographical location and occupation, while different occupational groups may be united in one overall tribal unit. Prime examples of this are the

1 Statistics on the actual numbers of members of nomadic tribes are by the nature of their way of life difficult to obtain and unreliable. However earlier writers such as DOUGHTY (1924) p.427 and LORIMER (1908)passim, reflect this numerical relationship. In the past the military superiority of the bedouins has rested on mobility and inaccessiveness rather than numerical superiority.

Muntafiq and Bani Ḥuchaim confederations of the lower Euphrates near Samāwa and Nāṣiriyya which include shepherd, sedentary and semi-nomadic marshmen groups. In these areas the main dialect division seems to be between marsh-dwellers (Mi'dān) and other rural tribal groups whether primarily shepherds (*shāwiya*) or settled agriculturalists (*ḥadhar*). Factors involved in this are certain distinctive Mi'dān characteristics such as the occurrence of /*ž*/ as a reflex of OA *j** rather than /*y*/ or /*j*/ and the occurrence of the negative particle -*š* as in *mūš* "not", *mā yfūtīš* "it doesn't pass".

For the main large bedouin tribes of the area on the other hand dialect corresponds to tribe in an easily distinguishable way and can be related to the history of the migration and ethnic makeup of the tribes. Going from north to south along the Euphrates, the first, the Sba'a and 'Amārāt groups of the 'Aniza, speak a Central Najdi type of dialect with some northern characteristics.(1) South of these from Najaf are the Shammar with their own distinctive North Najdi dialect. South of these from around Samāwa are the Ḍhafīr with a very mixed type of dialect, a combination of the North and Central Najd type. South of these again from the Bāṭin depression and in the vicinity of Kuwait are the Muṭair, again with a Central Najdi dialect but without the northern features of the 'Aniza dialect. These linguistic characteristics correspond closely to the original geographical location of these tribes. The 'Aniza originate in western Najd in the area of Khaibar and have spread out to the north of their originally northeastern neighbours, the Shammar. The Ḍhafīr are reputed to be of mixed origin combining Shammar and Central Najdi elements with, it seems, a high degree of ex-slave admixture who moved over to the south Euphrates in the early 19th century. The Muṭair in turn moved over to eastern Arabia from western Najd in the area of Madina in the 18th and 19th centuries. This type of close correspondence of dialect grouping to ethnic origin irrespective of present geographical location is similar to the picture of dialect geography held by the early neogrammarians, that of the "family tree" or Stammbaum Theory. In this view, as expounded by A. Schleicher, dialects are seen as moving through time and space with groups of people. We have therefore a linguistic mirror of the history of folk migration. The dialect geography of the sedentary population on the other hand is closer to the view presented by the "Wave Theory" (Wellen Theorie) of J. Schmidt and G. Wenker, namely that the linguistic features spread across geographical landscapes from centres of importance irrespective of the original geograph-

1 The features distinguishing these various dialects are described in detail in Chapter 7.

ical or ethnic origin of the population concerned.(1) We therefore have here an interesting example of how a different history of population movement can produce different types of linguistic landscape.

THE MULTIVALENCY OF DIALECT FEATURES

Within the basic framework of attributing social and geographical relevance to particular linguistic contrasts we have to make the qualification that the relevance of a contrast may be different from place to place, i.e. the valency of the contrast is stated for a particular sub-region of the total area. A prime example of this is the contrast */j/* vs. */y/* as a reflex of OA *j** mentioned above. In the context of Iraq the pronunciations */rayyāl/* "man" */yīb/* "bring" etc. are a mark of southern and therefore Shi'a speech as opposed to */rajjāl/ /jīb/* which are more characteristically Sunni pronunciation. The fact that the Sunni population of Zubair in southern Iraq and also Sunni speakers of Kuwait use the */y/* pronunciation is within the Iraqi context generally unknown or disregarded in the face of the predominant correspondence of */y/* with Shi'a identity. In Kuwait on the other hand and presumably also in the other Gulf states */y/* is the predominant form and characterises the sedentary population while */j/* is the pronunciation of the bedouins whether nomadic or settled. Similarly in southern Iraq the form */-u/* rather than */-ah/* for the pronominal suffix for "him" or "his" is along the Euphrates taken as a "bedouin" characteristic since the bedouin tribes of the area, namely Shammar, Ḍhafīr and other smaller tribes such as the Ḥumaid and Rufai', all show this form as opposed to the more usual southern Iraqi */-ah/*.

Within Najd however this */-u/* pronunciation is of geographical significance marking North Najdi dialects in contrast to Central ones and is not relevant to the nomad vs. sedentary division. Similarly in Kuwait the occurrence of */-k/* as the form of the pronominal "you" or "your" masc.s. is regarded as "bedouin" since it is characteristic of the speech of some important bedouin tribes of the area, i.e. Muṭair and 'Ajmān, also to a lesser extent the 'Awāzim and Rashāyida (see below, p.98.). Within Najd however the */-k/* form is geographically significant marking Central Najd and al-Hasa vs. the northern area. In Bahrain a complete reversal obtains since this */-k/* form is characteristic of the Shi'a population or Baḥārna vs. the later Sunni arrivals. Generally we see that what are geographically regional

1 See BYNON (1977) p.190-4 for a discussion of these views.

features within Arabia are transported with population movements to the outer area and there acquire occupational or social significance. This is a natural process insofar as the outer lands are in general ignorant of the geography and political divisions of Inner Arabia with which they have very little contact. To the people of these areas the main functional characteristic is that people coming from Inner Arabia are "bedouins" and contrast with themselves in their way of life. Within Arabia the contrast of nomad vs. sedentary is in many areas less important. The important factor is locality and tribal allegiance, since people will easily move from a nomadic to a sedentary way of life and vice versa(1) and dialect geography to a great extent reflects this. The word "bedouin" in fact in Arabia means "member of an established bedouin tribe" and does not necessarily imply a nomadic life-style.

1 See KATAKURA (1977) for a detailed and revealing account of this process, especially p.55-9.

3 Reductional changes in the dialects of Mesopotamia and the gulf

GENERAL

Comparison of the dialects of inner Arabia with those of the outer fringe, namely Mesopotamia and the Gulf, reveals a marked generalisation: that the outer dialects, and more particularly those of Mesopotamia, have reduced a number of contrasts still extant in the dialects of the interior. These operate at the grammatical, morphological and phonological levels, and in some cases, such as that of the verb transitivity system, it may involve more than one level at a time. In the main it is more accurate to regard the process as one of simplification than one of reduction, since the ability of the language to make grammatical distinctions is not reduced, but the method of doing it is simplified. Illustrative of this is the elimination of the so-called "internal passive" in the outer dialects. In these the contrast between */nišad/* "he asked" and */nšid/* "he was asked" is replaced by the forms */nišad/* "he asked" and */innišad/* "he was asked". Here the process of prefixing, which is the more general verbal inflection process in the dialects, replaces the process of internal vowel and syllable modification, which is not present to the same degree elsewhere in the verb system. The process of reduction can be seen to proceed along the parameters of identification or contact with the Najd or the outer regions, as outlined in Ch. 1. In general the most conservative dialects are those of Najd, whether of the Northern or Central type. Somewhat less conservative in some features are the dialects of the bedouin of the Syrian desert, followed by the bādiya dialects of Iraq. The least conservative are those of the riverine population of Iraq and the Gulf towns.

In some cases the features levelled are redundant(1)

1 The term redundant is used here in its technical sense, meaning "not signalling a grammatical distinction exclusively".

features, as in the case of the different morphological noun classes mentioned below (p.37) and in the simplification of the syllable structure types by the introduction of an anaptyctic between the two elements of a final cluster, as shown below (p.56f,60f). In others they are distinctive linguistic features which are replaced by some other feature which is of a type more extensively used within the language, such as in the reduction of the internal passive and the indefinite marker /*-in*/. Very rarely can it be said that a particular grammatical term is lost, although in some cases marking of it is lost in some word classes. In the case of the reduction of gender distinction in the plural, the verbal word class ceases to show this distinction in some dialects.

The use of the terms reduction and levelling perhaps necessitates some qualification. When one uses them in this sense, one does not mean to imply that the capacity of the language to express thought accurately is diminished. All that is implied is that the number of types of grammatical and phonological structures used to convey meaning is reduced. This process of reduction has been noted for a number of languages and standard English is perhaps one of the most well-documented examples.(1)

Compared to many English rural dialects, standard English has undergone considerable reduction in the stressed vowel system. Such reduction is in most cases correlated with mobilisation of the population, or with the influx of foreign groups into the speech community. The term mobilisation, as used here, denotes the entry of elements from the whole population into the activities of the community.(2) In the case in question we know that the Gulf ports, the area of Bahrain and al-Hasa and the Shaṭṭ al-'Arab region have for a long period been subject to immigration from central Arabia, from the Syrian desert and also from Iran. In Khuzistan and Bahrain, in particular, the Shi'a sect of Islam forms a link with Iran. In addition, a tradition of one-way intermarriage with the neighbouring Iranian populations is quite common among the Khuzistan Arabs, in which Arab tribesmen take Persian wives who are absorbed into the Arab population. It is important to stress that bilingual, rather than inter-racial, contact is the important factor here. Within central Arabia a high degree of intermixture with the slave population of African origin is present, although under somewhat restricted

1 See TRUDGILL & FOXCROFT (1978); also KURATH (1972) for simplification in Afrikaans as compared to Standard Dutch, p.116-18.

2 See in particular GUMPERZ (1962), p.36.

conditions. However the slave(1) population speak only "Arabic" with no discernible dialect difference, and no linguistic effect is evident from this mixture. The actual process by which language contact can lead to language change has been described in detail by other writers.(2) Since no actual comparison of bilingual and monolingual families was made in connection with this research I do not go into this here, but point only to the general correlation between linguistic conservatism in stable populations and linguistic levelling among populations of diverse origin. The two main areas in which this levelling can be seen here are in the verb transitivity system and in the reduction of the indefinite nominal marker /*-in*/. These are dealt with in detail below (pp.39-56). Certain other examples will now be given briefly:

1 Phonological merger of certain consonant elements has taken place in the periphery area and also in the dialect of Mecca. In the dialects of the Gulf litoral and much of Khuzistan and southern Iraq, /*j*/ and /*y*/ have merged to /*y*/. This is true in all of southern Iraq, up to about al-Baṭ̤ha on the Euphrates and Kūt on the Tigris, with the exception of the speech of the marsh-dwellers of the Haur al-Ḥuwaiza and Haur al-Ḥammār, who have /*ž*/ for OA /*j*/.(3) Isolated examples of this merger are also attested for the interior in the dialect of al-Ḥauṭa south of Riyadh and in the speech of the Sardiyya of the Syrian desert.(4)

Examples:

Retaining System (Central Najd)	Merged System (S. Iraq)	
yōm	*yōm*	"day"
yimīn	*yimīn*	"right"
yamm-	*yamm-*	"beside"
jāb	*yāb*	"he brought"
jimal	*yimal*	"camel"
jibal	*yibal*	"mountain"

In the dialect of the al-Hasa region and in the Shi'a dialect

1 The word "slave" is used here in direct translation of Arabic /*'abd*/ which is synonymous with "negro" and implies people of slave ancestry in Arabia, many of whom hold high social and financial status.
2 See in particular WEINREICH (1970) passim, but especially p.14-71.
3 JOHNSTONE (1967b) p.9-11; INGHAM (1976) p.67.
4 CANTINEAU (1937) p.137.

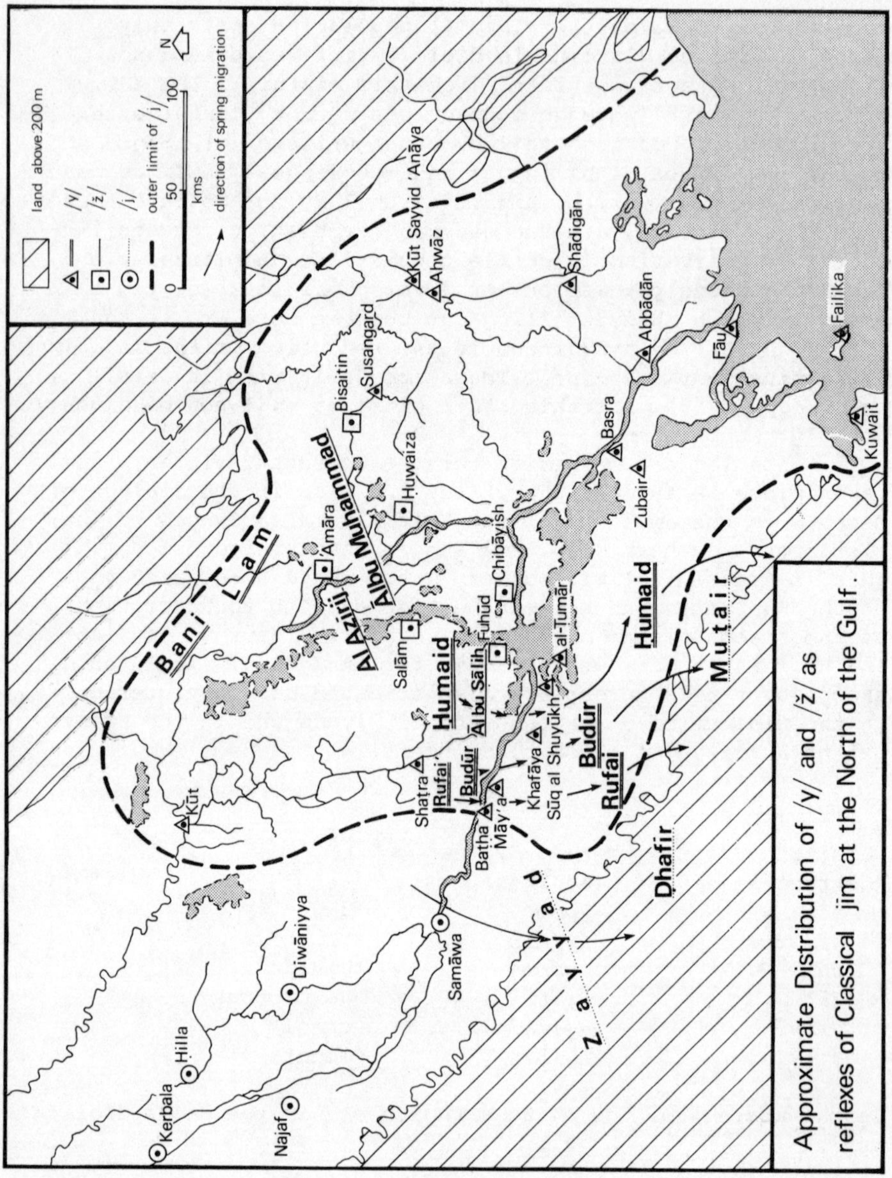

MAP 3: APPROXIMATE DISTRIBUTION OF /y/ and /ž/.

of Bahrain(1) */d/* and */ḏ/* have merged to */d/* while */ṯ/* and */f/* have merged to */f/*. Similarly in the dialect of Mecca(2) where again considerable immigration from outside Arabia has occurred the mergers */d/* and */ḏ/* to */d/*, and */t/* and */ṯ/* to */t/* have taken place.

Examples:

Retaining System (Central Najd)	Merged System (Meccan)	(Shi'a Bahrain)	
ṯalāṯah	*talāta*	*falāfeh*	"three"
ṯāni	*tāni*	*fāni*	"second"
ṯiźīl	*tagīl*	*fagīl*	"heavy"
dūn	*dūn*	*dūn*	"near to.."
bidāl	*bidāl*	*bidāl*	"instead of.."
hāḏa	*hāda*	*hāde*	"this"
axaḏ	*axad*	*axad*	"he took"

2 In a particular set of nouns reduction of morphological classes has taken place in the extreme Mesopotamian type, whereas in the Najdi type a more complex system is maintained. In the marginal Mesopotamian types also the more complex system is maintained. This set of contrasts obtains for nouns relatable to OA forms of the type: */fa'ala, fa'la, fi'la/* and */fu'la/*. In the Najdi type, the class *fa'la* has split into */fa'la/* and */f'ala/*, while */fa'ala/* has become */f'ila/*. */fi'la/* and */fu'la/* remain, although the contrast of */i/* and */u/* is now phonologically conditioned. In the Mesopotamian type */fa'ala/* has merged with the */fi'la, fu'la/* type, while the */fa'la/* type remains undifferentiated.

Examples:

Najdi Type	Mesopotamian Type	
tfuga	*tufga*	"rifle"
wruga	*wurga*	"leaf"
rguba	*rugba*	"neck"
gṣuba	*guṣba*	"reed, rifle barrel"
ġrufa	*ġurfa*	"room"
mruga	-----	"stew"
ḥṭuba	-----	"firewood"
šbića	*šibča*	"bird trap"
ḥurma	*ḥurma*	"woman"
fikra	*fikra*	"thought"
turba	*turba*	"earth"
zibda	*zibda*	"cream"
'idla	*'idla*	"basket"

1 PROCHAZKA (to appear).

2 INGHAM (1971) p.273.

ghawa	*gahwa*	"coffee"
n'aja	*na'ya*	"ewe"
nxawa	*naxwa*	"call for help"
ṣḥala	-----	"pot"
nxala	*naxla*	"palm tree"
lgaḥa	-----	"pregnant camel"
šaġla	*šaġla*	"work"
šanṭa	*šanṭa*	"suitcase"

3 In certain areas of the periphery, and also in certain large urban centres, the distinction of masculine and feminine in the 2nd and 3rd persons plural of the verbal and pronominal system is lost. Material for Iraq, Khuzistan, Kuwait and Northern Najd showed that the distinction was maintained almost everywhere, except in the urban centres of Zubair, Kuwait, Basra and Baghdad. Prochazka's material for Shi'a Bahraini and al-Hasa, and my own from the dialect of Mecca, also showed the reduced system. The affixes and pronouns concerned are shown below:

Retaining System

ktib-aw "they (m) wrote"	*ktib-an* "they (f) wrote"
kitab-tu "you (m p) wrote"	*kitab-tin* "you (f p) wrote"
yaktibūn "they (m) write"	*yaktibin* "they (f) write"
taktibūn "you (m p) write"	*taktibin* "you (f p) write"
ikitbu "write! (m p)"	*ikitbin* "write! (f p)"
intu/intam /intaw "you (m p subj)"	*intin/intan* "you (f p subj)"
hum "they (m)"	*hin* "they (f)"
-kum/kam "you (m p obj)"	*-kin/ćin/čan* "you (f p obj)"

Reduced System

kitb-aw "they (m/f) wrote"	*kitabtu* "you (m/f p) wrote"
ykitbūn "they (m/f) write"	*tkitbūn* "you (m/f p) write"
kitbu "write! (m/f p)"	*intu* "you (m/f p subj)"
hum "they (m/f)"	*-kum* "you (m/f p obj)"

The independent pronouns and objective suffixes are somewhat more resilient than the verbal subject affixes, and in some varieties these remain while the latter are collapsed.(1)

4 In some dialects of southern Iraq, Khuzistan and Bahrain there is a tendency to reduce the four morphological form classes of the perfective of verbs. Preceding certain subject suffixes a vowel /-ē-/ is inserted, while with the geminate verb class a vowel /-ā-/ precedes object suffixes with the third person singular. Both these features assimilate the Strong, Hollow and Geminate verb classes to the Final Weak Class.(2) This type of system is attested for the dialects of the Shaṭṭ al-'Arab and for the ~~Shi'a~~ Sunni dialect of Bahrain.

Examples:

	Retaining System	Reduced System	
Strong:	*kitabt*	*kitbēt*	"I wrote"
Hollow:	*nimt*	*nāmēt*	"I slept"
Final Weak:	*ligēt*	*ligēt*	"I found"
Geminate:	*šaddih*	*šaddāh*	"he tied it"
Final Weak:	*ligāh*	*ligāh*	"he found it"

THE VERB TRANSITIVITY SYSTEM

The old Arabic verb showed a system of stem vowel alternation which marked the active and passive voice distinction and also, in a somewhat less consistent way, the transitivity characteristics of the verb marking transitive, intransitive and causative types. In its classical form this is marked

1 JOHNSTONE (1967b), p.41.
2 INGHAM (1973) p.544; JOHNSTONE (1967b) p.92; PROCHAZKA (to appear).

mainly by vowel quality, but also involves syllable structure. The traditional interpretation separates the active/passive system from the transitive/intransitive/causative; since the first is regarded as being more strictly "grammatical" and applicable to any verb, while the second can be treated as a system of lexical derivation, since in many cases semantic modifications are also involved. This system can be illustrated by the following verb items:

Transitive Verb Type

katab	"he wrote"	*yaktub*	"he writes"
kutib	"it was written	*yuktab*	"it is written"

Intransitive Verb Type

sami'	"he heard"	*yasma'*	"he hears"
sumi'	"it was heard"	*yusma'*	"it is heard"

Causative Verb Type

asma' "he caused someone to hear"
yusmi' "he causes someone to hear"
usmi' "he was caused to hear"

The verbs showing the pattern */a-a/*, like *katab*, are fully transitive, while those showing the pattern */a-i/* or */a-u/* may be intransitive: like */ṣa'id/* "he ascended", */ḍabuṭ/* "it became firm"; or may express states or processes of sensory perception: like */sami'/* "he heard", */'alim/* "he found out". Here the subject is involved as the patient, or undergoer, of the action rather than as a strict actor.

The dialects of the Najd have preserved this old Arabic system to a great extent, while those of Mesopotamia have shown a tendency to level them, cutting out these distinctions as shown by the vowel pattern. Passivity and causativity are shown in these dialects by means of other morphological features connected with the "Measure" system of the verb. Various intermediate types are distinguishable, preserving part of the system. The degree of retention corresponds, to a large extent, with the degree of contact with Central Najd. Here the dialects of Qaṣīm (Midhnab) in Najd and the Shaṭṭ al-'Arab in Mesopotamia are taken as extreme types.(1)

1 In the following account of the verbal systems not all forms are given since the remaining forms can be predicted from those shown, i.e.*nšidaw* "they (m) asked", *nšidan* "they (f) asked", *nišadti* "you (f s) asked", *nišadtu* "you (m p) asked", *nišadtin* "you (f p) asked", *nanšid* "we ask", *tanšdūn* "you (m p) ask", *tanšdin* "you (f p) ask".

QAṢĪM

Transitive Verb Type

Active		Passive	
nišad	"he asked"	*nšid*	"he was asked"
nšidat	"she asked"	*nišdat*	"she was asked"
nišadt	"I asked"	*nšidt*	"I was asked"
nišadna	"we asked"	*nišidna*	"we were asked"
yanšid	"he asks"	*yinšad*	"he is asked"
tanšid	"she asks"	*tinšad*	"she is asked"
anšid	"I ask"	*inšad*	"I am asked"
yanšdūn	"they (m) ask"	*yinšdōn*	"they (m) are asked"
yanšdin	"they (f) ask"	*yinšdan*	"they (f) are asked"

Causative Verb Type

ablaš	"he involved somebody in something"
ablišat	"she involved somebody in something"
ablašt	"I involved somebody in something"
ablašna	"we involved somebody in something"
yibliš	"he involves somebody in something"
tibliš	"she involves somebody in something"
abliš	"I involve somebody in something"
yibilšūn	"they (m) involve somebody in something"
yibilšin	"they (f) involve somebody in something"

Intransitive Verb Type

Active		Passive	
simi'	"he heard"	*smi'*	"he was heard"
sam'at	"she heard"	*sim'at*	"she was heard"
simi't	"I heard"	*smi't*	"I was heard"
simi'na	"we heard"	*smi'na*	"we were heard"
yasma'	"he hears"	*yisma'*	"he is heard"
tasma'	"she hears"	*tisma'*	"she is heard"
asma'	"I hear"	*isma'*	"I am heard"
yasma'ūn	"they (m) hear"	*yisma'ōn*	"they (m) are heard"
yasma'in	"they (f) hear"	*yisma'an*	"they (f) are heard"

A property of this system is that a certain approximation obtains between the Passive and Intransitive patterns in the perfective, reflecting their semantic relationship as both involving a non-active subject. The resemblance is particularly close with the first and second persons, where they are separated only by the presence of one unstressed /*i*/, i.e. /*simi't*/ "I heard", /*smi't*/ "I was heard". In certain marginal types there is identity of form between these two (cf p.49 below).

SHAṬṬ AL-'ARAB

Active(1)		Passive	
nišad	"he asked"	*innišad*	"he was asked"
nišdat	"she asked"	*innišdat*	"she was asked"
nišadt	"I asked"	*innišadt*	"I was asked"
nišadna	"we asked"	*innišadna*	"we were asked"
yinšid	"he asks"	*yinnišid*	"he is asked"
tinšid	("you (m s) ask" ("she asks"	*tinnišid*	("you(m s) are asked" ("she is asked"
anšid	"I ask"	*annišid*	"I am asked"
ynišdūn	"they (m) ask"	*yinnišdūn*	"they (m) are asked"
ynišdan	"they (f) ask"	*yinnišdan*	"they (f) are asked"

As can be seen from the above examples, in the Najdi type, the patterns /*nšidat*/ and /*nišdat*/ have quite different functions: one being active, the other passive. Also, the imperfective patterns /*yaf'il*; *yif'al*/ and /*yif'il*/ mark active, passive and causative. In the extreme Mesopotamian type these internal vowel and syllabication contrasts are collapsed. Certain Mesopotamian perfective active forms such as /*nišdat*, *nišdaw*, *nišdan*/ resemble the corresponding Najdi passive forms. Further, in the imperfective the vowel of the stem is always /*i*/ or /*a*/, depending on certain phonological factors. This means that forms of the type /*yif'al*/ and /*yif'il*/ are both plain active with the vowel alternation being non-functional.

In the Mesopotamian type the passive function is served by the addition of the prefix *in-* to the stem. This prefix /*in-*/ is the mark of the seventh Measure. These "Measures" are forms showing modifications of the basic verb meaning. In all of these the modification is signalled by the addition of some consonant element, or by the lengthening of an existing consonant or vowel. The more common verbal Measures are illustrated below as extant in the Mesopotamian type.(2)

Measure

1 *fi'al yif'il*

nišad	*yinšid*	"to ask"

1 The Intransitive verb follows the same pattern as the Transitive in this system, i.e. *sima'*, *sim'at*, *sima't*.

2 The numbering of these Measures follows the traditional numbering employed in Classical Arabic Grammar. Measure 4 - /*af'al yif'il*/ - does not occur in the variety shown here.

2 *fa''al yfa''il*		
dawwax	*ydawwix*	"to confuse"
3 *fā'al yfā'il*		
ḥārab	*yḥārub*	"to fight"
5 *tfa''al yitfa''al*		
tkaṯṯar	*yitkaṯṯar*	"to increase"
6 *tfā'al yitfā'al*		
tbādal	*yitbādal*	"to exchange"
7 *nfi'al yinfi'il*		
nnišad	*yinnišid*	"to be asked"
8 *fta'al yifti'il*		
ntišal	*yintišil*	"to catch a cold"
9 *f'all yif'all*		
xraff	*yixraff*	"to panic
10 *istaf'al yistaf'il*		
istafham	*yistafhim*	"to enquire"

The meaning of Measure 7 in Classical Arabic is said to have been "reflexive"; however, it has clearly always had passive connotations. In Classical Arabic and modern Najdi speech the internal (vowel marked) passive serves as the basic productive passive form. Measure 7 is restricted to certain roots only, forming specific verbal items with passive or intransitive connotation, such as /*inqalab*/ "to be turned over", /*inkasar*/ "to be broken", /*insaḥab*/ "to retreat", /*inṭalaq*/ "to go out".

In the Mesopotamian varieties, this has become a productive passive form, also having the connotation of "possible" or "-able" in such structures as /*yinšāf*/ "it is visible", /*mā yinšāf*/ "it is invisible", /*yingiri*/ "it is legible". The /*in-*/ prefix is also attached to the other measures giving compound forms of the type /*mā yinḥārab wiyyāh*/ "he cannot be fought with", /*mā yinsōlaf wiyyāh*/ "he cannot be spoken with".

The move from the use of the internal vowel marked transitivity system to the use of the Measure 7 prefix /*in-*/ as the passive marker can be considered as a process of simplification. In the internally marked system the vowelling of all verbal forms except the Transitive Active type has to be stated as phonologically basic for the form. Only in the

Transitive Active form can the vowelling of many forms be stated as derivable according to the rules of verb phonology. Further, it stands out as exceptional in being the only word class in which internal short vowels are grammatically distinctive. In the typical Mesopotamian system the vowelling can, to a great extent, be stated as a part of the phonologipatterning of words in general, and the grammatical marking of the passive is effected by prefixing which is the main verbal marking system. The simplification, therefore, lies in the following factors:

1 Reduction of the features specified as underlying in the phonology, reducing much of the vowel phonology to the level of surface derivation.

2 Reduction of the number of verbal form classes: the original Transitive - Intransitive - Passive - Causative system being reduced to Active - Passive.

3 Analogical levelling of the morphology of the verbal grammar: internal vowel change being eschewed in favour of the more universal consonantal prefixing.

4 Simplification of the number of possible syllabic structures for verbal forms. This factor cuts across the verb/noun word class division. Its result is the elimination of structures of the type CCV(C(V(C))); i.e. those with an initial consonant cluster followed by a stressed short vowel. In the extreme Mesopotamian type this structure occurs only in a very few words, and is regarded as a mark of rural origin. The following list gives examples of the Najdi type contrasted with the extreme Mesopotamian type, i.e. that of the urban and some of the riverine population.

Najdi	Mesopotamian	
nšidat	*nišdat*	"she asked"
nšidaw	*nišdaw*	"they (m) asked"
nšidan	*nišdan*	"they (f) asked"
nšidih	*nišadah*	"he asked him"
rgubah	*rugba*	"neck"
xšibah	*xišbah*	"piece of wood"
wlidi	*waldi*	"my son"
wlidih	*waldah*	"his son"

A considerable number of tribal names of this pattern also occur in Najdi dialects, which of course have no equivalent in the Mesopotamian. Of these may be cited /*'nizah*, *rwugah*, *'bidah*, *ḥṣinah*, *sba'ah*, *xruṣah*/. There is some reason for thinking that structures of this type which distinguish the speech of Najd from other neighbouring areas, i.e. the west (Hijaz) and the north (Syria and Mesopotamia), may have been reinforced as a marker of Arabian identity.

Geographical Distribution of Transitivity Systems

As stated before, the full system outlined above is preserved to a greater or lesser degree in Najdi speech. Between this and the reduced Mesopotamian type there are various intermediary grades. The clinal nature of this contrast operates along a number of different parameters:

1 The use of the passive may be confined to the third person, or to the perfective tense.

2 The use of the passive may be reduced stylistically and become confined only to formal styles, such as narrative and poetry.

3 The passive and intransitive forms may show partial merger, becoming formally indistinguishable in certain persons. Similarly, the intransitive and transitive may merge in the imperfective, both showing the prefix /*yi*-/.

4 The passive, and also the causative, may become lexically reduced, occurring in only a number of lexical items. They then lose their grammatical significance as a form, and become purely somewhat irregular lexical items.

The following remarks on the distribution of these forms are, of necessity, somewhat incomplete, since they cover only the groups for whom material is available. However, they do show a definite correlation between maintenance of the old system and Najdi identity. Further, the material can only be considered as a sample of the whole dialect, showing a leaning towards the use of these forms or a relative reduction of them. The dialects can be grouped in terms of this type of variation into the following types:

Type 1

This is attested for Shammar, Sudair and Midhnab, and largely confirmed by Abboud's and Prochazka's material from Hail and Johnstone's material from 'Anaiza.

In these dialects the internal passive was at least potentially fully productive for all verb Measures of all classes, and the paradigms for these were easily elicited. Sudair also shows a very regular use of the internal passive. Here, however, the vowel of the imperfective prefix is /*i*/, with stems in /*a*/, giving such forms as /*nifham*/ "we understand", /*niṭ'an*/ "we strike" and /*yilbas*/ "he dresses". This means that the active and passive of such verbs are identical in form. These forms are, nevertheless, used with passive function, the passivity being apparent from collocation and context.(1) Such examples as the following illustrate this:

1 Another example of this sort of phonological merger in the speech of 'Aṣīr was given to me by T. Prochazka: /*šifthum ušift*/ "I saw them and was seen". Similarly, I

/halmawḍū' lāzim yibhaṯ/ "this matter must be investigated", */ḥaćyuhun mā yifham abad/* "their talk cannot be understood at all". Here the verbal form */yif'al/* is used with the passive function, while the same form is active in such cases as */yibga/* "he remains", */yiftaḥ/* "he opens", */yinsa/* "he forgets", */tigdar/* "you are able", */nilga/* "we find", */tišrab/* "you drink", */niṭla'/* "we go out", */niḏhar/* "we go out in the evening", */nisma'/* "we hear", */yiṣlaḥ/* "it is right", */yiṭbax/* "he cooks".

Having said that in these dialects the passive is fully productive for all persons, it must be mentioned that by far the most common use is with third persons. The forms for the other persons were readily given by my informants, but occur quite rarely in material as non-elicited forms, except in poetry and set phrases.

The only non-elicited first person passive was in an account of a dream: */šift nafsi agawwad firriyāḏ/* "I saw myself being led to execution in Riyadh", and */ti'iddīt/* "I was offended" (Shammar). Elicited examples included: */mita jībīt/* (1) "when were you born" (Shammar), */abinšad 'ank/* "I will be asked about you" (Midhnab), */iḏā nišidt 'anna/* "if you are asked about us" (Shammar), */ġilibt/* "you were deceived" (Shammar). Non-elicited third person passives were, however, far more frequent. The following are representative examples: */wildat/* "it (f) was born", */ḏbiḥ/* "he was killed", */binyat albeit/* "the tent was built", */wiš yigāl-lu/* "what is it called", */ṣilliḥ/* "it has been repaired", */yūxaḏ/* "it is taken", */mā yilga/* "it is not found", */rubṭat/* "it (f) was tied up", */ḏibḥaw/* "they (m) were killed", */wiźźfat u tirkat/* "it (f) was stopped and deserted", */guwwid/* "he was led to execution" (Shammar), */yibġā-lih/* "it is required for it", */širyat/* "it was bought", */rikkib/* "it was assembled", */xilluṣ/* "it was finished", */suwwiyat/* "it was done", */mā yšāl/* "it cannot be lifted", */mā yidra 'awāgbih/* "its results are not known" (Sudair).

The intransitive and causative conjugations are also fully operative in these dialects. The following examples are not differentiated for tribe or locality, but would seem to be general for this group.(2) The examples are given in the

have heard a Sudairi rendering of the well-known gaṣīda of Sājir al-Rfidi as */niṭ'an u niṭ'an/* "we strike and are struck at". In the 'Anizi dialect of the composer the two forms would be differentiated as */naṭ'an u niṭ'an/*.

1 Contrast 'Anizi (Sba'a) */wēn jābakk ummak/* "where did your mother bear you", where the passive is avoided for the second person.

2 The forms would apply to all dialects with the exception of that of Sudair in the case of the Imperfective Transitive in cases where the vowel of the stem is */a/*.

third person masculine singular. In the intransitive the vowel of the second syllable is */i/* or */u/*, depending on the factors mentioned earlier. The vowel of the first syllable is */i/*, except in the environment of the gutturals or preceding */l/*, */n/* or */r/*, with some exceptions.(1)

Intransitive

ġaluṭ yġaluṭ	"to make a mistake"
nisi yansa	"to forget"
ṭili' yaṭla'	"to come out"
rićib yarćab	"to mount"
ṣidig	"he was truthful"
fihim yafham	"to understand"
širib yašrab	"to drink"
gidir yagdar	"to be able"
libis yalbas	"to get dressed"
ćibir yakbar	"to grow"
nizil yanzal	"to descend"
ti'ib yat'ab	"to tire"
ḥalim yḥalim	"to dream"

Causative

ag'ad yig'id	"to wake"
anbat yinbit	"to make something grow"
adra yidri(2)	"to make someone know"
asga yisgi	"to water"
ablaš yibliš	"to cause someone to be involved"
amda yimdi	"to allow"(3)
axbar yixbir	"to inform"
arćab yirćib	"to cause to mount"
adrak yidrik	"to understand" (Sudair)
aṣbaḥ yiṣbiḥ	"to be in the morning"(4)
abhar yibhir	"to spice"
akram yikrim	"to treat kindly"
abga yibgi	"to make someone remain"
aflaḥ yifliḥ	"to enjoy oneself"
aš'ar yiš'ir	"to make someone feel"
aḏ̣neih tiḏ̣ni	"to bear (a child)" (Shammar)

1 See also JOHNSTONE (1967b), Appendix 1.
2 Occurring in the expression */wiš yidrīk/* "how do you know, what makes you know?".
3 Impersonal verb, occurring in such expressions as */yimdīk/* "can you?", */mā yimdīni/* "I cannot", and */mā amdāni/* "I couldn't".
4 Certain of these forms do not have causative significance; cf p. 50 below.

Type 2

This type comprises the speech of the Sba'a informants interviewed, from whom quite substantial data was obtained. Certain other groups interviewed seemed to have a similar system. However for these slightly less data was available and therefore the classification is less conclusive. These are the other 'Aniza groups, namely 'Amārāt and 'Awāja; also the Ḍhafīr. The system for Type 2 is identical with Type 1, except that the internal passive is confined to the third person except in certain set phrases and in poetry. The following Perfective passives are from the Sba'a unless otherwise marked. Examples are given showing masculine and feminine singular:

ḏbiḥ ḏibḥat	"he/she was killed"
ḏrib ḏirbat	"he/she was beaten"
šrib širbat	"it (m/f) was drunk"
ćtil ćitlat	"he/she was killed"
ġdir ġidrat	"he/she was deceived"
smi' sim'at	"he/she was heard"
ksir kisrat	"it (m/f) was broken"
wćil wićlat	"it (m/f) was eaten"
tirkat	"it (f) was deserted"
šīf šīfat	"he/she was seen"
ḥći 'alēha	"she was spoken about"
rmi rimyat	"he/she was shot"
lźi liźyat	"it (m/f) was found"
bni binyat	"it (m/f) was built"

Imperfect examples were fewer, namely: /*yūxaḏ*/ "it is taken", /*yūkal*/ "it is eaten" (Ḍhafīr), and /*ysamm*/ "he is poisoned"(1)

This slightly reduced system is consistent with the position of the groups mentioned who are emigree Najdi populations living in the Syrian desert, in closer contact with the settled populations of the outer areas.(2)

Type 3

The basic characteristics of this type are that the internal passive is lost except in a very few special usages and in

1 This occurs in the common ritual exchange /*samm!*/ "Call (on God)!", /*'aduwwak ysamm*/ "May your enemy be poisoned", appropriate on offering coffee to a guest.

2 In Landberg's 'Aniza material only two examples of the internal passive occur, namely /*ḏibiḥ*/ "he was killed" (/*ḏibeḥ*/ in his notation) and /*wuṣṣfat*/ "it was described". (1919)p.14-72. Examples of the Intransitive and Causative conjugations are fairly common, such as /*a'raḏ*/(p.14), /*rićib diri diryat*/(p7),/*biźi biźyat*/(p6), /*ćibir*/(p1).

narrative and poetry; also there is partial or total merger of the transitive and intransitive conjugations in the Imperfective. Here we have to consider two subtypes, a Najdi and a Mesopotamian one, based on the morphology of the imperfective causing this merger. However, functionally they are very similar. This type is shown in the speech of the Mesopotamian nomadic groups investigated, namely the Ḥumaid, Rufai', Budūr shepherds and Kawāwila; also the Bani Khālid and the Gulf dialects investigated, namely Kuwait town, Jahra, Zubair and Failika island. On the basis of Johnstone's Gulf material(1) and Meissner's material from Ḥilla, it would seem to be general for the Gulf coast with the exception perhaps of al-Hasa, for which our information is limited, and for large areas of rural southern Mesopotamia.

In this type Transitive and Intransitive are distinguished in the Perfective; however the Intransitive and the passives occurring in the same strong verb classes are identical, resulting in a functional eclipse of the passive as a separate type.(2) Examples:

Transitive (General)

kitab ktibat	"he/she wrote"
kisar ksirat	"he/she broke"
saḥab sḥabat	"he/she pulled"
ništad nšidat	"he/she asked"

Intransitive/Passive

Kuwait:

simi' sim'at	"he/she heard"
širib širbat	"he/she drank"
wiṣil wiṣlat	"he/she arrived"
fihim fihmat	"he/she understood"

Ḥumaid, Rufai':

ričib ričbat	"he/she mounted"
wirid wirdat	"it (m/f) came to water"
libis libsat	"he/she got dressed"
wiṣil wiṣlat	"he/she arrived"
čibir čibrat	"he/she grew up"

1 See particularly 1967b p.41-43.

2 The examples of the passive obtained were the following: Kuwaiti: /*wilid wildat*/ "he/she was born", /*xilig xilgat*/ "he/she was born"; Mesopotamian Kawāwila : /*čitil*/ "he was killed", /*ġidir*/ "he was deceived", /*ruwā-li*/ "there was seen by me (a dream)". /*wilid wildat*/ is marginal, and could be regarded as Intransitive depending on whether or not a form /*wlidat*/ "she bore" exists.

In the Imperfective the Mesopotamian type and the Bani Khālid show the vowel /*i*/ in the prefix in all cases. In the Kuwait type there is dissimilation of stem and prefix vowel, giving two types: /*yif'al*/ and /*yaf'il*/. The vowel of the stem is /*i*/ except where the stem involves one of the gutturals as second or third radical. Compare the following:(1)

Mesopotamian and Bani Khālid	Kuwait	
yinšid	*yanšid*	"he asks
yiksir	*yaksir*	"he breaks"
yidri	*yadri*	"he knows"
yibči	*yabči*	"he cries"
yirbuṭ	*yarbuṭ*	"he ties up"
yiṭbax	*yiṭbax*	"he cooks"
yiftaḥ	*yiftaḥ*	"he opens"
yiṭla'	*yiṭla'*	"he comes out"
yirja'	*yirja'*	"he returns"

A slightly more reduced, but related, system was recorded for the Kawāwila or gypsies of Iraq. This showed complete merger of transitive and intransitive in the perfective, giving /*sima' sma'at*/ "he/she heard", /*širab šrubat*/ "he/she drank", etc. for the intransitive items. This would seem to be also true of the Gulf dialects for some speakers, and a situation of instability exists as regards these forms.(2)

The position of the causative was not plain for the dialects in this system. The speech of the Ḥumaid and Rufai' showed the item /*amraḥ yimriḥ*/ "to rest in the evening". Meissner's material also shows some examples.

The speech of the Kawāwila showed /*aġma 'al-* / "to faint", /*agbal*/ "he approached", /*adbar*/ "he went" and /*aṣlaḥ*/ "he was encouraged". In the Mesopotamian type the Causative could only be distinguished in the Perfective, since in the Imperfective the prefix distinction /*ya-*, *yi-*/ is no longer present, all the verbs showing /*yi-*/.

In the Gulf dialects, since the vowel /*a*/ is preserved for prefixes of the Imperfective, a number of examples of the Causative conjugation are found.(3)

Examples: /*axbar yixbir*/ "to inform", /*arsal yirsil*/ "to send", /*aṣbaḥ yiṣbiḥ*/ "to be in the morning", /*amsa yimsi*/ "to spend the night", /*axla yixli*/ "to destroy".

1 A certain amount of variation occurs with a number of items, particularly /*yig'ad yag'id*/ "he sits", /*yiṭbax yaṭbux*/ "he cooks", /*yinzal yanzil*/ "he descends".
2 JOHNSTONE (1967b), p.42.
3 Ibid., p.73, 79.

Type 4

This type is attested for the Shaṭṭ al-'Arab, southern Khuzistan and the larger settlements and towns of southern Iraq. This is basically the type represented by standard Baghdad colloquial, although differing from it in terms of features not connected with the transitivity systems. In this system, as shown above, distinctions of transitivity are dealt with within the verbal Measures system, using consonantal morphology. The causative is expressed by Measure II using gemination of the medial radical. The distinction of transitive and intransitive is not morphologically marked in the verb, all verbs being of the pattern /fi'al yif'il/ or /yif'al/.(1) Verbs which in the other dialect types have the form /af'al yif'il/ are either not extant or use the forms /fi'al yif'al/ or the Measure II, /fa''al yfa''il/. Examples:

Najdi	Mesopotamian	
akram	karram	"he treated kindly"
ablaš	ballaš	"to involve"
arkab	rakkab	"to cause to mount"(2)
ag'ad	ga''ad	"to waken"
axbar	xabbar	"to inform"
asga	siga	"to water"

Summary

The above shows a definite correlation between geographical and ethnic closeness with the populations of central Arabia, and preservation of the system of transitivity as marked by internal vocalisation. Within Mesopotamia nomadic populations, or those more recently sedentarised such as the Kawāwila and bādiya population, show a higher degree of conservatism in this respect. The dialects of the Gulf area are in general closer than those of Mesopotamia to the Najd.(3)

1 In some marginal types, verbs of the form /fa'al/ are encountered as in Types 1-3, the vowel being determined by phonological factors; see JOHNSTONE (1967b) p.257, INGHAM (1973) p.540.
2 In the Najdi type /rakkab/ means "to mount or erect" a thing on another, ie "to fix, build". In the Mesopotamian type it has both the constructional and the equestrian meaning of "mount".
3 However, as Johnstone mentions, the dialect of the Shi'a population of Bahrain shows a similarity to the Mesopotamian type in a number of respects (1967b, p.92-94). The dialect of Bahrain has no */af'al yif'il/* form and shows */yif'il/* for */yaf'il/* in some varieties.

TABLE 1: INTERNAL VOWEL MORPHOLOGY OF THE VERB AND POPULATION GROUPS

	Najd settled population & Shammar bedouin	Sba'a & Ḍhafīr	Gulf States	Euphrates bedouin & shepherds	Mesop. Kawāwila	Mesop. bādiya	Mesop. ḥaḍhar
Internal Passive 1st & 2nd persons *d̲biḥt*, *d̲biḥna* etc.	✓	o	o	o	o	o	o
Internal Passive 3rd person *d̲biḥ*, *d̲ibḥat* etc.	✓	✓	sporadically	?	sporadically	o	o
Intransitive Perfective *simi'*, *sim'at* or *sam'at*	✓	✓	✓	✓	o	o	o
Causative Imperfective *yismi'*, *tismi'* etc.	✓	✓	✓	o	o	o	o
Causative Perfective *asma'*, *asmi'at* etc.	✓	✓	✓	✓	✓	✓	o
Transitive of the form *fi'al*, *f'ilat*	✓	✓	✓	✓	✓	✓	o
Transitive of the form *fi'al*, *fi'lat*	o	o	o	o	o	✓	✓

Table 1 shows the distribution of the different morphological forms for the main population groupings. The Mesopotamian bādiya and ḥaḍhar groups show functionally the same system, having only one verb class. However, the bādiya population in some cases show the pattern */fi'al f'ilat/* as the form of the verb corresponding to the Najdi type which has */fi'al f'ilat/* as the major type.

The Noun Indefinite Marker

In Classical Arabic a system of indefinite marking existed associated also with the case system. Indefinite nouns, adjectives, and particles took the endings *-un* (nominative), *-an* (accusative), *-in* (genitive). These collectively were referred to as *tanwīn*(adding the letter *nūn* "n"). The definite noun added the article *al-* and dropped the *n* of the ending. This produces the following paradigm:

nom.	*kitābun*		*alkitābu*	
acc.	*kitāban*	"a book"	*alkitāba*	"the book"
gen.	*kitābin*		*alkitābi*	

In pausal position the case endings *-un*, *-an*, *-in*, or *-u*, *-a*, *-i* were freely elidible giving *kitāb* and *alkitāb*. In the modern dialects the case distinctions have been completely lost. The distinction between definite and indefinite is, however, retained. In the majority of dialects outside the Arabian Peninsula the distinction is born purely by the presence or absence of the definite article *al-*, the indefinite being formally "unmarked". In some areas of central Arabia however a modified form of indefinite marking is retained. In this system one suffix *-in*(1) remains to mark the indefinite with, however, no distinction of case. The occurrence of this marker is governed by syntactic, grammatical and stylistic factors and not all nouns lacking the definite article *al-* show the suffix *-in*. Therefore the present system may be represented as:

definite:	*alkitāb*	"the book"
indefinite:	*kitābin* or *kitāb*	"a book"

The factors governing the occurrence of this marker are not altogether clear. However it is plain that certain syntactic structures favour its occurrence without regard to semantic considerations of "definiteness" and "indefiniteness" in any general sense. In other cases also the marker has an adverbial function reminiscent of the accusative ending *-an* in Classical Arabic. The only case in which it may be that the

1 Phonetically */-in/*, */-un/* or */-$^{\partial}$n/* depending on the preceding consonant. See also p.xvii.

occurrence of the marker signals some measure of "indefiniteness" or "vagueness" in a semantic sense is where a noun occurs as the sole constituent of a nominal phrase. In this case it seems that the occurrence of *-in* signals something of the semantic value of "a certain...", "a particular...", i.e. one single but undefined member of a class, whereas the absence of the marker means purely "a member of the class in general", as in the following two sentences:

(a) *nidawwir sāyig*
"we are looking for a driver

(b) *ligēna sāygin ... wlidin ḥarbi*
"we found a driver ... a Ḥarbi boy"

In the example (b) a particular member of the class of "drivers" is referred to known to the speaker, but unknown to the addressee. In the first sentence the class of "drivers" in general is referred to; any driver will be sufficient and no specifications are made. It must be said however that it is difficult to establish this since numerous exceptions occur and perhaps even more importantly because the occurrence of *-in* seems to be a definite marker of Najd/bedouin identity and is thus socio-symbolic. In certain contexts the occurrence of *-in* may therefore be increased in order to emphasise this social identity. For the moment, if we disregard semantic and socio-symbolic factors, syntactic structures favouring the ending *-in* are the following:(1)

1 Nouns followed by a qualifying element which may be an adjective, a verb phrase, or a sequence of preposition and pronoun suffix. Examples:

mā yḥāćīna alla bnafsin šēn
"he only talks to us with an unpleasant expression"

rūtinin m'ayyan
"a definite routine"

maṭ'amin t̠āni
"another restaurant"

nōbtin t̠ānya
"another time"

ma'raktin ṭuwila
"a long battle"

'ala mōgfin t̠ābit
"in a firm position"

rifīźin-li
"a friend of mine"

jiz'in minh
"a part of it"

fōḏ̣an mā-lih ṭaraf
"chaos unlimited"

1 CANTINEAU (1937) p.204-5, gives almost the same environments, but differently grouped. Compare also BLANC (1970) p.143 *[32]*.

azmitin mā lih ṭaraf
"an extreme crisis"
kalmitin gālōhāli
"a word which they had said to me"
mištāgin-lik
"anxious (to see) you"
mā fīh ḥadin jayyin
"there is no one coming"
haguwtin-li
"a thought of mine" (Sudair)
bīrin bu-ma
"a well with water in it" (Shammar)
gahawtin abahayyilha
"some coffee which I want to mix cardoman with"('Awāja)

2 Verbal participles occurring with verbal function in the sentence and not followed by an object suffix. Here the ending *-in* may have the function of separating verbal from non-verbal use of the participle. In particular where the participle is followed by the sequences */li/* "to me", */lak/* "to you", */lih/* "to him", etc. the occurrence of the marker is obligatory. Examples:

min jāyibin hu
"whom has he brought"
whu 'ārifin inn-
"and he knew that ..."
jīt mbaććirin
"I came early"
māhu gāṣdin iḥtiyāl
"he did not intend any deception"
uhu gāylin-lik...
"and he had said to you ..."
hāḏi mnawwirtin albalad killih
"this has lit up the whole city"
hu āxḏin ṭurīgathum
"he had adopted their ways"

3 Certain adverbial expressions show the ending *-in* reflecting the classical use of *-an* for this purpose:

ġaṣbin
"by force, of necessity"
hagwitin
"it seems"
gōltin
"it was said, as you would say"
'ugbin
"afterwards"
ġazwin
"on a raid"
ḥirwitin
"approximately"
dōrin
"once upon a time"

nōbtin
"one time" (Shammar)
snitin min hā-ssnīn
"one of these years" (Muṭair)

Certain expressions are more commonly heard with the ending *-an*, which probably reflects borrowing from classical, i.e. */tagrīban/* "approximately", */abdan/* "at all",(1) */kullan/* "in toto",(2) */jimī'an/* "all together".

It can be seen from the above that in environment 1 the retention of -in can be said to have phonological causes, i.e. it may have the function of effecting a juncture between a noun and a following qualifying element. In 2 and 3 however it has specific grammatical function as the marker of verbal function in the participle in 2 and as the marker of adverbial function in 3.

Occurrence of the marker *-in* in a similar way to that noted above was recorded for the dialect of Qaṣīm, Sudair, Shammar, 'Aniza and Ḍhafīr. In the speech of the Euphrates bedouin it occurred in poetry and was recognised as a syntactic possibility. It occurred less however than in the more central Najdi dialects, but this may be a reflection of the more limited material. Examples include:

'isbin lā yṭūl
"grass which will not last" (Text 7)
lu šāwrin bah čīs
"he has a tobacco box with a pouch"
čabdin tyabbisah u čabdin tibillah
"you dry one heart (lit.liver) and moisten another" (Text 9)

In the Gulf dialects it occurs only rarely and that mostly in set expressions. It was not recorded at all for the non-bedouin dialects of Mesopotamia and in fact in these dialects a preposed indefinite marker */farid/* or */fad/* has been evolved. The use of */fad/* is equally a marker of Mesopotamian identity and occurs in all varieties examined.

The Treatment of Final Clusters

General

A phonological feature of high incidence which separates Mesopotamian and Nadji varieties is the treatment of underlying consonant clusters in word and stem final position. In brief the difference is that in the Mesopotamian type an anaptyctic vowel is introduced between the two consonants when in pause or preceding a consonant while in the Najdi type this happens in a more restricted set of cases. Taking

1 But also */abad/* without nunation, and */labdin/*"not at all".
2 The dialect form */killin/* would mean "each one".

a fairly generally applicable example the contrast is as follows:

	Mesopotamian	Najdi	
1	*šifit*	*šift*	"I saw"
2	*šifitha*	*šiftaha*	"I saw her"
3	*šiftah*	*šiftih*	"I saw him"

In forms 1 and 2 the Mesopotamian variety shows a vowel /*i*/ between the two elements of the final cluster /*-ft*/. In form 3 this is not present as the cluster is followed by the initial vocalic suffix /*-ah*/. In the Najdi variety no such anaptyctic occurs although in form 2 /*siftaha*/ a different type of anaptyctic occurs between the stem /*sift-*/ and the suffix /*-ha*/ preventing the junction of three consonants, which is non-permissible in certain environments.

These contrasts occur with (a) nominals of the form CaCC or CiCC /*galb*/ "heart", /*bišt*/ "cloak"; verbal forms with the suffix /*-t*/, /*riḥt*/ "I, you m.s. went"; and (c) a small number of imperatives of final weak verbs such as /*imš*/ "walk*!*", /*iḥć*/ or /*iḥč*/ "talk*!*".(1) In these three cases the underlying form can be regarded as identical so that the contrast is one of surface derivational phonology as revealed by the total scatter of forms such as those shown above. There are also certain other structures involving the suffixes /*-k*/ and /*-ć*/ where some Najdi varieties show a final cluster, i.e. /*anšiḍk*/ "I ask you m.s.", /*anšidć*/ "I ask you f.s.".(2) These forms do not have corresponding underlying structures in the Mesopotamian type where the suffixes are /*-ak*/ and /*-ič*/ giving /*anišdak*/, /*anišdič*/. However the existence of these various final cluster forms in the Najdi varieties taken as a whole constitutes a defining characteristic in contrast to the Mesopotamian type.

The contrast between the two varieties is of a clinal nature rather than being a straightforward contrast between the presence and absence of final clusters. This clinality is due to the following factors:

1 An anaptyctic vowel of this type does occur in the Najdi varieties associated with certain consonant cluster types. Particularly relevant to this point are those anaptyctics associated with voiced plosives and the liquid group *l*, *n*, *r*, *ġ*, *m*.

1 This contrast is not relevant to all Mesopotamian dialects since in some a form with a final vowel occurs for these imperatives, i.e. /*imši*/, /*iḥči*/.

2 See page 96-7.

2 In the Mesopotamian variety where the anaptyctic occurs, it is, at least in the extreme type, regarded as a full vowel from the point of view of stress placement and syllabication. In the Najdi varieties however it does not count as a full vowel for stress placement.

3 In general the nature of the transition from consonant to consonant in certain consonant sequences differs in the Najdi and Mesopotamian types. Particularly with voiced consonants a definite vocalic transition of a shewa type is heard in the Central Najdi varieties which is absent in the Mesopotamian type, giving contrasts of the type:

Mesopotamian	Najdi	
dgārabna	*tigārabəna*	"we became relatives"
hubaṭna	*hubaṭəna*	"we went down"
baṭni	*baṭəni*	"my stomach"

This is clearly reflected in the transcriptions of earlier linguists. It seems that speakers of these varieties do not themselves perceive this as a vowel, but regard it as a feature of the release of the consonant. The existence of these highly non-structural vocalic features in the variety makes the status of the final cluster anaptyctics of less structural importance than in the Mesopotamian type.

This vocalic transition is heard with sequences of voiced consonants and also with the /ṭ/ particularly where the first consonant is a plosive or the second is /r/. The inclusion of /ṭ/ among this group of otherwise voiced consonants is interesting. Instrumental investigation(1) has shown that the segment of voicelessness in /ṭ/ is shorter than for the other voiceless plosives and it may be that in many environments it is in fact voiced. In these dialects the voicelessness feature is not essential since it contrasts with /ṣ/ and /ḏ/ only, not /ṣ/ and /ḍ/ as in the dialects of the West. It is also relevant that the Arab phoneticians classed /ṭ/ as /majhūr/ "loud, sonorant" a class which otherwise includes voiced consonants.(2) Examples are given below from the speech of various Najdi groups. The 'Utaiba, Qaṭari and Dawāsir examples are from Hess and Johnstone retranscribed into my own notation.

'UTAIBA: /*'aṭəni*/ "give me", /*wizərih*/ "his loincloth", /*mišibərih*/ "his staff"; QAṬARI: /*'awwadəna*/ "we returned"; DAWĀSIR: /*bakəratna*/ "our camel", /*gidərin*/ "a pot", /*igṣarəna*/ "our neighbour"; SHAMMAR: /*rijəlu*/ "his leg", /*faxəḏu*/ "his thigh", /*naṭəla'*/ "we come out", /*mintaṯərih*/ "broken f.", /*baṭəni*/ "my stomach", /*sumaṭəri*/ "perfume from

1 MARÇAIS (1948), p.21-6.
2 SA'RĀN (1951), p.218-30.

Sumatra", /*wajᵊdi*/ "my heart", /*aṣġarᵊham*/ "the smallest of them"; ḤUMAID: /*xēzᵊrānih*/ "staff, stick", /*igᵊḏub*/ "hold!"; RUFAI': /*tigārabᵊna*/ "we became relatives", /*nijərin*/ "coffee pot"; MUṬAIR: /*ḥajᵊra*/ "room", /*zuġᵊba*/ "slut"; ḤARB: /*hubaṭᵊna*/ "we came down"; SBA'A: /*axaḏᵊna*/ "we took"; ḌHAFĪR: /*nišadᵊni*/ "he asked me", /*'išᵊb*/ "grass".

Bearing in mind the occurrence of the above type of vocalic transition in the Najdi dialects we can now examine the stem final clusters in which differences of syllabication occur. In terms of their general phonological behaviour these fall into two classes: (1) those involving a liquid as the second element; (2) other types. Type 1 differs in terms of stress assignment, while type 2 involves different syllabic structures in the majority of cases.

1 Clusters involving nominals of the structure CaCC or CiCC in which the first element of the cluster is not one of the guttural group *h*, *ḥ*, *x*, *ġ*, *'*, and in which the second element is one of the liquids *m*, *l*, *r*, *n*, *w* and *y* show an anaptyctic *i* or *u* in all dialects. There are a number of exceptions with *m* which do not show the anaptyctic. Examples:

SBA'A: /*źidir*/ "pot", /*ḥadir*/ "under", /*sagur*/ "hawk", /*fikir*/ "thought", /*sitir*/ "curtain", /*ṣabur*/ "patience", /*ḥisin*/ "beauty", /*ṭiliy*/ "lamb", /*ṭagum*/ "set", /*xaṣum*/ "enemy", /*ragum*/ "number"; ḤUMAID: /*zamur*/ "rifle hammer", /*zamil*/ "camels", /*ačil*/ "food", /*ḥabil*/ "rope"; SHAMMAR: /*badir*/ "full moon", /*matin*/ "back", /*baṭin*/ "stomach", /*ġuṣin*/ "branch", /*baduw*/ "bedouins", /*ġazuw*/ "raiding party", /*giruw*/ "girl", /*ḥazim*/ "hill", /*rijim*/ "cairn of stones", /*xaṣum*/ "enemy", /*wagul*/ "dried yoghurt cakes"; 'AWĀZIM: /*iṯil*/ "Ithil, a plant", /*wabil*/ "Wabl, a plant", /*ḥijil*/ "anklet", /*hijil*/ "young camel", /*'ijil*/ "young camel", /*'adil*/ "straight"; RWALA(1): /*iḏin*/ "ear", /*jifin*/ "eyelid", /*ifim*/ "mouth"; ḤARB: /*gabil*/ "before"; MESOPOTAMIAN: /*ṣuġur*/ "smallness", /*kubur*/ "size", /*šibir*/ "a span", /*xamur*/ "wine", /*xuṣur*/ "blood money", /*šuġul*/ "work", /*miṯil*/ "like", /*šibil*/ "lion cub", /*haḏum*/ "digestion", /*xaṣum*/ "enemy", /*wazin*/ "weight", /*dihin*/ "oil", /*gabul*/ "before".

With a following initial vowel suffix or before a vocalic initial word, both types have elision of the anaptyctic. However in the Najdi type, as a number of these forms contain combinations of voiced consonants, the vocalic transition is often heard. This is absent in the Mesopotamian type, giving contrasting sets of the type:

1 CANTINEAU (1937), retranscribed into the present notation system, p.216-7.

Mesopotamian	Najdi	
miṯil	*miṯil*	"like"
miṯli	*miṯ*^{ə}*li*	"like me"

With a following consonantal suffix both types in general retain the anaptyctic vowel. However while in the Mesopotamian type the vowel counts as a full vowel for stress assignment, in the Najdi type it is disregarded for this purpose giving contrasting sets of the following type:

Mesopotamian	Najdi	
miṯílhum	*míṯilhum*	"like them"
wazínha	*wázinha*	"its weight"
gabúlha	*gábulha*	"before it f."

In some cases also in the Najdi type these forms act like the non-anaptyctic forms in this structure giving forms of the type: *miṯl*^{ə}*hum*, *miṯ*^{ə}*l*^{ə}*hum*.

With the final *y* and *w* especially Najdi dialects show the non-anaptyctic forms occasionally:

ġazw^{ə}*na*	"our raiding party"
badw^{ə}*na*	"our bedouins"
ḥaćy^{ə}*kum*	"your talk"

2 Other cluster types. It is with clusters not involving combinations of the type mentioned under 1 above that a clear contrast is seen between the Najdi and Mesopotamian types. In the Najdi type as a rule no anaptyctic occurs although there are cases where a sporadic vocalic transition occurs of the type described above. In the Mesopotamian type, however, the anaptyctic *i* or *u* always occurs. Examples:

MUṬAIR: /*'išb 'iš*^{ə}*b*/ "grass", /*wagt*/ "time", /*zibd*/ "cream", /*ġand*/ "lump sugar", /*barg*/ "lightning", /*libs*/ "clothing", /*najd*/ "Najd", /*šams*/ "sun"; ḤARB: /*ig*^{ə}*ṭ*/ "dried yoghurt cakes", /*galb*/ "heart", /*bišt*/ "cloak"; AHL AL-SHIMĀL:[1] /*galb*/ "heart", /*'abd*/ "slave", /*šift*/ "I saw"; ḤUMAID: /*xurb*/ "knot of the tent rope", /*ḥarb*/ "war", /*rimḏ rim*^{ə}*ḏ*/ "Rimth, a type of desert plant", /*šams šamis*/ "sun"; 'AWĀZIM: /*ṣid*^{ə}*g*/ "truth", /*ćiḏb*/ "lying", /*ćalb*/ "dog", /*ćabd*/ "liver", /*katf*/ "shoulder", /*'ijizt*/ "I became tired", /*'iš*^{ə}*g*/ "love", /*darb*/ "path", /*ḥad*^{ə}*b*/ "camel hump", /*ams*/ "yesterday", /*ḥabs*/ "prison"; SHAMMAR: /*wagt*/ "time", /*'aṭ*^{ə}*š*/ "thirst", /*tifaṭṭant*/ "I remembered", /*riḥt*/ "I went", /*širibt*/ "I drank", /*rimṯ*/ "Rimth, type of desert grass" (compare Ḥumaid /*rimḏ*/); MESOPOTAMIAN: /*'išib*/ "grass", /*wakit*/ "time", /*zibid*/ "cream", /*ġanid*/ "lump

1 See below Text 9.

sugar", */barug, baruġ/* "lightning", */libis/* "clothing", */šamis/* "sun", */galub/* "heart", */bišit/* "cloak", */'abid/* "slave", */šifit/* "I saw", */ḥarub/* "war", */sidig, sidij/* "truth", */čiḏib/* "lying", */čalib/* "dog", etc.

With the vocalic beginning suffixes as with type 2 above, both varieties show elision of the anaptyctic giving forms such as */'abdi/* "my slave", */bištik, bištak/* "your cloak", */darbuh, darbah, darbih/* "his road". With the consonantal beginning suffixes in the Mesopotamian variety the anaptyctic is maintained. As with type 1, it counts for stress in the extreme Mesopotamian type. In the nomad-influenced type it can in some cases be disregarded for stress. This gives variants of the type: */wákitna, wakítna/* "our time", */šífitha, šifítha/* "I saw her", */gálubha, galúbha/* "her heart". In the Najdi type there are two possible structures, one with a further anaptyctic separating the stem and the suffix, one with a tri-consonantal cluster. Here it seems that the speech of the north of Najd and the Syrian desert favoured the introduction of this second anaptyctic while the southern area, i.e. Muṭair, 'Awāzim, Rashāyida and Sudair showed a heavier incidence of the triconsonantal cluster type. Examples:

'AWĀZIM: */rimšha/* "her eyelash", */milkhum/* "their property", */šifthum/* "I saw them", */istašartni/* "you asked my advice"; MUṬAIR: */galbaha/* "her heart", */šuftahum/* "I saw them"; 'AWĀJA: */abhartaha/* "I have put spice in it", */kitabtaha/* "I wrote it"; SUDAIR: */nuṭgaha/* "its f. pronunciation", */darsina/* "our studies", */wagtukum/* "your m.p. time", */nafsaha/* "her self", */harjhum/* "their talk"; AHL AL-SHIMĀL: */šiftakan/* "I saw you f. pl."; KUWAIT: */galbha/* "her heart", */šifthum/* "I saw them".

Summary

The different treatment of stem final clusters and the associated function of stem and affix is one of the clearest, most generally recognised variables separating the speech of Mesopotamian and Najdi populations. Najdi speakers, when presented with forms with the anaptyctic, usually recognised them as Iraqi, while Iraq bedouins regarded them as a Mi'dān characteristic. Iraqis usually regarded the non-anaptyctic form as "Kuwaiti" or "bedouin". The vocalic transition between stem and affix was, however, not widely perceived as a dialect marker and informants felt that the difference between such forms as */bētha/* and */bētaha/* was unimportant and non-significant. The only exception to this was that certain informants involved in local folk culture and oral poetry in Kuwait were aware that the forms such as */bētaha/* were characteristic of certain important local bedouin tribes, namely Shammar, Ḍhafīr and 'Aniza.

Forms with the anaptyctic of the type */gilit/* "I said" were used by all Mesopotamian groups including the nomadic shepherd tribes of the Euphrates and southern desert, but excluding the Euphrates bedouin groups Rufai', Ḥumaid and Ahl al-Shimāl. These last did show some sporadic occurrences of it in my material, which may be the result of assimilation to a Mesopotamian type. In terms of their general characteristics, however, they were clearly distinguished from them, showing in addition the highly idiosyncratic Northern Najdi features mentioned in Ch.4.

In the speech of the population of the Najd itself, in general no examples of anaptyxis with type 3 clusters were found except that some Shammar informants gave sporadic examples of it in interrogatives */šifit?/* "did you see?", */inbuṣaṭit?/* "did you enjoy yourself?". On this point my material is inconclusive.

4 Non-reductional changes in the North Najdi dialects

As was mentioned in Chapter 1, in the dialects of the North Najdi type, exemplified particularly by the speech of the Jabal Shammar and the Shammar bedouin of the Syrian desert and the Jazīra, the process of linguistic change has produced a somewhat idiosyncratic(1) morphological and phonological system. The term idiosyncratic is used here to denote that there are more features distinguishing these from the various neighbouring dialects than there are distinguishing neighbouring dialects from each other. These features are non-reductional in that they do not constitute mergers of distinct items but changes in the form of particular items. In some cases they result rather in an increase in complexity. Further, they can in most cases be characterised as analogical in nature, i.e. resulting from structural pressure within the language and in no sense due to extralinguistic factors of the type suggested for the reductional changes described in Chapter 3. The core dialect of the group is the speech of the Shammar nomads whose dīra extended traditionally north from the Jabal Shammar across the Nafūd and along south of the Darb Zubaida, reaching the Euphrates between Najaf and Samāwa. North of this was the area of 'Aniza but both met in the Ḥajara, which they disputed. To the south they extended to the area of their cousins, the Ḍhafīr, with whom they were intermingled with no definite boundary, roughly along the line from Samāwa to Līna.(2)

1 CANTINEAU (1937) also remarks on the idiosyncratic type of the Shammari dialect when compared with 'Aniza type, p.230 and 234;

2 For details of the Shammar tribal area and their neighbours, see PHILBY (1922) Ch.VI p.248; MUSIL (1928b) p.32-33; LORIMER (1908) "Shammar" (Southern) p.1749; GLUBB (1960) passim. DOUGHTY (1964) p.329 also mentions the Shammar colony of Taima and refers explicitly to their dialect: "their fathers came to settle here, by their saying, not above two hundred years past... Theirs is

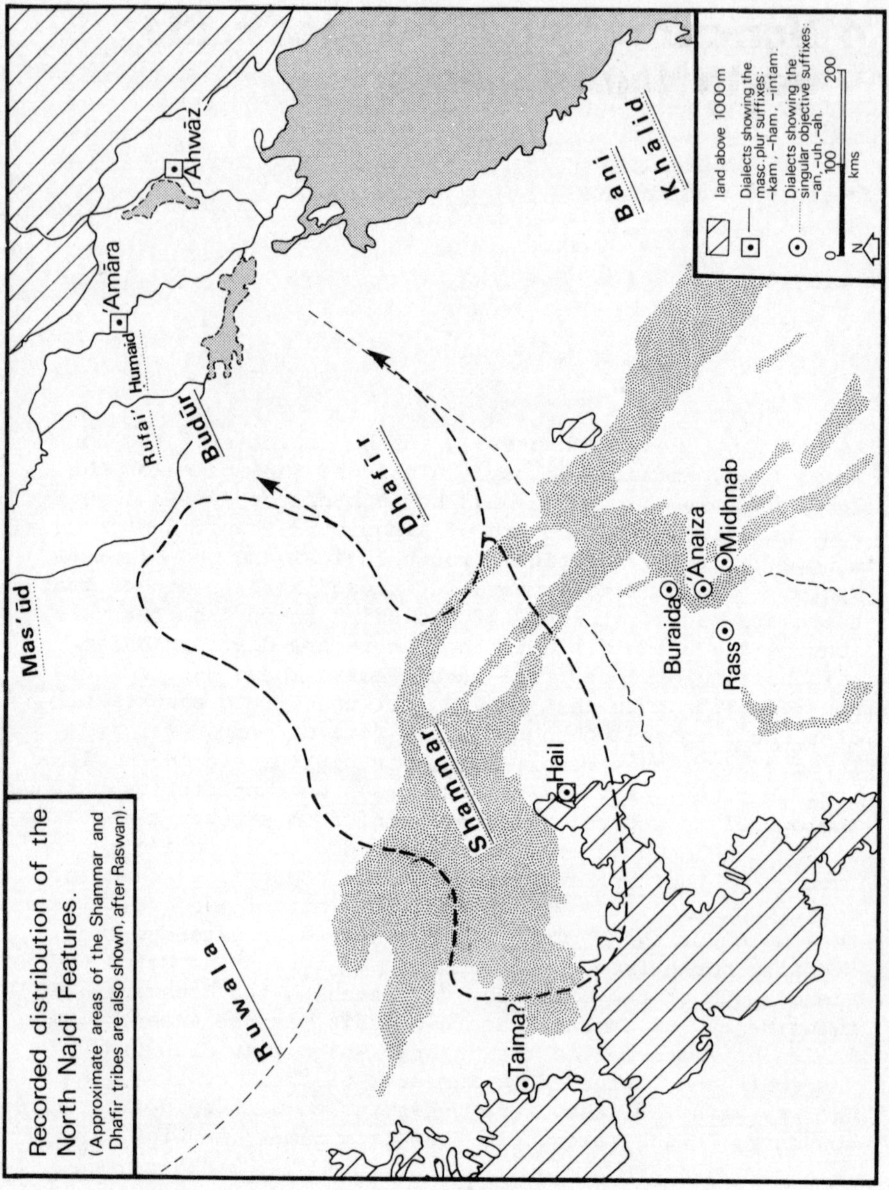

MAP 4: RECORDED DISTRIBUTION OF NORTH NAJDI FEATURES

This group were known as the Najd Shammar and owed a vague suzerainty to the Rashīd dynasty of Hail, themselves of the Shammar. Another group, the Shammar Jarba or Shammar of the Jazīra, are split off from this group and occupy the northern Jazīra between the Euphrates and Tigris. From the point of view of dialect there seems to be little difference between these two groups(1) and I will concentrate here on the Najd Shammar from whom I have first-hand material. Fringe dialects showing only some features of this type are, to the south, the dialect of the settled population of Qaṣīm, the Quṣmān; to the east the dialects of the Ḍhafīr and Bani Khālid; and to the north the dialects of the Euphrates bedouin Ḥumaid, Rufai' and Ahl al-Shimāl.

The Bani Khālid are a tribe al-Hasa of whom large sections are now found in the area of Kuwait. The previous ruling dynasty of Kuwait, the Āl-'Arai'ir,(2) were from the Bani Khālid. As a tribe of al-Hasa the north Arabian dialect type may seem at first difficult to explain. However, a number of links exist between them and the more northerly groups. A clan of the Bani Khālid, the Āl Kathīr, is mentioned by Lorimer (1908, p.1014) as migrating with the Ḍhafīr. 'Azzāwi (1956, III-IV, p.76) also mentions that the Ajwad group of the Muntafiq were once ruled by the Āl Ḥumaid of the Bani Khālid. However none of the sources mention whether the latter have any connection with the present Āl Ḥumaid of the Euphrates. A further Bani Khālid tribe was investigated by Cantineau in the Syrian desert also showing the North Najdi features mentioned here (1936, p.232). These he regards as identical with the eastern Bani Khālid (1936, p.11). Unfortunately, the sum of his material and mine are not sufficient to demonstrate this. None of the sources is very illuminating on the present position of the Bani Khālid or their origins; however the connection of the Āl-Kathīr section to the Ḍhafīr may explain to some extent the North Najdi dialect of my informants in the Kuwait area. These various links between the Bani Khālid with the Ḍhafīr on the one hand and the Muntafiq on the other make it possible to surmise that, in their original position occupying al-Hasa and stretching north to the Iraq borders, they formed part of a general North Najdi block (see Map 5). They were then cut off from them as a relic area in al-Hasa after the westward drive of the Muṭair which separated them. The Muṭair defeated them in the 'Arma plateau in 1823 with the help of the 'Ajmān.(3)

even now in another dîra, the speech of Shammar."

1 But see also MONTAGNE's (1935) remarks on the assimilation of the speech of Shammar to the Iraqi type, p.37.

2 See Text 9.

3 PHILBY (1955), p.156.

In dress also the nomadic Bani Khālid informants resembled the northern tribes wearing *ghutra* and *'agāl* and having short groomed beards in contrast to the Ḥarb and Muṭair of the area who very often have no *'agāl* and wear long untrimmed beards. Other fringe dialects are the Syrian desert nomads mentioned by Cantineau, i.e. the 'Umūr, Ṣlūṭ, Sardiyya, Sirhān, western Bani Khālid and Bani Ṣakhar. These are outside our area but represent a parallel type. One particular feature, feature 4, has an even more extensive distribution and is found in the dialect of al-Jauf, in the speech of the Ruwala, a branch of 'Aniza in the Syrian desert, and also across the Euphrates in the areas of Kūt, 'Amāra and Ahwaz.

The North Najdi features are described below giving the geographical distribution of each as far as possible in order of greatest generality.

1 The form of the third masculine singular object suffix has an inherent bilabial feature and is basically *-u(h)* with positional variants */-u/* or */-uh/* postconsonantally, */-w/* after */a/* and */-h/* after other vowels. The form in the rest of the area is */-ih/* in Central Najd and */-ah/* in the Gulf area and Mesopotamia. A complication of our model is that the form */-u/* is general to the whole of the area to the west, i.e. Hijaz and the dialects of Syria, Lebanon, Palestine and Jordan. However in these the post-vocalic form */-w/* does not occur so that the differentiation is maintained at least for the core type, while features 2 and 3, which also occur in the Syrian desert dialects, separate them from the above western sedentary dialects. Contrasting types are shown below from the North Najdi and more general types:

North Najdi	Other Areas	
bētu(h)	*bētah, bētih*	"his house"
šāfu(h)	*šāfah, šāfih*	"he saw him"
bu(h)	*bih, bīh*	"in it"
šifnāw	*šifnā(h)*	"we saw him"
wiyyāw	*wiyyā(h)*	"with him"
rumāw	*rumā(h)*	"he shot it (m)"
xadāw	*xadā(h)*	"he took it (m)"
jāw	*jā(h)*	"he came to him"
māw	*mā(h)*	"its water"(1)

Following other vowels the North Najdi and other types agree showing */-h/* and lengthening of the preceding vowel as in */'alē(h)/* "on it", */ligō(h)/* "they (m) found him", */šūfū(h)/* "look (m.pl.) at it (m)", */šūfī(h)/* "look (f.s.) at it (m)",

1 In many dialects the basic form of this item is */māy/* "yielding" */māyah/* as in the Mesopotamian type.

/šūfī(h)/ "look (f.s.) at it (m), */yḥāčī(h)/* "he speaks to him".

The core dialect, that of Shammar, shows both */-uh/* and */-w/* variants as also do the dialects of the Ḍhafīr and of Qaṣīm. My material from the Euphrates bedouin and Ahl al-Shimāl shows a mixed type with */-uh/* postconsonantally and */-h/* postvocalically, i.e. */ismu/* "his name", */'indu/* "he has", but */sammāh/* "he called him", */anṭāh/* "he gave him". Cantineau (1936, p.104) gives similar mixed systems for the 'Umūr, Ṣlūṭ and Sirḥān. My material for the Bani Khālid does not show examples of this suffix in post-vocalic position.

2 The form of the third feminine singular suffix is */-a(h)/* with the positional variant */-h/* following the vowel */a/*. The form in the rest of the area is */-ha/* in all positions. Associated with the form */-ah/* forms ending in the vowels */-i/*, */-ay/*, */-u/* and */-aw/* show */-y/* and */-w/* for these vowels thus giving a quite different syllabication for the forms concerned. Compare the following examples:

North Najdi	Other Areas	
šāfah	*šāfaha*	"he saw her"
baytah	*baytaha*	"her house"
ligāh	*ligāha*	"he found her"
abyah	*abīha*	"I want it (f)"
'alyah	*'alēha*	"on it (f)"
šilyah	*šilīha*	"take (f.s.) it (f) away"
tilyah	*tillīha*	"pluck (f.s.) it (f)"
idbaḥyah	*idbaḥīha*	"kill (f.s.) it (f)"
abwah	*abūha*	"her father"
škumwah	*škimōha*	"they (m) bridled it (f)"
sāgwah	*sāgōha*	"they (m) drove it (f)"
sigwah	*sūgūha*	"drive (m.pl.) it (f)"
ajjalwah	*ajjalōha*	"they (m) postponed it (f)"
a'ṭyah (Ḍhafīr)	*a'ṭīha*	"I will give it (f)"

Forms with */-ah/* and forms with the semi-vowels */-y/* and */-w-/* preceding such as */'alyah abwah/* are attested in my material for the Shammar and Ḍhafīr and for Qaṣīm. The form */-ah/* is also shown for the Bani Khālid, Ahl al-Shimāl and Euphrates bedouin, although no instances of the type */'alyah abwah/* occurred. The form */yinṭī-ha/* "he gives her" occurs in the Ahl al-Shimāl text rather than the North Najdi type */yinṭy-ah/*. A similar mixed type is given by Cantineau (1937 p.183-4 and 232) showing both */-ah/* and */-ha/* for the Bani Ṣakhar and Bani Khālid. Examples of */-h/* are attested for Shammar, Qaṣīm, and Ḍhafīr only in my material.

3 The form of the first person singular is */-an/*(1) post-consonantally, */-nan/* post-vocalically, contrasting with */-ni/* in all positions elsewhere. Compare the following:

North Najdi	Other Areas	
šāfan	*šāfani, šāfni*	"he saw me"
tirkan	*itrikni*	"leave me!"
ysubban	*ysibbini, ysibbni*	"he insults me"
tḥabsan	*tḥabisni, tiḥbisni*	"you imprison me"
xallōnan	*xallōni*	"they left me"
itnan	*itnini* (Ḍhafīr)	"wait for me"
'aṭan	*'aṭni* (Ḍhafīr)	"give me"

This feature is less widespread than those mentioned above. It is attested for the Shammar, for Qaṣīm and for the Euphrates bedouin. The Ḍhafīr and Ahl al-Shimāl showed */-ni/* in all cases, i.e. Ḍhafīr */'aṭni/* "give me", */itnini/* "wait for me", */ṭaggini/* "he hit me", */'aṭāni/* "he gave me", */nišadni/* "he asked me"; Ahl al-Shimāl */'aṭni/* "give me", */'ayyarōni/* "they insulted me". The Euphrates bedouin showed */-an/* but */-ni/* post-vocallically, i.e. */yāni nšidan/* "he came to me and asked me", */m'allman buh ant?/* "did you teach me it?". Cantineau (1937, p.176, 232) shows a similar system for 'Umūr, Ṣlūṭ and Sirḥān and Bani Khālid.

4 Certain masculine plural morphemes show an open vowel */a/* in contrast to the more usual */u/* in the following forms:

intam	"you (m.pl.)"	independent pronoun
-kam	"you (m.pl.)"	suffixed
ham	"they (m.pl.)"	independent pronoun
-ham	"they (m.pl.)"	suffixed

These contrast with the more usual */intu, -kum, -hum, hum/*. They are attested for the Shammar, Ḍhafīr, Bani Khālid and also for certain areas of Mesopotamia, namely 'Amāra, Kūt and Ahwaz. It also occurs in the dialect of the Ruwala investigated by Prochazka and in the speech of Cantineau's Shammar sattelite tribes of the Syrian desert, namely the Sardiyya and Bani Ṣakhar (1937, p.185). This is one of the most widespread of the North Najdi features and can be more accurately described as a Syrian Desert characteristic. It is also the only one adopted by an 'Anizi tribe of the Syrian desert,

1 A suffix */-an/* also occurs as a non-obligatory subject marker for the first person singular in the dialects of Southern Mesopotamia (see p.83). It may be that there is a connection between these two as a number of other connections also exist (see p.87-94).

namely the above-mentioned Ruwala.(1) Informants from other 'Aniza sections, namely the Sba'a, Ṣugūr and 'Awāja, showed the more expected forms, as also did other Najd bedouin informants from the Ḥarb and Muṭair tribes. Inexplicably the Euphrates bedouin who exhibit feature 3, one of the less-widespread North Najdi features, did not show these forms. Neither did the Ahl al-Shimāl.

5 Fronting has taken place with certain feminine suffixes and */-y/* replaces an original */-t/* in pausal position, giving */eih/* or */-ih/* for the feminine singular nominal suffix, */-āy/* for the feminine plural nominal suffix, and */eih/* for the feminine singular verbal suffix in place of the more usual */-ah, -āt, -at/*. Fronting of the nominal feminine singular is the most common and is attested for the Shammar, Euphrates bedouin and the dialects of Qaṣīm. In the dialects of Qaṣīm, the Euphrates bedouin and the speech of Hail the form is */-ih/*.(2) In the speech of my Shammar informants it was usually */-eih/*, but */-h/* in non-pausal positions. With the Shammar it occurred following all consonant types, whereas with the Euphrates bedouin it occurred mostly following non-guttural consonants. Examples:

SHAMMAR: */mareih/* "woman", */sinjāreih/* "Sinjāra", */gwāreih/* "hillock", */ṯimīleih/* "well", */ṭrugeiḥ/* "journey", */nāzyeih/* "sand dune", */maršaḥeih/* "saddle", */faj'eih/* "suddenly", */musābleih/* "expedition", */šičīmeih/* "bridle", */tal'eih/* "a pass", */birčeih/* "well", */luġweih/* "language", */širriyyeih/* "small pass".

EUPHRATES BEDOUIN: */mallih/* "boredom", */sāḥi/* "tent curtain", */dīrih/* "tribal area", */ghawiḥ/* "coffee", */šibāyih/* "gunsight", */riblih/* "type of grass", */siyyādih/* "prayer carpet", */miḥīlih/* "drought", */yizīrih/* "Jazīra", */nhēdih/* "breast", */ṯamānyih/* "eight", */xēzarānih/* "camel stick", */dōlih/* "state; but */ṣaffārah, šiggāra, gfē'a /* "types of grass".

Contrast the following forms from the dialect of the Ḍhafīr: */ṯimānyah/* "eight", */ghawah/* "coffee", */laġa/* "language", */sāḥa/* "tent curtain", */markābah/* "fireplace frame".

1 Landberg's 'Aniza material also shows forms of this type as optional variants, i.e. */likam/* "for you", */laham/* "for them" (1919 p.71). My Sba'a informants also gave sporadic examples of */ham/*, i.e. */hāḏōḷa ham/* "there they are!" The Budūr shepherds of the Nāṣiriyya area also show */intam/* and */-kam/*, but not */-ham/*. Wetzstein regards these forms as characteristic of "bedouins" in general as opposed to sedentaries (1868 p.196), presumably as a result of the selection of his bedouin informants.

2 The form */-ih/* also occurred in fronting environments in a somewhat more restricted fashion in the speech of the

Fronting of the other two suffixes occurred only in the dialect of the Shammar. Examples:

Shammar	Other Areas	
ṣalāy	*ṣalāt*	"prayer"
sayyārāy	*sayyārāt*	"cars"
dārāy		"curved sand dunes"
thādāy		"pegs for hobbling camels"
ṭaggāgāy	*ṭaggāgāt*	"drills, borers"
kalimāy	*kalimāt*	"words"
baṭārāy	*baṭārāt*	"batteries"
ḥwēṭāy	*ḥwēṭāt*	"Ḥuwaiṭāt (tribal name)"
ḥurmāy	*ḥurmāt*	"women"
banāy	*banāt*	"girls"
dukturāy	*dukturā*	"Doctorate"
inglubeih	*inglubat*	"it overturned"
ṭāḥeih	*ṭāḥat*	"it (f) fell"
xluṣeih	*xluṣat*	"it (f) finished"
mišeih	*mišat*	"she went"

A further difference connected with the feminine suffixes is that in the Shammar dialect the final */-t/* is present in non-pausal position. This agrees with the more general type in the verbal form and in the feminine plural, but in the nominal feminine singular contrasts, since the rest show */-ah/* except where suffixed. Contrast the following:

SHAMMAR

1 *yōm waṣlat ittal'at u ti'aṭṭilat issayyāreih*
2 *yōm waṣlat ittal'at w assayyārat ti'aṭṭileih*
"When it reached the pass, the car broke down."
3 *'abdat u sinjāreih* "'Abdah and Sinjāra (tribal names)"
4 *'itēbat u ḥarb* "'Utaiba and Ḥarb (tribal names)"
5 *halfēḏat hāḏi* "this hollow"
6 *lighawt aṣṣaḥīḥeih* "the correct coffee"

OTHER AREAS

1 *yōm waṣlat ittal'ah u ti'aṭṭilat issayyārah*
2 *yōm waṣlat ittal'ah w assayyārah ti'aṭṭilat*
3 *'abdah u sinjārah*
4 *'itēbah u ḥarb*
5 *halfēḏa hāḏi*
6 *lighawh iṣṣaḥīḥah*

Sudair informants, i.e. */ṯimānyih/* "eight", */ṯalāṯih/* "three", */ṭayyibih/* "good", */'ārfih/* "knowing", */ḥāḏrih/* "ready", */ćiṯīrih/* "many".

The following table shows the distribution of the North Najdi features examined. The most widespread general features are the third person pronouns /*-ah*/ and /*-uh*/. The masculine plural forms /*-kam*/, *-ham*, *-intam*/ have a more northerly distribution but do not occur in the dialect of Qaṣīm.

TABLE II

	Shammar	Qaṣīm	Ḥumaid & Rufai'	Ḍhafīr	Bani Khālid	Ahl al-Shimāl	'Amāra Ruwala
-ah as 3 f.s. obj.	✓	✓	✓	✓	✓	✓	o
-uh as 3 m.s. obj.	✓	✓	✓	✓	✓	✓	o
-kam, *-ham* *intam* m.pl.	✓	o	o	✓	✓	o	✓
-eih or-*ih* as f.s. nominal ending	✓	✓	✓	o	?	o	o
-an as 1st s. object	✓	✓	✓	o	?	o	o
-āy as f.pl. nominal ending	✓	o	o	o	o	o	o
-eih as f.s.	✓	o	o	o	o	o	o
-nan 1st s. obj.	✓	✓	o	o	o	o	o

As can be seen from the maps on p.64 and p.78 , before the movement of the 'Aniza tribes to the Syrian desert and the subsequent move of the Shammar Jarba to the Jazīrah, the North Najdi dialect features formed a distinct enclave covering the North Arabian desert or Bādiya centred on the Jabal Shammar and surrounded on all sides by dialects which, although not identical, nevertheless were similar in certain features which contrast with the North Najdi type. These latter features are in fact those common to the majority of Arabic dialects and similar to the form of Classical Arabic.

It seems likely that this widely divergent form has grown up as a result of isolation from the surrounding settled areas and as the speech of the Syrian desert nomadic area or the historical Arabia Deserta. In the surrounding areas concentrations of settlements form a zone of communication which stretches from the settled areas of the Mediterranean coast down to the Hijaz across the Arabian peninsula from the Hijaz to Qaṣīm and the Jabal Ṭuwaiq, al-Hasa and the Gulf Coast, the Gulf being then linked to the Shaṭṭ al-'Arab and Mesopotamia by sea or from Kuwait via Zubair to Basra. The circle is then completed by the towns of the northern Euphrates which are linked to northern Syria.(1) Although when compared with the more populous areas of the world such as western Europe none of these constitute a continuous band of settlement, except perhaps the rivers of Mesopotamia, and are in places separated by quite extensive desert tracts,(2) nevertheless it seems that contact has always been maintained. The old trade routes also reflect this, going from Yaman northwards via Hijaz to Syria or northeastwards up the Jabal Ṭuwaiq to the Gulf Coast and Mesopotamia, also joining Mesopotamia to Syria along the north of the Syrian desert. (3) The exception to this is the Darb Zubaida pilgrim road from Najaf, via Hail, to Mecca. However this is not a natural route and had to be maintained by specially constructed water cisterns across the desert region. Large bedouin tribes of these areas have similarly been in close contact with these settled areas in a consistent way which is reflected in the less idiosyncratic type of their dialect. The 'Aniza, although now spreading north into the Syrian desert, were originally a tribe of the Haj road of Hijaz, stretching up from the Holy Cities to the towns of

1 The resemblance of the dialects of northern Mesopotamia to northern Syria is described in full by BLANC (1964) p.7-10.
2 This particularly between Najd and the Hijaz in the 'Utaiba steppe. See DOUGHTY (1924) p.367.
3 See BLÜME (1976), p.93; also GRANT (1937), p.258.

Syria. The Ḥarb were a tribe of the Hijaz closely connected with the town of Madina and whose dīra stretched from Madina eastward to Qaṣīm. The 'Utaiba similarly are closely connected with the town of Mecca and spread eastward to the Qaṣīm and al-'Āriḍh.(1) The Muṭair, also originally from western Najd, now have their main central area from Qaṣīm to Kuwait and were originally of great influence in Kuwait. The 'Awāzim and Rashāyida tribes of the Gulf Coast have for centuries been intimately connected with the town of Kuwait and have had settled sections in that region since the 15th century.(2) In the central area, however, the old Arabia Deserta, nomadism on the grand scale has been possible. As was outlined earlier in Chapter 1, the Shammar tribes occupy a self-enclosed area utilising the grazing of the Nafūd and the Syrian desert in the spring and relying on the wells and settled areas of the Jabal Shammar in summer. We know that in the past the Shammar held sway over the greater part of the Syrian desert, probably since the middle ages.(3) We can presume that the North Najdi type of dialect became in that epoch the symbol of nomadic identity. Subsequently fringe dialects of the type of the Ahl al-Shimāl, Ḍhafīr, Euphrates bedouin and Bani Khālid developed. These parallel exactly the fringe dialects of the desert of Syria mentioned by Cantineau.(4) Since then, probably between the 17th and 18th centuries,(5) the 'Aniza have forged up from western

1 See DOUGHTY (1924) p.331, 366-67, for the relation of Muṭair and 'Utaiba to the towns of Hijaz and Qaṣīm. Another explanation of this relative uniformity of the central Najdi type may be that the constant and gradual movement of populations northward and eastward across the peninsula recorded by tradition and toponymy which was referred to in Ch.1 maintained a constant contact and renewing of the central Najdi type from a possible source in the southwestern Najd area. The Jabal Shammar, as mentioned earlier, would have been isolated from this.

2 See 'UBAYYID (1971) p.28.

3 Authorities differ on the date of their initial expansion but probably in the 16th and 17th century. See in particular CANTINEAU (1937) p.233, DICKSON (1949) Appendix I, MONTAGNE (1935) p.37, 47.

4 CANTINEAU (1937) p.233 talks of "tribus peut-être d'abord géographiquement voisines des Šammar, peut-être satéllites des Šammar, peut-être apparentées indirectement aux Šammar," namely 'Umūr, Ṣlūṭ, Sardiyya, Sirḥān, Bani Khālid and Bani Ṣakhar.

5 For the arrival of the 'Aniza see PHILBY (1922) p.108,249, 288; MUSIL (1928b) p.112; MONTAGNE (1935) p.40; CANTINEAU (1937) p.122; PHILBY (1955) p.6; OPPENHEIM (1939) p.68; Encyclopaedia of Islam, "'Anaza", p.482.

Najd and taken over the central Syrian desert, splitting the Shammar into two, those of Najd and the Jarba Shammar across the Euphrates. This has complicated the dialect map somewhat insofar as a central Najdi dialect, that of the 'Aniza, is now spread over wide areas north of the North Najdi type. It has however not affected the core area of the North Najdi dialect type, the Jabal Shammar, which still stands apart from the other settled areas and from the nomad tribes of the Syrian desert. Although 'Aniza, Shammar, Ḍhafīr and Muṭair all border closely on each other in the spring grazing grounds, in the summer the Shammar in the main contract inwards to the Jabal Shammar, while the others move outwards to the settled lands. The Wild Sulaimān and Wild 'Ali go towards the Hijaz, the Ruwala towards Syria, the Sba'a, 'Amārāt and Ḍhafīr towards the Euphrates.(1)

THE ANALOGICAL BASIS OF THE NORTH NAJDI FEATURES

If we compare the pronoun system of the North Najdi with the Central Najdi type, it can be seen that although both show a modification of what we presume to be the OA system, the North Najdi type has gone further and the modifications can be characterised as resulting from structural pressure within the language based on analogy with other forms. The following shows Old Arabic, North Najdi and Central Najdi forms.(2)

	OA	CENTRAL NAJDI	NORTH NAJDI
"me"	*-ni*	*-ni*	*-an/-nan*
"you m.s."	*-ak*	*-(i)k/(a)k*	*-ak*
"you f.s."	*-ik*	*-(i)ć*	*-ić*
"him"	*-uh*	*-(i)h*	*-uh*
"her"	*-ha*	*-ha*	*-ah*
"us"	*-na*	*-na*	*-na*
"you m.pl."	*-kum*	*-kum*	*-kam*
"you f.pl."	*-kunna*	*-ćin*	*-ćin*
"they m.pl."	*-hum*	*-hum*	*-ham*
"they f.pl."	*-hunna*	*-hin*	*-hin*

1 This pattern is contradicted to some extent by the Muṭair who occupy their own summer wells in the desert between Kuwait and Qaṣīm, DICKSON (1949) p.563. However, their central dialect type can be related to their earlier location in western Najd.

2 The forms given are those appropriate to forms with a final consonant such as */anšid/* "I ask", */yanšid/* "he asks", i.e. */anšidk/* Central Najdi, */anšidak/* Northern Najdi "I ask you m.s."; */yanšidni/* C.Najdi, */yanšidan/* N.Najdi "he asks me".

Both types show the split of OA */k/* to */k/* and */ć/* and the specialisation of */i/* and */u/* for separate consonantal environments. Thus the Central Najdi forms */-kum/* and */-ćin/* and */-hum/* and */-hin/* at a higher level of analysis share the same vowel, i.e. */-kIm, -ćIn, -hIm, -hIn/*. In the North Najdi type it would seem that the development of the forms */-kam/* and */-ham/* also */intam/* is by analogy with the */a/* of */-ak/*, giving a system of the following type:

		Sing.	Plural	
masculine (vowel *a*)	2nd person	- *ak*	*intam*	*-kam*
	3rd person		*ham*	*-ham*
feminine (vowel *i*)	2nd person	- *ić*	*intin*	*-ćin*
	3rd person		*hin*	*-hin*

The development of the forms */-an/* "me" and */-ah/* "she" seems to represent levelling of the syllabically diverse OA set to the pattern */-vc/*in conformity with the majority of the set, i.e. */-ak, -ik, -uh/*. This produces a system where singular affixes are of the form */-vc/* and plural affixes of the form */-c v (c)/*.

The fronting of the feminine suffixes */-at/* and */-āt/* to */-eih/* and */-āy/* can be considered to be by analogy with other feminine pronominal elements all of which have a front vowel feature, i.e. */-i/* f.s. imperative, */-īn/* f.s. imperfective, */-ti/* f.s. perfective, */anti/* 2nd f.s. pronoun, */hi/* 3rd f.s. pronoun. A parallel development has occurred in Hebrew where the old Semitic 3rd f.s. pronoun suffix */-at/* has been changed to */-ā/* by analogy with the feminine ending of the noun.(1)

Although most of the developments shown here are regularizing and levelling in nature in terms of the individual systems in which they operate, nevertheless in terms of the inventory of items involved in each case they either retain the same level of complexity or increase it, i.e. in producing more forms to be learnt in each case. This can be seen by comparing certain of the units concerned with those of the Central Najdi type. In each case it will be seen that the North Najdi is the more complex. This is in contrast to the levelling and reductional changes outlined in Chapter 3 for the periphery dialects.

1 See MOSCATI (1969), p.137.

	North Najdi	Central Najdi
1st sing. object	*-an / -nan*	*-ni*
3rd m.s. object	*-uh / -w / -h*	*-ih / -h*
3rd f.s. object	*-ah / -h*	*-ha*
3rd f.s. subject	*-eih / -at*	*-at*
3rd f.pl. nominal	*-āy / -āt*	*-āt*

A similar case of increase in complexity occurs in some of the Central Najdi type, namely the development of two forms for the third masculine plural perfective suffix /*-aw*/ and /*-am*/.(1) The form /*-am*/ occurs when final in the form, and /*-aw*/ when followed by a further suffix, e.g. /*šāfam*/ "they m. saw", /*šāfawk*/ or /*šāfōk*/(2) "they saw you". Some dialects also show / *-um* ~ *-ū* / for the masculine plural imperative /*tfaḍḍalum*/ "come in (m.pl.)". These are presumably on analogy with the masculine plural forms /*-tum, -kuṁ, antum, hum*/ etc. These forms are attested for a group of geographically central dialects, i.e. the Ḥarb, 'Awāzim, Rashāyida and some 'Aniza groups of the Syrian desert, namely Sba'a and Ruwala. It does not occur in the Shammar dialects or in the dialect of Muṭair and Ḍhafīr or in the 'Utaiba dialect as described by Hess. This makes it geographically North Central. This is still consistent with our model since the Central Najd area is still relatively isolated although, as we have tried to point out above, less so than the Northern Najd area.

1 See also CANTINEAU (1936) p.80, who gives examples of this suffix for the 'Umūr, Ṣlūṭ and Manāḍhra. LANDBERG (1919) gives such examples as *gālom, šāfom*.

2 The existence of the forms /*aw*~*ō*/ and /*u*~*ū*/ in the rest of the area is not regarded as of parallel complexity since the sounds /*aw*~*ō*/ are in many areas in complementary distribution and can be regarded as related, as also can the alternation final /*-u, -i, -a*/, non-final /*-ū, -ī, ā*/. This however is not true of /*-am*~*-aw, ō*/.

5 General isogloss distribution of the area

A set of important lexical and phonological isoglosses separates the area running in an east-west direction and separating it into northern and southern blocks. However the distribution is generally of the non-territorial type(1) and does not divide the region into distinct sub-areas but shows a gradual spread out from the Central Najd to the other regions. A number of contrasts separate Mesopotamia from the Arabian peninsula, while a further group separate Mesopotamia and Northern Najd on the one hand from the rest of the Arabian peninsula on the other, with the majority of Syrian desert bedouin dialects falling in with the northern area. A further set separate Najd and the bedouin dialects from the outer rim, i.e. Mesopotamia and the Gulf. As was shown with the reductional changes, the Euphrates bedouin and Ahl al-Shimāl are grouped sometimes with Mesopotamia and sometimes with the Arabian area. This is also true of the Budūr shepherds who show a basically Mesopotamian type with some general Arabian and some specifically North Najdi features. There are, however, significantly, no isoglosses which group North Najd with the Gulf against the rest, or which group Inner Arabia with Mesopotamia against the Gulf. The isogloss structure therefore corresponds to the general history of population movement in the area out from Central Arabia to the Gulf and to Mesopotamia in successive waves with a subsidiary division into a generally northern and a generally southern peninsular area. Of the bedouin dialects studied, the Muṭair, 'Awāzim, Rashāyda and Central Ḥarb(2) show an

1 These terms are used by IVIĆ (1962) p.34-7.
2 Central Ḥarb designates the Ḥarb informants from the Wādi Turmus area who were of the Bani 'Amr and Bani Sālim. These differ in some respects from my main Ḥarbi informant, Ḥamza Muzaini, who was from the Hijaz, and from Ḥāzmi's informants, also Hijazis. Qaṣīm denotes the dialect of my main Qaṣīm informant, Abdallah Tamīmi, from

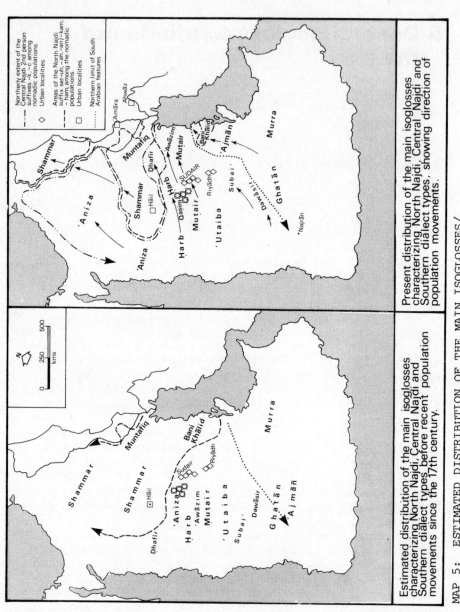

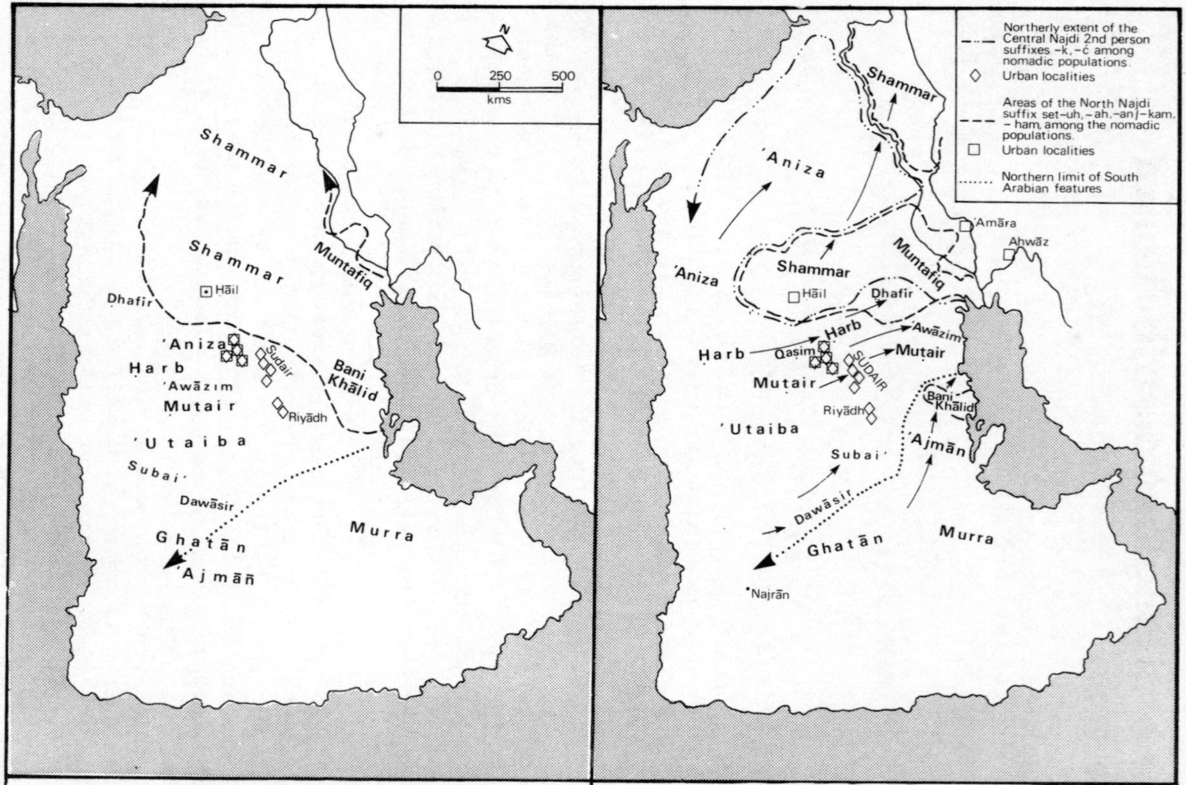

Estimated distribution of the main isoglosses characterizing North Najdi, Central Najdi and Southern dialect types before recent population movements since the 17th century.

Present distribution of the main isoglosses characterizing North Najdi, Central Najdi and Southern dialect types, showing direction of population movements.

MAP 5: ESTIMATED DISTRIBUTION OF THE MAIN ISOGLOSSES/
PRESENT DISTRIBUTION OF THE MAIN ISOGLOSSES

affinity to the dialects of Central Najd investigated, i.e. Riyadh and Sudair. The 'Aniza, although in their basic structural features of the same type, show some affinity to the northern area as regards the features mentioned under 2. The Ḍhafīr show a very mixed dialect type divided between a North and a Central Najdi type similar to that of the 'Aniza and with sporadic addition of Mesopotamian features. The place of the Bani Khālid is not entirely clear due, in part, to the scantiness of my material. However they seem to be of a type similar to the Euphrates bedouin. The features looked at here are lexical, phonological and morphological and in one case syntactic. In the main I concentrate on the form of lexical and functional elements of high frequency of occurrence which are the ones most apparent to a foreign investigator. These differ in some cases in the choice of a completely different element, as in the case of the verb "to want" */rād, yrīd/* in Mesopotamia vs. */baġa, yabi/* in Arabia. In other cases they differ in the phonological form of what is in essence the same element, i.e. Mesopotamian */man/* "who" vs. Arabian */min/*. One important syntactic difference is mentioned, namely the structure of interrogative sentences which shows an important difference between Mesopotamian and Arabian types. The features are listed under the main contrastive cleavages, i.e. Mesopotamia/Arabia, Northern/Southern, Inner Arabia/Outer Fringe. A number of other features of more restricted distribution are also mentioned connected with a North Central Najdi type and with the central marshland area of Southern Mesopotamia.

FEATURES SEPARATING SOUTHERN MESOPOTAMIA FROM ARABIA

1 In the Mesopotamian type the reflex of OA */ay/* in certain consonant environments(1) is a close front gliding vowel of the type *[ɩə]* or *[ɩɛ]* contrasting with *[ɛː]* or *[ei]* in the rest of the area. In the Arabian type the distribution of the pure vowel *[ɛː]* and the glide *[ei]* differs somewhat from place to place.(2) In general the pure vowel

Midhnab. 'Aniza, unless otherwise stated, denotes the dialect of my Sba'a informants in Kuwait. The Sudair material is from my informants in Saudi Arabia. Zayyād denotes Rākān al-Zayyādi, an attendant of Muḥammad al-Sudairi in Qaṣīm. 'Utaiba denotes Hess's material. All other sources were informants in the place of origin.

1 In general those in which the initial consonant is not a guttural or r and the following consonant is not r.

2 See in particular LEHN (1967), p.129; also INGHAM (1979) p.28.

occurs preceding the emphatics *ṭ, ṣ, ḍ*, the gutturals *', ḥ, h, ġ, x* and also the apical continuants *l, n, r*. In other environments the glide occurs. The vowels *[ɩə]* and *[ɩɛ]* are symbolised */ie/*.

MESOPOTAMIAN: */biet/* "house", */liel/* "night", */bien/* "between, */zien/* "good", */šien/* "bad", */šiex/* "sheikh", */ties/* "goat", */ḥsien/* "Ḥusain", */ligiet/* "I found", */ligiena/* "we found", */šiel/* "loading", */zied/* "Zaid", */kiliet/* "I ate", */yieb/* "pocket", */ziet/* "oil", */lieš/* "why", */'alieh/* "on him", */sief/* "sword", */'aliek/* "on you".

ARABIAN (SHAMMAR): */zēn/* "good", */šēn/* "bad", */bēn/* "between", */bētēn/* "two houses", */šēl/* "rain, flood", */'alēh/* "on him", */blēhi/* "Blaihi (p.n.)", */šeix/* "sheikh", */ligeit/* "I found", */zeid/* "Zaid", */kaleit/* "I ate", */jeib/* "pocket", */zeit/* "oil", */leiš/* "why", */seif/* "sword", */'aleik/* "on you", */leit/* "would that", */jeiš/* "troup of camels", */feid/* "Faid (n.loc.)", */xḷeif/* "Khulaif", */ćeif/* "how", */wġeid/* "young boy".

The Mesopotamian type is recorded for the core of the Mesopotamian dialect area, namely the banks of the Shaṭṭ al-'Arab up to Gurna, Shādigān, Ahwaz, Ḥuwaiza and Khorramshahr in Khuzistan, the settlements of the southern Euphrates near Sūq al-Shuyūkh, Nāṣiriyya and Samāwa, Dīwāniyya, Najaf Karbala and Baghdad, and also for Mi'dān informants in the area of Chibāyish, Fuhūd and Butaira. Groups showing the Arabian type were the Euphrates bedouin and Ahl al-Shimāl, the Budūr and Zayyād shepherds, also some parts of the 'Amāra area. In these the vowel */ē/* occurred but not */ei/*.

EUPHRATES BEDOUIN (RUFAI'): */čēf/* "how", */šēl/* "rain", */bētana/* "our house", */zēn/* "good", */lēl/* "night", */'alēman/* "about who", */ḏōdēn/* "two herds", */šēl/* "moving camp", */gfē'a/* "gufai'a (plant name)".

AHL AL-SHIMĀL: */klēb/* "kulaib (n.p.)", */nihētak/* "I forbid you", */bētēn/* "two verses".

In the 'Amāra type */ē/* and */ī/* occur as distributional equivalents of the usual Mesopotamian */ie/*. The variant */ē/* occurs in final weak verb forms of the type */ižēt/* "I came", */ligēt/* "I found", */kilēt/* "gate", */xaḏēt/* "I took", while */ī/* seems to occur in non-verbal forms */bīt/* "house", */xīl/* "horses", */ḥsīn/* "Ḥusain" , */čīf/* "how, what", */wīn/* "where", */'alīš/* "why".(1)

1 A similar type of system is shown for the Negev bedouins by BLANC (1970) p.118. He suggests that this type of system may be general to much of the Syrian desert area. 'Anizi forms such as *zīn* "good", *šīn* "bad", *gīḏ* "summer" seem to support this. This shows a connection between the Syrian desert and the bādiya area of Iraq between the Euphrates and Tigris. See also INGHAM (1976) p.68-9. Also Shammar *bwīrag* "flag", *zīneih* "good", *šīneih* "bad", *ġīr* "other than me". MONTAGNE (1935) p.85, 102.

In other consonantal environments the distinction between the two types is only maintained in cases where the Arabian type shows the glide */ei/* which contrasts with */ē/* in the Mesopotamian. In the majority of cases however both show */ē/* as in */hēl/* "cardoman", */ḥēl/* "strength", */xēl/* "horses", */xēr/* "good", */wēn/* "where", */fēḏah/* "hollow", */gēḏ/* "summer", */fēṣal/* "Faisal", */ġēr/* "except".

But compare Shammari: */ṣeif/* "summer", */ṣeid/* "game", */breićeih/* "well", */ḏ̣eif/* "guest", */'eib/* "shame", */sawweit /* "I did"; Mesopotamian: */ṣēf, ṣēd, ḏ̣ēf, 'ēb, sawwēt/*.

However it seems that particularly in the Syrian desert area the vowel */ē/* may be general to all environments. This was the case with some of the Sba'a informants who gave */lēt/* "would that", */ligēt/* "I found", */waddētih/* "I brought it", and regarded the pronunciation */leit, ligeit, waddeit/* as characteristic of "Southern" tribes such as the Muṭair.(1) The main distinction therefore between the Mesopotamian and Arabian type remains that of the characteristic gliding vowel of Mesopotamian *[ɩə]* or *[ɩɛ]* in anterior consonantal environments vs. the *[ē]* or *[eɩ]* of the neighbouring areas.

2 Certain feminine plural pronominal elements show a segment */-an/* in the Mesopotamian type but */-in/* in the Arabian type. These are */-čan/* "you (f.pl.obj.)", */-tan/* "you (f.pl.subj. perfective)", */intan/* "you (f.pl.)", also */-an/* "f.pl. suffix of the imperfective and imperative". These contrast with */-ćin, -čin, -kin, -tin, intin* and *-in/* in the rest of the area. Compare:

S. MESOPOTAMIAN (KAWĀWILA): */intan ḏibban arwāḥčan 'alieh/* "you (f.pl.) throw yourselves upon him", */'yūni yhimlan/* "my eyes are watering", */yōm alba'ārīn yšīlan rūshin/* "and when the camels lift up their heads";

ḌHAFĪR: */yšūfin/* "they (f.) see";

SHAMMAR: */ydillinihin/* "they (f.) know them (f.)", */hāḏōlinć ilyamšin/* "those (f.) who walk", */alḥīrān ynūḥin/* "the yearlings call for their mothers", */mā yšālin/* "they cannot be removed,(2) */šuftin/* "you (f.pl.) saw" */šuftinnu/* "you (f.pl.) saw him", */ašūfakin/* "I see you (f.pl.)";

MUṬAIR: */y'āydinnih/* "they (f.) visit him";

QAṢĪM: */antin šiftinnu/* "you (f.pl.) saw him", */hin yašrabin/* "they (f.) drink", */hin yanksin/* "they (f.) go back", */antin tanšdin/* "you (f.pl.) ask".

1 On this point see INGHAM (1979) p.28. This was also recorded for the area of Kūt Sayyid 'Anāya in N. Khuzistan in such forms as *sigēt* "I watered", *jalēt*"I polished", *gatlēt* "I killed", *ligēt*"I found", *štaġlēt*"I worked".

2 This is unexpected in view of the normal *-an* of the passive. It may be that in these forms the open vowel of the stem *šāl* - is sufficient to mark the passive and therefore the more common *-in* is used.

In the Arabian type the form */-an/* does occur in the imperfective structures but under more restricted conditions. Where there is an internal passive it is the normal feminine plural suffix as */yinšdan/* "they (f.) are asked", */tinšdan/* "you (f. pl.) are asked", It also occurs in the V and VI Measures of the verb which are intransitive in nature: Qaṣīm */ytigahwan/* "they (f.) take coffee", Muṭair */ytisābigan/* "they (f.) compete". In the dialect of the Sudair it occurs with final weak verbs in */-a/*, i.e. */yilgan/* "they (f.) find", */yibgan/* "they (f.) remain", */yibdan/* "they (f.) begin". The Sba'a material showed examples of a type which seemed to operate with a vowel harmony system(1), i.e. */y'aṭan/* "they (f.) give", */irtaćan/* "lean (f.pl.)", but */taktibin/* "you (f.pl.) write", */yḥasbinhin/* "they (f.) think them (f.)", */gūmin/* "rise (f.pl.)", */baḥḥrin/* "look (f.pl.)", */irtać/* "lean (m. s.)", */irtići/* "lean (f.s.)", */irtućum/* "lean (m.pl.)". The Ruwala dialect showed the form */-in/* in the expected places, but for the second feminine plural */-tan/* and */intan/*, i.e. */intan libistan/* "you (f.pl.) dressed". Also */-an/* in certain final weak verbs, i.e. */ićwan/* "brand (f.pl.)", */yalwan/* "they (f.) twist", */yamšan/* "they (f.) walk", */yaćwan/* "they (f.) brand", */insan/* "forget (f.pl.)". In this they resemble the Sba'a.

The Gulf dialects group more closely with the Arabian type showing */intin, -kin, -tin/* but also with */-an/* as the suffix of the imperfective and imperative */yaktban/* "they (f.) write", */yišrban/* "they (f.) drink", */iktban/* "write! (f. pl.)"(2) The Euphrates bedouin show the Arabian type: Ḥumaid */yirčibin/* "they (f.) mount", */yiktibin/* "they (f.) write", */šūfin/* "look (f.pl.)", */intin/* "you (f.pl.)" */yḥasbinni/* "they (f.) consider me"; Rufai' */yidrin/* "they (f.) know", */yimšin/* "they (f.) walk", */mā yin'addin/* "they (f.) are uncountable". The Budūr also show this type */intin/* "you (f.pl.)" and */yšūfin /* "they (f.) see". The Ahwaz informant who was from the Zuhairiyya, a branch of the Budūr, also gave */aṭṭīčin/* "I give you (f.pl.)". The Ahl al-Shimāl showed the Mesopotamian type in */šiftakan/* "I saw you (f. pl.)", */šiftanni/* "you (f.pl.) saw me", */tḥatban/* "they (f.) cut wood", */intan/* "you (f.pl.)". The position with the imperative is not completely clear however as examples with */-an/* occur in non-conditioning environments in some examples: Rufai' */ibnan ibsā'/* "build (f.pl.) the tents quickly"; Qaṣīm */šfan/* "look (f.pl.)", */šfannuh/* "look (f.pl.) at him".

The above shows a generally wider distribution of the form */-an/* in the Mesopotamian type with some overlap in

1 A similar system occurs for the Negev bedouin, see BLANC (1970) p.136, *yikitbin, yugu'din, yimšin*, but *yašraban, yansan*.

2 JOHNSTONE (1967b) p.42-50. Zubair shows *intin* also.

the dialect of the Sba'a, northern 'Aniza of the Syrian desert.(1) In the more southerly Najd dialects */-in/* is even more widespread. One Ḥarb informant gave */šāfin/* "they (f.) saw" */šāfinnih/* "they (f.) saw it". It is interesting that as with a number of other features the North Khuzistan informant from the area of Kūt Sayyid 'Anāya showed the feature appropriate to the Euphrates nomadic type.

3 The feminine plural demonstrative also shows an element */-an/* as with 2 above in the forms */hāḏanni/* "there (f.)" */ḏannīč/* "those (f.)" in contrast to forms of the type */hāḏōlīć/* 'Aniza, Central Najd, */hāḏōlin, hāḏōlinć/* Shammar. The Ḍhafīr show */hāḏōlin/*, but also */hāḏalli/* and */ḏallīć/* approximating to the Mesopotamian type. The forms */ḏanni, ḏannīč/* were also used by the Budūr and the Ḥumaid and Rufai'. In Zubair the form */ḏannay/* occurs showing the common East Arabian feature of */-ay/* for */-i/* in final position.(2) The forms */ḏanni, hāḏanni/* were confirmed for all dialects of the South Mesopotamian area. Sporadic examples of */hāḏōlīč/ḏōlīč/* were recorded in al-Fao.

4 A non-obligatory suffix */-an, -ann/* occurs in the first singular imperfective in much of the South Mesopotamian area. This occurs most commonly with the hollow and doubled verb types. This is not found outside the area and is recognised as a specifically South Mesopotamian feature. Examples: */arūḥan/* "I go", */ašūfan/* "I see", */anāman/* "I sleep", */aṣubban/* "I pour", */ašūfanna/* "I see him", */arīdanna/* "I want it", */aġasman-ilkam/* "I divide it up for you!" (Ahwaz) */ayībanhin/* "I bring them (f.)". This feature did not occur in the speech of the Euphrates shepherds Budūr and Zayyād who regarded it as a Mi'dān characteristic.

5 The form of certain interrogative structures is quite different in these two types. In the Mesopotamian type the element */-man/* "which or who" can follow a verb preposition or noun as an enclitic often fusing with it by certain sandhi processes. The element */-š-/* "what" can also follow prepositions or nouns, although it also precedes verbs, as in the area generally. The element */wēn/* "where?" also can occur following prepositions.

This gives the following types of forms: */mnēn/* "where

1 CANTINEAU (1936) p.80 shows similar forms for the 'Umūr of the Syrian Desert, i.e. *ygūman* "they stand", *tgūman* "you (f.pl.) stand".

2 See particularly PROCHAZKA (to app). This is also mentioned by JOHNSTONE (1967b) p.71-72, who gives *daxlay* "enter (f.s.)!", *sim'ay* "listen (f.s.)".

from?", */'ala wēn/* "where to?", */luwēn/* "where to", */'alēman/* "on whom, which", */ilman/* "to whom, which?" (also */ilnan/* 'Amāra), */mimman/* "who from, from which?", */bīman/* "who by or with, by which", */'idman/* (for */'ind-man/*) "who with?", */wiyyāman/* "who with?", */ibin-man/*"whose son?", */māl-man/* "whose property?" */šifit-man/* "whom did you see?", */šāfat-man/* "whom or which did she see?", */xiḏēt-man/* "whom or which did you take?", */mšānēš/* "what for?", */bēš/* "what by?", */māltēš/* "belonging to what?", */liwēš/* "what for?", */ktāb-ēš/* "a book of what?".

In the Arabian type the question word precedes and may be reflected following the noun, preposition or verb by the *Ḍamīr al-'Āyid* or "returning pronoun". Where the preposition */l-/* "to" or */b-/* "with" occur, the independent pronoun */hu/* "he", */hi/* "she" are often introduced with, it seems, the function of giving phonological substance to the form. */min'anh/* "who about?", */min 'alēh/* "who on?", */min wiyyāh/* "who with?", */min 'indih/* "who with?", */min hu minh/* "who from?", */min hu-lih/* "who for?", */wēn minh/* "where from?", */wēn hu-lih/* "where to?", */wēn fīh* or *wēn hu-buh/* "in, at where?", */wiš 'alēh/* "what about?", */wišhu-lih/*"what for?", */wiš 'anh/* "what about?", */min ibnih/* "whose son?", */wiš ḥaggih/* "belonging to what?", */min jāyibtin hi/* "who has she brought?", Sudair; */min ant šāryinluh ḏa?/* "who have you brought that for?", Qaṣīm. With longer sentences the order of the elements is variable. The interrogative complex may precede the verbal as a unit as */wēn minh jīt?/* "where did you come from?" or the preposition and object pronoun may follow the verb as in */wēn jīt minh/*.

SUDAIR: */wēn yiji lhawa minh/*"where does the air come from?", */min hu 'indih alfaras/* "who is the horse with?" */wēn rihtu-lih/* "where did you go to?", */wēn antum mṭillīnin 'alēh/* "where do you look out upon?", */wiššu 'anh yḥaćūn/* "what are they talking about?".

QAṢĪM: */min taktib lammu/*(1) "who are you writing to?", or */min hu-lih taktib/*; */min ittigahwa 'indu/* "who are you going to drink coffee with?"

SHAMMAR:*/min nimt 'indu bal-ḥafar /* "whose house did you sleep in at al-Ḥafar?", */min ana bwajhu/* "under whose protection am I?"(2)

ḌHAFĪR: */hāḏa wiš ṣōtuh/* "what is this the noise of?"

In the area studied the Arabian type of structure was exemplified for the Najd localities, Ḍhahrān, Kuwait and also Zubair. The Budūr and Euphrates bedouin showed the Mesopotamian type of structure while, however, the Rufai' showed */min/* for "who" rather than the usual */man/*.

1 For the distribution of the preposition *lamm* see p.101.
2 MONTAGNE (1935) p.76.

RUFAI': */šift-min/* "who did you see?", */'inn-min yis'al/* "who or what is he asking about?"(1)

ḤUMAID: */yinšid 'alēman/* "who is he asking about?", */lwēn riḥt/* "where did you go to?"

BUDŪR: */'alēman nišad/* "who did he ask about?", */hāḏa ilman/* "what is this for?", */wāyahit-man/* "who did you meet?"

6 The use of the terms translatable as "also", "more", "still", "yet" separates Mesopotamia from the rest of the area. In all of the area the word */ba'ad/* has the general meaning of "more" as in */ba'ad wāḥid/* "one more". The meaning "after" is served by */'ugub/* as in */'ubgin/* "afterwards", */'ugub ma-/* "after ...". Examples of this use of */ba'ad/* are */jōna ba'ad ṯalāṯah/* "there came to us three more", */'aṭni ba'ad wāḥid/* "give me one more"; Mesopotamia: */ba'ad sōlif/* "tell us more!"; Sudair: */u fīh ba'ad anwā'in ṯānyih/* "and there are also other types", */aḏinn fīh ba'ad/* "I think there is still more". In negative sentences it gives the meaning "yet" in such examples as Sudair: */ma ba'ad jāna ssēl assanah ḏi/* "this year no rain has come to us yet", */ana mā ba'ad šiftih/* "I haven't seen him yet". In the Mesopotamian type */ba'ad/* is also used with the meaning "no longer" in negative sentences, while in the Arabian type the particle */'ād/* is used; contrast:

MESOPOTAMIAN: */ba'ad mā nrīdah/* "we don't want it any more", */hāḏanni ba'ad mā yfīdannah /* "these (f.) are no use to us any more", */ba'ad ma yiḥṣal min hāḏa nnō'/* "that type is no longer available".

SUDAIR: */mā 'ād bagi lha lzūm/* "there is no need for it any longer", */mā 'ād šiftih/* "I have not seen him any longer", */mā 'ād yimdīhum/* "they can no longer do it", */mā 'ād bagi 'indana illa yōmēn ṯalāṯih/* "we have no longer any time except two or three days".

In affirmative sentences it gives the meaning "still", */wa law ḥinna 'ād naṣbir 'alēh/* "although we would still be patient with him", */ba'dēn 'ād fīh/* "and again there is still something left". The most striking difference however is in sentences where the meaning "also" is given. In the Arabian type */ba'ad/* may be used or also one of the adverbs */zoudin, zād/* "in addition".(2) In many examples "also" is expressed

1 Compare also Ahl al-Shimāl *min tabūn min albadu* "which of the bedu do you want?" This may have been under the influence of Kuwaiti interlocutors.

2 This may also be the meaning of *zīd* (*yazīd*) as given by JOHNSTONE (1964) and glossed "another time" p.92. An example of *zād* occurs in MONTAGNE (1935) p.108 *hin rāḥan lahalhin u hu zād rāḥ mi' iṯarhin ilhaluh* "they went to their families and he also went on their tracks to their family".

by a special syntactic construction of the type "X, he and Y" with the meaning "X and also Y". Examples: Shammar: */jāna rākān hu wuswēlim/* "Rakan came and also Suwailim", */u galaṭ ibn ḥmeid wu wijmā'tuh /* "Ibn Ḥumaid came into camp and also his followers", */want ba'ad ṭayyib/* "and you also are a good person", */jāna xleif u ba'ad (zoudin)* (1) *'rēfij/* "Khulaif came to us and also 'Uraifij". In the Mesopotamian type an element */ham/* of Persian origin is used. In initial position */hammēn/* or */hammēna/* occurs. This is also common in the dialect of Kuwait, but is completely absent in the Arabian dialects. It was recorded also in the speech of the Ahl al-Shimāl: */u gliṭaw ham ma'zūmin/* "they came into camp as well, as guests", */ham šift wāḥid akram minni/* "have you also seen anyone more generous than me?" The following examples from the dialect of the Kawāwila illustrate the use of this particle: */ham iya sabi' 'alīh ham ḏabbaḥa/* "another lion came at him and he killed that one also", */ḏāk ham libas u širad/* "that one also got dressed and fled", */ham 'ēnha šab'āna u ham 'idha ḥalāl wāyid/* "she is both contented and has (also) much property", */waddaw innōb 'alīh xayyāl ham mā rāḥ/* "they sent again a rider against him and again he didn't go".

7 Certain common lexical items separate the two groups. In some cases an area of vagueness occurs in so far as a particular item may be used in one area but infrequently, whereas in the other area it is the most common term. This is the case with the word for "now". In the Mesopotamian type this is */hassa/* or */hassā'/*. In the Arabian type it is */halḥīn/*. However */hassā'/* is also found in the Shammar and 'Aniza dialects but with the more emphatic meaning "at this instant". (2) Similarly with the verb "to want". In Mesopotamia it is always */rād, yrīd/*. In the Arabian dialects the most common verb is */baġa,yabi /* but */rād,yrīd/* also occurs in the northern bedouin dialects as a less common alternative.(3) The following are the clearest contrasts:

1 Also in MONTAGNE (1935) p.77: *lēh taṭlub 'ala xūy albil walfaras zoudin 'alayy* "why do you ask from my brother camels and a horse in addition to me?"
2 MONTAGNE (1935) p.106: *igṣid hassā'eih* "compose a poem on the spot". In the dialect of the Rufai' *hēḥīn*, Budūr *halḥīn*.
3 MONTAGNE (1935) in the texts from the Khruṣa p.99, 104, 106; also *baġa/yabi* p.108 from the Khruṣa. No examples of *rād/yrid* occur in the 'Abda texts, but *baġa/yabi* p.82, 90, 92, 95. LANDBERG (1919) p.4, 7, 9, 10.

Mesopotamian	Arabian	
yamta	*mita*	"when"
yāhu	*min*	"who"
yāhu	*ayy*	"which" (1)
māl-	*ḥagg-*	"belonging to"
la'ad (2)	*ajal*	"so, then, therefore"
šin- (3)	*wiš*	"what"
lo ... lo	*yā ... yā* (4)	"either ... or"
kaḏ̣ḏ̣/ykuḏ̣ḏ̣	*jawwad/yjawwid* *giḏ̣ab/yagḏ̣ub* (5)	"to grasp"
ḏabb/yḏibb	*jida'/yajda'* (6)	"to throw"
ča, wilak, wilič wilkum, wilčan	no equivalent	expletives (7)
hāwan (8)	*nijr*	"pestle"
bāwa'/ybāwi'	*baḥḥar/ybaḥḥir* (9) *faććar/yfaććir*	"to look at"
čann-	*ćinn- činn-* (10)	"as though"
lo	*walla*	"or"

FEATURES SEPARATING THE NORTHERN AND SOUTHERN AREAS

A number of contrasts link Northern Najd with Mesopotamia and in some cases with a more general northern area as against Central Najd and the Gulf to the south. In general the isoglosses seem on the basis of the evidence available to

1 BLANC(1970) also notes *yāt* "which" for the Negev, p.144.
2 WETZSTEIN (1868) also gives *la'ad* "then, so" for the 'Aniza, p.126, 127.
3 *wišhu* was regarded by my Budūr informants as "bedouin"; they used *šinu* "what is it". See also CANTINEAU (1936) p.108 who gives forms of the type *šinu,šinhu,wišinhu* for the 'Umūr, Ṣlūṭ, Bani Khālid and Mawāli. The Ḍhafīr also used *šinhu, šinhi* etc. as well as *wišhu*.
4 Also in the Ahl al-Shimāl, Text 9.
5 *yawwad/yyawwid* in the Rufai' dialect; also Zubair who show *giḏ̣ab* as well.
6 Also in the dialect of Zubair *yida'/yiyda'*.
7 Kawāwila: *wilak ča yahaw ilšāf martah ykuḏ̣ḏ̣un bīha wiyġādūn bīha jiddāmak winta xāyif.* "Look, really, who could watch his wife being pulled and dragged about in front of your eyes and you are afraid (to do anything)." *wak* in the dialect of the Zubair.
8 Persian *havang*
9 *baḥḥar* also in the dialect of the Rufai' and Ḥumaid.
10 *činn* in the Ḥumaid dialect.

run between the Jabal Shammar and the northern Qaṣīm area in Central Arabia for the sedentary dialects. As regards the nomads, those regarded as "southern", i.e. Ḥarb, Muṭair, 'Awāzim, Rashāyda, 'Utaiba, 'Ajmān and Dawāsir have the southern form, and those regarded as northern, i.e. 'Aniza, Shammar, Ḍhafīr, Bani Khālid and Euphrates bedouin, have the northern form.(1) The Ḥarb are divided for feature 1 into Hijazi and Najdi types. The Hijazi type show the northern feature which is also the form for the Hijaz urban dialect. (2) The Najd Ḥarb showed the southern feature. The 'Aniza although northern show the southern feature for feature 4 and for one of the cases mentioned under 3. The dialect of my Qaṣīm informant showed the southern form for all cases except 2 where it seems to have the northern type. However my material on that point was not complete. In general the isogloss distribution reflects the view of a later emergence of the various 'Aniza dialects into the northern area as they show considerably more southern characteristics than the Najd Shammar and Ḍhafīr dialects although now more northerly in location.

1 The form of the second person masculine singular object suffix is basically */-ak/* in the north, */-ik/* in the south. In the southern area the two suffixes of the singular are distinguished for gender purely by the nature of the consonant, i.e. */-ik, -iċ/* Qaṣīm and Central Najd, */-ik, -ič/* the Gulf area, and */-ik, -iš/* Southern Najd and Oman.(3) In the northern type the realisation of the */k/* consonant in the masculine suffix is often a very back velar i.e. */-aḳ/*. The Inner Najdi type dialects also show */-uḳ/* or */-iḳ/* [-ɤḳ] while the Gulf type has */-ik/* [-ɪk]. In my material */-ak/* is recorded for all of Khuzistan and South Iraq, the Euphrates bedouin, Shammar, Ḍhafīr and all 'Aniza dialects investigated, that is: Ṣgūr, Sba'a, Ḥiblān and 'Awāja. The 'Awāja are the southernmost group, being a branch of the Wild Sulaimān west of Hail. It seems that the Bani Khālid also show this form.(4)

1 Interestingly DICKSON (1949) p.155 gives almost the same division for the wearing of the *burgu'* or women's face mask. This is worn only among the southern tribes, which include however the Bani Khālid, southern by location but not by dialect.
2 See INGHAM (1971) p.289.
3 See JOHNSTONE (1967b) p.14.
4 My information on the Bani Khālid was inconclusive, as one informant also gave *-ik*, but Shammar informants were agreed that *-ak* was the most common form among the Bani Khālid.

SBA'A: /tabīni agūlha lak/ "would you like me to recite it for you?", /niṣīhti lak/ "my advice to you".
ṢGŪR: /wišbālak/ "what's wrong with you", /ummak/ "your mother", /wišbak/ "what's wrong with you".
SHAMMAR: /anšidak/ "I ask you", /mṛutak/ "your wife", /wlidak/ "your son", /mnak/ "from you", /yidak/ "your hand".
ḎHAFĪR: /šlōnak/ "how are you", /'indak/ "you have", /'aṭeitak/ "I gave you".
AHL AL-SHIMĀL: /axbirak/ "I tell you", /'abdak/ "your slave", /š'alāmak/ "what's wrong with you".
RUFAI': /a'allmak/ "I will tell you", /xallak hnayya/ "stay here!"
ḤUMAID: /anšidak/ "I ask you".
ḤARB (Bani 'Amr): /'induk/ "you have".
MUṬAIR: /ašūfuk/ "I see you", /rawwiḥlik/ "send for yourself".
'AWĀZIM: /liḥyitik/ "your beard", /waguftik/ "your position", /šōfuk/ "your sight", /ša'bik/ "your people".
RASHĀYIDA: /abanšdik/ "I will ask you", /liḥālik/ "for yourself", /y'āwnik/ "he helps you", /wajhik/ "your face".
FAILIČA: /šāfik/ "he saw you", /bagūllik/ "I say to you", /šāfitik/ "she saw you", /wlāyhimmik/ "let it not concern you".
QAṢĪM (Midhnab): /wišnōḥik/ "what's wrong with you?", /byāltik/ "your cup", /buh 'indik ghawa/ "have you any coffee", /bintik/ "your daughter".
SUDAIR: /ana jayyin lammik/ "I am coming to see you", /nḥawwilhā-lik/ "we will transfer it to you", /mištāgillik/ "looking forward to seeing you".
'AJMĀN: /dūnuk/ "before you", /kānuk/ "if you are...", /'induk/ "you have".
ZUBAIR: /bētik/ "your house", /anšdik/ "I ask you".
'UTAIBA: /xallik/ "leave yourself", /jārik/ "your neighbour", /xawiyyik/ "your companion", /'irfik/ "your knowledge".
'AWĀJA: /xawiyyak/ "your companion".

Dialects showing /-ik/ are the Gulf, Sudair, Qaṣīm and Riyadh; also the Muṭair, 'Awāzim, Rashāyida, Najdi Ḥarb,(1) 'Utaiba, 'Ajmān and Dawāsir.

2 In the northern type the prepositions /fi/ and /bi-/ have merged leaving only /bi-/ as a general locative and instrumental preposition. In the south /fi/ remains with the meaning "in" while /bi-/ designates "at" or "by". The distribution of this contrast seems to be identical with 1 above. Although the evidence for the 'Aniza dialects is not absolutely clear, both Landberg's and Wetzstein's material

---

1 The Ḥarb of Hijaz also show -ak. This is true of the dialect of my informant and also of el-Ḥāzmi's.

and my own suggest that */fi/* is replaced by */bi-/* in these dialects. In neither Landberg's nor Wetzstein's material are there examples of */fi/*. In my own Sba'a material */fi/* occurs but this may be under the influence of the more common type. A factor which supports this interpretation is that the word for "here" is */bihāḏa/* "in this place" and the word for "there is" is */baha/* or */bih/* "in it". In some other dialects with */fi/* the word for "there is" is */fīh/* and "here" is */fīḏih/*.(1) Sentences suggesting this interpretation from the texts are the following: (Landberg, 1919): */xašš bwusṭ halġanam/* "he entered into the middle of these sheep" (p.2); */wilyā lḥadid brijlēn azzlima/* "and there were the irons on the legs of the man" (p.5); */yimalli lźirbah ukullma yḥuṭṭ baha šwayyat ma/* "he filled up the skin and every time he put some water in it" (p.7); */walā titwāṣa lgahawa ibbētak/* "and you will not order coffee in your tent" (p.6); */hu bak ši wuja'/* "is there some pain in you" (p.6); */ṣār ibbēt ibn swēṭ/* "he came into the tent of Ibn Suwaiṭ" (p.8); */al'ūd yinbut ibmaćānu 'ūd/* "a stick grows up as a stick in its own place" (p.10); */rakaz arrumḥ bilbalad/* "he stuck the lance in the earth" (p.13). From my own material we find: Ṣgūr: */halmukān alli ḥinnā-bha/* "this place which we are in"; Sba'a: */mā ligeitkum ibbeitkum/* "I didn't find you at your house". In the Shammar dialects and those of Iraq and Khuzistan the non-existence of */fi/* is well known. Consider the following: Shammar: */laffuh balhiẓām/* "he wrapped it in the belt"; */ga'ad balgaṣur/* "he stayed in the castle" (Montagne, 1935, p.176); */šāl ġadfituh uḥaṭṭah balxarj/* "il enleva son voile de tête et le mit dans son bissac" (Montagne, 1935, p.91). Kawāwila: */irrumḥ ṭāf 'ala baṭn ilfaras winšijax birričāb/* "the lance went around the stomach of the horse and stuck into the saddle"; */u šaggah bwaṣt iddarwāza mālt ilġaṣur/* "and he stuck it in the middle of the gate of the castle"; */asma' bilbīr ḥiss ixtibāṭāt/* "I hear the sounds of movement in the well". Zubair: */bilbēt/* "in the house"; */bilġrufa/*"in the room".

In contrast the following examples show the use of */fi/* in the more southern dialects:

MUṬAIR: */wara mā rićibtum min dīratkum all antum fīha gabul/* "why did you not set out from your dīrah in which you were before?"; */twallawh min najd u min hāk alkasrah mā šabb fīha nār/* "they drove him out of Najd and after that defeat he did not light a campfire there"; */lēh mā simaḥt libin ḥmeid yrabbi' fi najd/* "why did you not permit Ibn Ḥumaid to graze in Najd?"

1 However it seems that some dialects which show *fi* also have *bih*, cf. JOHNSTONE's Hājiri text (1967b, p.226).

'AWĀZIM: */wuṭanna alli ḥinna fīh/* "our homeland which we are in"; */min istišārik daxal fi ḏimmitik/* "he who asks your advice enters into your protection"; */ana a'allmik fīh/* "I will teach you about it"; */wagūl fi wāḥdin mnal'iyāl/* "and I say about one of the family".

'AJMĀN: */doulat alatrāk falḥasa/* "the government of the Turks was in al-Hasa"; */'indi lkum sālfa lṯāmir ibn s'ēdān issbē'i fisābg izzimān/* "I have a story for you about Thāmir ibn Su'aidān the Sbai'i in earlier times"; */ḥāṭṭīnin firjīlih ḥadid/* "and they had put chains on his legs"; */arrajjāl dāxlin 'alēha filġrufah alli hi fīha/*"the man entered in to see her in the room which she was in"; */ṣōb ahalih fil'āriḍ/* "towards his family in al-'Āriḍh".

ḤARB: */baġat tiži fīha rgāb umaṣāyib/* "there was going to come in it rivalries and problems"; */u tisawwagna fassūg/* "and we did our shopping in the market"; */utidaxxaḷ waḷḷah fīha 'beid/* "and 'Ubaid interceded in the matter".

3 A number of lexical items have somewhat different forms distributed roughly north and south although they are obviously cognate, unlike the non-cognate items mentioned above for the Mesopotamian/Arabian contrast. These are the following:

Northern	Southern	
anṭa yinṭi	*'aṭa y'aṭi*	"to give"
kala/yākil	*akal/yākil*	"to eat"
xaḏa yāxiḏ	*axaḏ yāxiḏ*	"to take"
hēč, hīč, hīć	*čiḏa,ćiḏah,ćiḏīh,čiḏi*	"thus, so"

The division into Northern and Southern for these features is the same as the general division outlined above except that the 'Aniza and Shammar seem to show both types for the verb "to give", while some 'Aniza show the northern and some the southern type for "to take" and "to eat". My Shammar material gives */yi'ṭūn/* "they give", */'aṭeitūni/* "you gave me". Cantineau (1937, p.231) mentions the northern forms for the two items, while Montagne gives nasalised forms in */'āṭīk/* "I will give you". For the 'Aniza my Sba'a and 'Awāja informants gave */'aṭa y'aṭi/* and said that */niṭa yanṭi/* meant "to weave". However both Landberg (1919) and Wetzstein (1868) give numerous examples. Landberg (p.4): */tanṭīh/* "you give him", */anṭīk/* "I give you"; Wetzstein (p.80): */anṭāhin/* "he gave them(f.)". For the verbs "to take" and "to eat" Cantineau, agreeing with my Sba'a informants, states that the 'Aniza show the southern type of form (p.234), while both Landberg and Wetzstein give examples of the northern. Landberg: */kala/* (p.5); */xaḏa/* (p.6,7), */xaḏēna/* (p.80), */xaḏāh/* (p.14) passim. Wetzstein: */kala/* (p.5), */xaḏa/* (p. 6,7) passim. The Ḍhafīr surprisingly show the southern type for all three cases: */'aṭāni/* "he gave me", */almiṛa 'aṭatni/*

"the woman gave me", */a'ṭyah/* "I give her", */'aṭni/* "give me", */axaḏt/* "I took", */akaltah/* "I ate it (f.)".

Apart from the above the distribution is as expected for these items: Iraq and Khuzistan */niṭa, yinṭi/* "to give", */xiḏa, yāxiḏ* or *xaḏa/* "to take", */kila*(or *kala*) *yākil/* "to eat"; all Arabian dialects investigated (1) */'aṭa y'aṭi* (or *yi'ṭi*)/, */axaḏ,yāxiḏ/*, */akal, yākil/*. The Ahl al-Shimāl gave */anṭīk/* "I give you" but also */'aṭni/* "give me". However it seems that */'aṭni/* as an imperative is used in dialects where the normal form of the verb is */niṭa, yinṭi/* as this was also the case in the dialect of 'Amāra. With the word for "thus, so" the north/south division is easily established. All 'Aniza dialects investigated have */hīć/*; Khuzistan and Iraq have */hīč/* except for the Shaṭṭ al-'Arab and Kārūn which have */hēč/*. The Bani Khālid, Euphrates bedouin and Budūr have */hīč/*. From my Shammar informants I heard */hīć/* and */hāć/*, though far more commonly */hallōn/* which is also heard in Iraq. The Ḍhafīr accepted */hīć/* but gave as more typical */hassuwa/* or */hassuwayya/*. In the south */ćiḏa/* was the most widespread, common to Rashāyida, Ḥarb, Muṭair, Sudair, Riyadh and Qaṣīm. The 'Awāzim show the form */ćiḏīh/*, the East Coast and Zubair */čiḏi/*.(2) A feature with corresponding distribution to this is the occurrence of */ḏa/* or */ḏi/* as a form of the demonstrative. All dialects of the area show */hāḏa/* "this (m)", */hāḏi/* "this (f)", but dialects of a southern distribution also show */ḏa/* and */ḏi/* as an alternative form. The 'Aniza, Shammar and Ḍhafīr informants regarded this as "southern"; however it does occur in restricted conditions in the 'Aniza material of Landberg and Wetzstein: Landberg (1919, p.6, 59, 72, 79) */min 'ugub ḏa/* "after that"; Wetzstein (1868, p.179, 78) */ḏil wćēt/* "at that time", */yōm min ḏāt ilayyām/* "one of those days".(3) Examples from the southern dialects include:

ḤARB: */hāḏ al yaḏhar min ḏah/* "this is what appears from that", */aṭṭurīgah ḏi/* "that matter".

MUṬAIR: */fḏa lfēḏah/* "in that hollow", */u šlōn aljiha ḏa, ćiḏah?/* "and what about in that direction, like that?".

SUDAIR: */fḏa lisbū'/* "that week", */tabi hāḏ walla ḏah/* "do you want this or that?", */wana ḏa lli ana sām'ih/* "and that is what I have heard", */alwruga ḏi/* "that paper", */alḥarakih ḏi/* "that action".

1 One exception outside our area is the Dawāsir who show *xaḏa* (JOHNSTONE, 1964, p.97).

2 In the West *hēk* is common to most of Syria and Lebanon, while *kiḏah* or *kida* is the form in the Hijaz. BLANC (1970) gives *kiḏiy* or *kiḏi* for the Negev bedouins, p.35, 146. See BERGSTRASSER (1915) for details of the situation in Syria.

3 JOHNSTONE (1967b) also mentions that phrases like *ḏalḥīn*

QAṢĪM (Midnab): /*mnant šāryin luh ḏah*/ "who have you bought that for?"

RIYADH: /*albēt ḏa*/ "that house",/*aššijarah ḏi*/ "that tree", /*wiš ḏa*/ "what is that?", /*wēn tabūn ḏi walla ḏi*/ "which do you want, this or that?"(1)

DŌSIRI: /*wiš hu ḏa ššayy li mḏ̣ayyigiš* / "what is that thing which has upset you (f.s.)?", /*ma' il fintōg-ḏa*/ "through that pass", /*ma' ḏa ljabal*/ "across that mountain"(2) /*li'irg ḏa*/ "that sand dune".

QAṬARI: /*ḏah min aḷḷah mu mink*/ "that is from God not you".

HĀJIRI: /*ḏa ygūlih*/ "that is what he said", /*wlē ḏa B mitlāgīhu N*/ "and there was B and N who had met B".(3)

4 A further feature which seems to have a north/south distribution, but which is somewhat more difficult to establish exactly, is the form of demonstratives cognate with OA /*hunā*/ "here". In the north the forms /*hnā*/ or /*hna* / and /*hān*/ occur; in the south /*hnayya*/ or /*hni*/. The problem in determining this is that in the inner Najd and bedouin dialects alternative forms of the type "in this (place)" have developed (see following section) and the reflexes of /*hunā*/ are not always used. Forms of the type /*hnayya*/ are found only in the southern area and also in some 'Aniza dialects. Landberg gives it for the Wild 'Ali, but only one occurrence (/*hĕneyya*/). Blanc gives /*hni*/ and /*hniyya*/ for the Negev bedouins. Examples from my notes include Sba'a, Ṣgūr, Ḥarb, Muṭair: /*hnayya*/; 'Awāzim: /*hniyya, hnīh*/; Kuwait, Zubair: /*hni*/. The Shammar and Ḍhafīr said that they did not use /*hnayya*/ and regarded it as "southern". The form used in Iraq and Khuzistan is regularly /*hnā*/, with /*hān*/ also used in the areas of North Khuzistan and 'Amāra.(4) The Euphrates bedouin showed both forms; Rufai': /*xallak hnayya*/ "stay here", /*hni yāy*/ "in this direction", /*hān*/ "here"; Ahl al-Shimāl: /*minu hnā*/ "who is here?". The form /*hna* / is used in the central dialects but with a less deictic function, corresponding to "there is", in such examples as:

ṢGŪR: /*hna ṯnēn jaw*/ "there are two people coming".(5)

ḏilayyām "those days" are common to dialects which do not normally show *ḏa* (p.118).

1 BADAWI (1965) p.216, 214)

2 JOHNSTONE (1964) p.98, 101, 103, 102.

3 JOHNSTONE (1967b) p.119, 122.

4 Also in many of the "petits nomades" of the Syrian desert, CANTINEAU (1936) p.110.

5 But also Dōsiri *hnā*, JOHNSTONE (1967b) p.17.

RIYADH: /*mā hna mrāja'a*/ "there is no blasphemy", or even meaning "there".

ḌHAFĪR: /*ruḥ hna*/ "go there!"

And in combination with /*min*/:

SHAMMAR: /*šiddaw min ihna*/ "load up and move away (from here)".

'AWĀJA: /*mišaw min ihna*/ "they went from here".

The form /*hān*/ is used by the Shammar in /*min hān*/ "from here". Generally then /*hna*/ is used in most of the area as a general demonstrative, but only in Iraq and Khuzistan as "here". /*hnayya*/ and /*hni*/ are used in the so-called southern dialects but also among the 'Aniza.(1)

5 The occurrence of the negative construction with /*mā b-*/ is generally distributed to the south. To the north the plain negative /*mā*/ occurs. The construction with /*bi-*/ was recorded for Riyadh, Sudair and for the dialects of the Ḥarb, Muṭair and 'Awāzim. It does not occur in the dialects of Mesopotamia, Kuwait or Zubair or in the dialects of the Ḍhafīr, Shammar and 'Aniza.(2) My material for the Qaṣīm is inconclusive on this feature. Examples:

ḤARB: /*mā hu b'indak*/ "it is not with you", /*mā hum biygaṣṣirūn*/ "they will not let us down".

MUṬAIR: /*mā hi bhi*/ "it is not so", /*zimānhum wagt ma hu bṭayyib*/ "there was a time of drought, it (was) not good".

'AWĀZIM: /*mā hu biššiʼr ilawwal*/ "it is not (like) the early poetry", /*māhu bṣidź*/ "it is not the truth", /*māni bnāsin*/ "I have not forgotten", /*māhi bḥilu*/ "it is not nice".

SUDAIR: /*manta bjayy*/ "you are not coming", /*mā hum biyjūn*/ "they will not come", /*māni bbalḥēl*/ "I am not so well", /*mā ḥinna bmiḥtājīnillihum*/ "we are not in need of them", /*mā hu biyxālif*/ "it doesn't matter".

RIYADH: /*mā hi biḥkūmiyya*/ "they are not from the government", /*mā hu bma'gūl*/ "it is not reasonable", /*ana mā bb'arif illa hal 'arabi*/ "I know nothing except this (language) Arabic", /*māhu bilyōm*/ "not today".

1 It may also be relevant that a form /*hna* / seems to be used meaning "bravo" in some 'Aniza dialects; see LANDBERG (1940) p.91.

2 None of my 'Aniza informants gave forms of this type and in the material of Landberg and Wetzstein it is absent except for one instance in a poem in LANDBERG (1919) p. 123. *māni bšaggām* "je ne mangerai pas pour soutenir ma vie".

FEATURES SEPARATING THE CENTRAL AREA FROM THE OUTER FRINGE

A number of features not connected with the reductional changes mentioned in Chapter 3 separate the interior from the outer fringe, i.e. Mesopotamia and the Gulf. For a number of these features, namely 2 and 3, the outer bedouin tribes (Euphrates bedouin and the 'Awāzim and Rashāyida) group with the outer region. For feature 1 also the Euphrates bedouin group with the outer region, while the 'Awāzim and Rashāyida group with the inner tribes, i.e. 'Aniza, Shammar, Ḍhafīr, Muṭair and Ḥarb. The distinction is somewhat obscured in respect of 2 and 3 by the fact that the Shammar also show the form characteristic of the outer region to the west, i.e. Hijaz and the East Mediterranean lands. In 3 the Ḍhafīr also show similar forms. However this does not invalidate the inner/outer distinction but only relates to a rather more restricted inner area.

1 One of the most widely recognised features and one amply described elsewhere (1) is the type of fronting which has occurred with OA */kāf/* and */qāf/* in fronting environments. In the interior type these have been fronted to */ć/* [ts] and */ź/* [dz], while in the outer type they appear as */č/* [tʃ] and */j/* [dʒ]. In this feature the Euphrates bedouin and Bani Khālid and the shepherds group with the outer area, while the Muṭair, Rashāyida, 'Awāzim, Shammar, 'Aniza, Ḍhafīr and Najd Ḥarb group with the inner area. Within the peninsula Qaṣīm, Sudair and Riyadh are recorded as showing the */ć,ź/* forms while the Gulf dialects (2) show */č/* and */j/*. The 'Ajmān, who originate in Southern Najd, do not have affricated forms of */kāf/* and */qāf/* and show */k/* and */g/* in all reflexes of these units.(3) Examples:

MUṬAIR: */rićib/* "he rode", */sīźān/* "legs", */tafriź/* "it is different", */ḥāćim/* "ruler", */yadć/* "your hand (f.s.)", */ćima/* "like, as", */ćiḏah/* "thus, so", */rīź/* "spittle", */aźźāblah/* "tomorrow evening".

'AWĀZIM: */yabći/* "he cries", */faććir/* "look!", */yaćḏib/* "he lies".

RASHĀYIDA: */ṯiźīl/* "heavy", */źīl/* "talk", */xālźik/* "your creator".

ḤARB: */smāć/* "period after the rain season", */ćannah/* "summer", */marāći/* "cushions", */mrēćib/* "fire hearth frame", */ṯalīź/* "tent pole", */aćil/* "food".

1 See JOHNSTONE (1967b) "Affrication", p.2-6; CANTINEAU (1937) p.139-43).
2 See JOHNSTONE (1967b) p.4.
3 See JOHNSTONE (1964) p.84-6; also see Text 1.

SHAMMAR: */šićīmeih/* "bridle", */rifīź/* "friend", */ḥći/* "it was said", */wiźźifat/* "it (f.) was stopped", */birćeih/* "well", */banādić/* "guns", */yinwićil/* "it is edible", */niź'idu/* "we will make him sit", */ćabd/* "liver, small hill", */ćitād/* "thorny tree".

SUDAIR: */mbaććirin/* "early", */asā'idć/* "I will help you (f.s.)", */źid/* "verbal particle", */ḥaćyikum/* "your talk", */ćid̲b/* "untruth".

ḌHAFĪR: */rićibt/* "I mounted", */tarćab/* "you mount", */šjarāt ćitīrāt/* "many trees", */ćeif int/* "how are you?"

QAṢĪM: */hād̲ōlīć/* "those (f.)", */ćibab/* "rope fixing to well bucket", */dannaź/* "he bent down".

'ANIZA: */fārić/* "tent-dividing curtain", */hīć/* "like this", */liḥiź/* "he followed", */irtać/* "lean!", */lźi/* "it was found", */wćil/* "it was eaten", */ćīs/* "bag purse", */mwarrić/* "sitting cross-legged", */mṣaźźil/* "polished".

EUPHRATES BEDOUIN: */čōl/* "desert", */jilīb/* "well", */čīs/* "tobacco pouch", */hīč/* "thus", */čitab/* "camel saddle", */čabd/* "liver", */činn-/* "as if", */yirčib/* "he rides", */čēf/* "how".

2 In the central area, except Northern Najd, the object suffixes */-ak* or *-ik*, *-ić* and *-ih/* lose their vowel in structures in which they follow a syllable of the type -VC. The */-t/* of feminine suffixes is often assimilated to */k/* and */ć/* giving */-kk/* and */-ćć/* for */-tk/* and */-tć/*. In the outer area and in Northern Najd the vowel is retained more frequently. Although the Northern Najdi type does not show this feature it is nevertheless characteristically a feature of the inner area rather than "southern", as in general the Gulf dialects (1) and also the dialects of the 'Awāzim and Rashāyida do not show it. (The vowel of the third person masculine singular suffix */-ih/* also loses its vowel under similar circumstances.) Dialects showing this feature are the 'Aniza, Ḍhafīr, Ḥarb, Muṭair, 'Utaiba, 'Ajmān and Dawāsir for the bedouin, also the dialects of Riyadh, Sudair and Qaṣīm. As mentioned by Cantineau, in the Syrian desert area this had become a prestige marking feature as characteristic of the powerful 'Aniza tribes of the area and as such was adopted by certain sedentary groups.(2) Examples:

ḤARB: */lizmatk/* "your promise", */naxalk/* "your palms", */yadk/* "your hand", */yadć/* "your (f.) hand", */waladk/* "your son", */wilyā minh.../* "when he...", */anšidk/* "I ask you", */mā jābh ḏ̣harih akalih baṭnih/* "what his back brings, his stomach eats", */mādri 'anh/* "I don't know about him", */salāmatk/* "your health".

1 An exception to this is the Shi'a dialect of Bahrain and the dialect of al-Ḥasa; see PROCHAZKA (to appear).
2 CANTINEAU (1937) p.236.

'ANIZA (Sba'a): */jābakk/* "she bore you", */ghark aḷḷah yā šīn/* "God abhores you, O evil one! (an expression used to a person of great cleverness)", */aḥasibć/* "I think of you (f. s.)", */ćinh.../* "as though he...", */jābh aḷḷah/* "God brought him".

DHAFĪR: */sa'alk 'anni/* "he asked you (m.s.) about me", */mā trūḥ lahalk/* "aren't you going home to your family?", */wilyā mink.../* "and when you have..." */sā'atk mbāraka/* "your hour is blessed (an expression of welcome), */aḷḷa yḥafuḏk/* "God preserve you", */a'allimk/* "I will tell you", */saḥḥāraćć/* "your (f.s.) suitcase", */xallah 'ank/* "leave it alone".

'UTAIBA:(1) */rgubatk/* "your neck", */ana baṯawwirk/* "ich möchte dich einschreiten lassen gegen", */yarḥamk aḷḷa/* "God have mercy on you", */'iyāli wudā'atk/* "my family are your ransom", */'iyālć/* "your (f.s.) family".

QAṢĪM (Midhnab): */akramk aḷḷah/* "God reward you", */simi'k/* "he heard you", */nšiditan 'ank/* "he asked me about you", */'ajabk/* "it pleased you", */anšidć/* "I ask you (f.s.)".

SUDAIR: */wāldakk/* "your mother", */sayyārakk/* "your car", */gōlakk/* "as you say", */axābirk/* "I will telephone you", */ḏeifk alli 'indik/* "your guest who is with you", */jiz'in minh/* "a part of it", */asā'idć/* "I will help you (f.s.)", */yḥaḏḏirūnh ilna/* "they will prepare it for us", */yirsilūnh ilna/* "they will send it to us", */'aṭeitk/* "I gave (it) to you".

MUṬAIR: */alla birxuṣtin minh/* "except by permission from him", */salāmatk/* "your health", */šālh azza'al/* "anger drove him away", */rajilć/* "your husband (f.s.)", */ḏimmatk/* "your protection".

In the outer type the vowel is retained in these forms. In the north, i.e. the Shammar dialect and the Mesopotamian type, the vowel of the second masculine singular is */-a/*, while in the Gulf area peninsular type it is */i/*. Examples:

SHAMMAR: */šāfitak/* "she saw you", */mrutak/* "your wife", */ḥurmitak/* "your wife", */anšidak/* "I ask you (m.s.)", */ wlidak/* "your son", */yidak/* "your (m.s.) hand", */yidić/* "your (f.s.) hand", */'nuh /* "from him", */mnuh/* "from him", */mnak/* "from you (m.s.)", */mnić/* "from you (f.s.)", */abanhabić/* "I am going to elope with you", */mnuh/* "from him".

MESOPOTAMIA (bādiya): */šāfitak/* "she saw you", */frusak/* "your house".

RASHĀYIDA: */wlidik/* "your son", */salāmtik/* "your health", */tanglik/*"she carried you", */waguftik/* "your situation", */haguwtik/* "your thought", */y'āwnik/* "he helps you", */abanšdik/* "I will ask you", */wāldik/* "your father".

1 HESS (1938) p.97, 94, 155, 94, 155.

'AWĀZIM: */šāwarik/* "he consulted you", */d̲immitik/* "your protection", */a'allmik/* "I will tell you", */liḥyitik/* "your beard". (1)

3 The form of the third person masculine singular suffix is */-ih/* in the inner area, */-ah/* in the periphery with the exception of areas with the North Najdi form */-uh/*. The form */-ih/* is attested for the Muṭair, 'Aniza, Ḥarb, 'Ajmān and Dawāsir, also for Riyadh and Sudair. The form */-ah/* is found in the Gulf dialects, al-Hasa and Mesopotamia and also in the dialects of the 'Awāzim and Rashāyida. In dialects where the form is */-ih/* the vowel is regularly elided when followed by vowel initial forms giving similar forms to those mentioned under 2 above, even where the form */-h/* would not normally occur, i.e. following syllables of the type Cv:C. Examples:

'AJMI: */yagd̲i lizūmh imn issūg/* "he completes his errands in the market".

SUDAIR: */yḥaḍḍirūnh-ilna/* "he prepares it for us".

'ANIZA: */jābh aḷḷah/* "God has brought him".

MUṬAIR: */šālh azza'al/* "anger carried him away".

ḤARB: */mā jābh d̲harih akalih baṭnih/* "what his back brings his stomach eats".

'UTAIBA: */alxāyin yxūnh aḷḷah/* "May God betray the betrayer".(2)

4 In the inner dialects alongside reflexes of OA */hunā/* "here", expressions of the type "in this (place)" occur. These are used commonly with the meaning "here" and are more common than the reflexes of */hunā/* which have lost some of their deictic function and can be used as purely syntactic elements (see 5 below). The forms occurring are */bhād̲a/* 'Aniza, Shammar, Ḍhafīr; also */bhāh/* Shammar; */bd̲a/* Qaṣīm; */fīd̲ah/* Sudair; */fīd̲ih/* Riyadh. The form */bhād̲a/* is also recorded for the Syrian desert 'Aniza by Landberg (1919, p. 2). */fīhād̲a/* or */bhād̲a/* is recorded by Blanc (1970, p.146) for the Negev bedouins. Examples:

SHAMMAR: */baġeit ašūf anta bhād̲a walla mānta bhād̲a/* "I wanted to see if you were here or not", */ligēnāw bhād̲a/* "we found him here.

ḌHAFĪR: */ta'āl bhād̲a/* "come here".

QAṢĪM: */atnāk bd̲a/* "I will wait for you here", */gim min d̲a/* "go away from here", */šiddu min d̲a/* "move away from here!", */šufēhum bd̲a/* "see (f.s.) them here!".

1 But also *'ank* "from you", *mink* "from you". It seems that this form of the suffix is common with these prepositions even in dialects where it is not common in other structures.

2 HESS (1938) p.155.

SUDAIR: */ywaggifūn fīḏah/* "they park (their cars) here", */want fīḏah/* "so you are here!".

RIYADH: */'abd il'azīz fīḏih/*"is Abd el'Azīz here?"(1)

'ANIZA: */ig'idum bihāḏa/* "sit here".(2)

My notes do not reveal whether or not these expressions are used by the Euphrates bedouin or by the 'Awāzim, Rashāyida, Muṭair or Ḥarb.

5 In the inner dialects the existential predicate is conveyed by an expression of the type "in it" or by the word */hna/* "here". In the north the form is */bah, buh* or *baha, bih/* depending on the dialect. In the central area */fīh* or *fīha/*. Expressions with */hna/* "here" also occur. The forms */bah* or *buh/* etc. are recorded for Qaṣīm and for the Shammar, 'Aniza, Ḍhafīr and Euphrates bedouin. The form */fīh/* is recorded for the Muṭair, Ḥarb, Dawāsir, 'Awāzim and Rashāyida and for the Sudair and Riyadh. In the outer dialects the form */aku/* is common, which may be derived from */yakūn/* "it is", and also */hast/* or */hassit/* from Persian */hast/* "there is".

a) Expressions with *fi-* or *b-*

'ANIZA (Sba'a): */wišbaha? baha l'išb u baha ra'i wājid/* "What is there there? There is grass and much pasture."

EUPHRATES BEDOUIN: */abašširkum bēh xēr u baha 'išbin lā yṭūl/* "I give you good news. There is good fortune and grass which will not last."; */addinya sāḥi u lā bah ġēm/* "The weather is clear and there is no cloud."; */addinya maḥal u gaḥaṭ mā buh ši/* "The world is in drought, there is nothing."

SHAMMAR: */addyār gṭū' mā bah ḥad/* "The area was deserted. There was no one there."; */bīrin bu ma/* "A well with water in it."

QAṢĪM: */aźźilīb bah ma? īh bah/* "Is there water in the well? Yes there is."; */buh 'indik ghawa? ī buh. lā mā buh, mā buš/* "Is there any coffee with you? Yes there is. No there isn't, there is nothing." */iććān darb alhawa buh 'ēb.../* "If there is any shame in the way of love..."

MUṬAIR: */fīh giṣāyid wājid/* "There are many Qaṣīdas (odes)."; */wadarrša fīh sabi' alḥmuḏāt u mrabbi/* "In Wādi al-Risha there are the seven ḥamaḏhat (saline plants) and it is in flower."

'AWĀZIM: */albil fīha nāgah u fīh mwaṣṣaṭa u fīha ḏilūl/* "Among camels there are racing camels, ordinary camels and guide camels."; */fīh ġāḏi yimīl u ġāḏi yicḥif/* "There are judges who are dishonest and some who are honest."

1 BADAWI (1965) p.78.
2 LANDBERG (1919) p.2.

DAWĀSIR: /*mā fīha ḥaḏarin aṣīlīn*/ "There were no original settled people there."; /*willēl muġdar mā fīha gamrā*/ "The night was dark. There was no moonlight in it."(1)

b) Expressions with *hna*

'ANIZA: /*hna iṯnēn jaw axāf in minhum*/ "Here are two (people) coming. I think they are from them."
RIYADH: /*mā hna murāja'a*/ "There is no blasphemy."; /*mā hna bnayyāt*/ "Are there no daughters?"(2)

c) Expressions with *aku or hast*

MESOPOTAMIAN (Kawāwila): /*mir'i ḥāss aku rbīd bilbīr*/ "Mur'i sensed that there was a snake in the well."; /*waḷḷa māku bdīratna hna*/ "There are none in this dīrah of ours here."; /*gāl: māku 'amal, šayy baṣīṭ*/ "He said: there is not (much) work, it is a simple thing."; /*halyōm ba'ad māku aḥad*/ "Today there is no one any longer."; /*bḥīn mā dašš ḥabīb māku bīda ṭaḥīn*/ "When Ḥabib entered there was no flour in his hand".
SHAṬṬ AL-'ARAB: /*māy hassit*/ "There is water."
GULF (Kuwaiti): /*mā hast šayy ṯāni*/ "There is nothing else."(3)

As can be seen from the above examples the interior type continues the system of Classical Arabic insofar as there is no existential verb "to be". Expressions of the type /*buh ma*/ "there is water" are extensions of the ordinary prepositional use of /*b-*/ in /*aẑẑilīb buh ma*/ "the well (there is) in it water". The /*-h*/ of /*buh*/ or /*fīh*/ is a dummy object referring perhaps to "the world" or "the place" so that /*buh ma*/ is at a higher level of analysis, "In it (the world) (there is) water." In the outer type on the other hand actual existential verbal particles have developed.

6 A number of lexical differences also follow the lines of those mentioned above. However, in the main, lexical differences separate Mesopotamia from Arabia and fall under "Features Separating Southern Mesopotamia from Arabia" (see p.79 ff.). In the main these differences consist of special lexical usages developed in the central area and differentiating it from the area outside Arabia in general. The most easily statable are shown below. Not all of these have been checked for all inner dialects, but can be expected to occur generally. However the dialects for which they are attested are marked.

1 JOHNSTONE (1964) p.97, 108.
2 BADAWI (1965) p.291, 293.
3 JOHNSTONE (1967b) p.155.

/balḥēl/ "good, well so good" normally occurring in the expression */māhu balḥēl/* "not so well" Shammar, Muṭair, 'Aniza, Sudair; */wara/* "why" in negative expressions i.e. */wara mā rićibtum/* "why did you not set out?", */haḻḻahaḻḻa/* "exactly, that is so!" Sudair, Muṭair, 'Aniza, Shammar; */bnōb/* "at all" (in negative expressions) Sudair, Shammar; */hagwiti hagwitin/* "it seems, I think, it appears" Shammar, Sudair, Euphrates bedouin; */mār, mēr/* "but" Muṭair, 'Aniza, Shammar, Ḥarb; */lamm-/* "towards" 'Aniza, Shammar, Sudair, Muṭair; */nikas, yankis/* "to return" Shammar, 'Aniza, Qaṣīm; */ḏahar, yaḏhar* (or *yiḏhar*)/ "to go out at evening" 'Aniza, Sudair; */źid/* emphatic verbal particle preceding the perfective, as */źid riḥt/* "I did go" 'Aniza, Sudair, Qaṣīm; */galaṭ, yagluṭ*(or *yigluṭ*)/ "to come in, approach" 'Aniza, Euphrates bedouin, Muṭair; */dūn- dūr-/* deictic particle as in */dūnak/* "here it is" Muṭair, 'Awāzim, Sudair, Shammar, Euphrates bedouin, 'Aniza,(1) also in some Bādiya areas of the Euphrates; */kūd/* "except" 'Aniza, Shammar, Sudair. This particle also passes into the meaning "must" (2) by the extension "There is no alternative but that..." In this meaning it has spread into Southern Mesopotamia in the form */kūn/* or */wākūn/*. Compare Shammari */kūd/* or */yakūd/*; */yad/* "hand" contrasting with */īd/* in the outer area Shammar, Ḍhafīr, 'Aniza, Sudair, Qaṣīm, Riyadh, 'Awāzim, Rashāyida; (3) */aġadi, aġadē-/* "perhaps, lest", Muṭair, Ḍhafir.

1 *dūr-* among the 'Aniza and Euphrates bedouin, *dūn-* elsewhere.
2 See also 'ABBOUD (1964) p.89; LANDBERG (1919) p.8,15; MONTAGNE (1935) p.77.
3 See also CANTINEAU (1937) p.200.

6 Texts with translation, background notes and information on sources

The texts which follow are divided into two groups: Najdi (Arabian) and Mesopotamian, although there is some difficulty in assigning some of the more marginal types, such as Text 8, Shammar Mas'ūd, to any of the groups. The division is therefore designed mainly for the guidance of the reader and does not constitute a classification system. The arrangement of the texts is generally in order of the degree of relationship to the speech of inner Najd and therefore proceeds in a general northerly and easterly direction.

Two of the texts, Text 3 Ḥarb and Text 4 'Aniza, are not strictly north-eastern in terms of their main location. However the Ḥarb tribe are distributed in a north-easterly line from Hijaz to Ḥafar al-Bāṭin, while 'Aniza dialects similar to the one shown are found to the east well within our area. They therefore participate in a linguistic continuum which centres on our area and are in any case of comparative interest.

TEXT 1

'AJMĀN: THE STORY OF THĀMIR IBN SU'AIDĀN

This text was given to me by the Kuwait radio service and is an excerpt from the radio programme Diwān al-Bādiya. The speaker is Māni' ibn Dhanbūḥ al-Shāmiri (abu Fahhād) of the 'Ajmān tribe. The 'Ajmān are a tribe of the Eastern region but originating in the Southern Najd in the area of Najrān. The dialect is very similar to that of T.M. Johnstone"s two texts in "Some Characteristics of the Dōsiri Dialect of Arabic as Spoken in Kuwait" (1961) and "Further Studies on the Dōsiri Dialect of Arabic as Spoken in Kuwait" (1964), which are of mixed 'Ajmān-Dawāsir origin, but basically 'Ajmān. Features marking it as Southern are the absence of the affricated variants of *kāf* and *qāf*. Otherwise it is very similar to the Central Najdi type of my Sudair informants.

TEXT 1

'indi lkum alyōm sālfah whiyya lṯāmir ibn s'ēdān issbē'i fi sābg izzimān. ṯāmir hāḏa ḥanšūli u nahhāb rajjāl ṭammā'. u gisam aḷḷah annahu ḏāk alwagt alatrāk / dōlat alatrāk falḥasa. 'indihum ixburih wa ḥāṭṭīn 'alēh 'yūn ytiṣayyidōl-lih u gulubōh wiḥbisōh. u 'ind ma-ḥbisōh ḥāṭṭīnin firjīlih ḥadīd. f-taṛaggab aṛṛajjāl ilfuraṣ waḷḷa hayyālih furṣah u ṭala' min issijin. wa bēt imḥammad ibin imsāmiḥ mn āl slēmān falḥasa' u gāl: "ana mā li illa 'āzmin bēt imḥammad" u yōm axaḏat uxt imḥammad / u hi fi bētaha 'ugb il'aṣir lā waḷḷa aṛṛajjāl dāxlin 'alēha filġrufah alli hi fīha. u gālat: "yā walad, kānuḳ ḏēf šuf al / ġrufat arrjāl warāk." gāl: "ana halḥīn māni baġiy (1) rjāl. ana bġi lmukān xāṣṣin xṣūṣ" (zābin) ay na'am! yōm axaḏat imḥammad 'ind ṣuḥbānillih

1 *baġi* < *bāġi*. This shortening of the vowels is more common in the Central and Southern Najd area. See also INGHAM (1979) p.28. Interestingly this was also noted

min tijjār ilḥasa lēn jāt il'aṣēr u yōm axaḏih, lā waḷḷah jayy imrawwiḥ yōm ja axūha gālat: "yā mḥammad šuf ḏa-lḥṣān (1) illi dūnuk, ṣawwitlih 'induk u yōm ṭalla' 'alēh, lā waḷḷah hāḏa ṯāmir ibn s'ēdān." gāl: "ibn s'ēdān!" gāl: "na'am." gāl: "ug^{ə}*luṭ jayy!"(2) u yōm ja lā waḷḷa fi rjīlih ḥadīd u mḥammad xābr innih masjū̄ - haḏōḷāk, yōm ivgudōh(3) arkubōlhum xayyāl yabḥaṯ 'annih. u 'ayyanih 'ind ibn imsāmiḥ gāl: "'aṭna-yyāh yā bn imsāmih." gāl: "alḥīn arrajjāl ḍeif, waḷḷah b'adik ilkarāmtih, u 'indi kunnih 'indukum hafūḍ." ilmuhimm yōm aṣbaḥ iṣṣubḥ ḥalaf 'alēh inn yrūḥ il-issūg u yagḏ̣i lizūmih imnissūg. gāl ibn s'ēdān: "axāf asabbib 'alēkum" gāl: "abdan!" wa 'ugbin yagḏ̣i lizūmh imnissūg uyzammlih g'ūdin-lih i'māni ṣōb ahalih fil 'āriḏ̣ 'ugub mā wiṣl - ihnāk arsal-lih kam bēt yahni bilma'rūf yigūl:*

yā rākbin min 'indina fōg faddād
mā fōgha illa lxarj mi' jā'd iššdād
yasraḥ min il'āriḏ̣ mi' iṣṣubḥ ilā ngād
wal'aṣir bilḥabil ḥirwitin m'aššāh
yalfi 'ala 'amr manā'īr wajwād
zabn ilḥuṣān ilyā wugaf sēr 'ilbāh
wilēh jīt bēt imḥammad innih fahhād
garm il'iyāl la'all alarḏāl tifdāh
mḥammad ibn imsāmiḥ garm al awlād
bētih kibīr u sālmin min tanaṣṣāh
wilēh wiṣlih ilmaṭrūd mašyitih bi'dād
yagḏ̣i lġaraḏ̣ fissūg walā ḥadin jāh
rab'ih mṭawwi't aṣṣa'āb lēn yangād
yuwwābrin wirṯat fuhūdin mfaḏḏāh
garmin ilyā min jaraḥ algiṣa yraxxṣ izzād
ugarmin šijā' u tarfig issamin yamnāh
yistāhl albēḏa 'ala rūs alašhād
mḥammad almašhūr mā -bih maġawāh

by the traveller PALGRAVE (1865) I, p.463. He refers here to the vowels *ā, ē, ū* being "starved down" to *a, e, u* in Riyadh and Southern Najd. The existence of the *ġ* in the form /*abġi*/ "I want" is also characteristic of the southern region. In the north /*abi*/ is more common. See also JOHNSTONE (1964), p.99 and passim, which gives /*abġei*/, /*tabġei*/.

1 /*ḏa*/ "this, that", a southern characteristic. See p.92-3.
2 *ivgudōh* < *ifgudōh*
3 /*jayy*/ characteristic of the south; northern /*jāy*/.

TEXT 1 ('AJMĀN) TRANSLATION

Today I have a story for you and it is about Thāmir ibn Su'aidān the Subai'i.(1) This man Thāmir was a lone robber and raider. He was an ambitious man, and God made it his fate that at that time the Turks / it was the rule of the Turks in al-Hasa,(2) and they had information on him. And they set spies out to hunt for him and they overcame him and imprisoned him. And when they had imprisoned him, they put chains on his legs. And the man watched his opportunities and God gave him an opportunity and he got out of the prison. And the house of Muḥammad ibn Musāmiḥ of the Āl Sulaimān(3) was in al-Hasa. And he said: "I have no alternative except to go to the house of Muḥammad." And when Muḥammad's sister began to / and she was in her house in the evening, no by God there was the man coming in to approach her, in the room which she was in. She said, "Oh boy,(4) if you are a guest see the / the men's room is behind you." He said: "I don't want to see the men now. I want a special private place." (Seeking refuge) Yes! And when she found Muḥammad with some friends of his, some of the al-Hasa merchants, when she came in the evening and when he began, no by God he was coming home. When her brother came, she said: "Oh Muḥammad, see that horse which is in front of you, call it to you!" And when he looked at it, no by God it was Thāmir ibn Su'aidān. He said: "Thāmir ibn Su'aidān!" He answered: "Yes!" He said: "Come here!" And when he came (he saw that) no, by God, he had chains on his legs and Muḥammad realised that he was an (escaped) prisoner. Those others (the Turks) when they realised that he was missing, sent off a horseman to search for him. He saw him with Ibn Musāmiḥ and said: "Give him to me Ibn Musāmiḥ!" He said: "At the moment the man is a guest, and by God you must treat him kindly and he is protected with me as he is with you."(5) The result was that he (ibn Musāmiḥ) adjured him (the horseman, to let ibn Su'aidān) go to the market and get his provisions from the market. Ibn Su'aidān said: "I'm afraid I will cause (trouble) for you." He said "Not at all!" And afterwards he got his provisions from the

1 Subai', a tribe of Southern and Eastern Najd.
2 The Ottoman Turks occupied al-Hasa in the 17th and 19th centuries.
3 The Āl Sulaimān are a section of the 'Ajmān of which the Ibn Musāmiḥ clan are the head; DICKSON (1949) p.569.
4 The word */walad/* "boy" is often used in addressing grown men.
5 The meaning of this section is unclear. However he seems to be saying that as a guest, he is dear to both of us by the laws of hospitality.

market and mounted him on a 'Omāni camel(1) (to ride) towards al-'Āriḏ.(2) After he had arrived there he sent him a few lines of poetry thanking him for the favour, saying:

O rider going from us on a strong mount
   on which there is nothing but the sheepskin cover and saddleframe
Riding out from al'Āriḏ with the morning when it breaks
   arriving at dusk at al-Ḥabl,(3) probably at evening
He comes in to the 'Amr(4) strong and generous men,
   coming in like a stallion when it arches its neck.(5)
If you come to the house of Muḥammad, he is
   the hero of the valiants, may all treacherous men die in his place.
Muḥammad ibn Musāmiḥ hero of the young men.
   His house is large, and he who seeks refuge with him is safe.
When the refugee reaches him his step becomes firm (in confidence).
   He carries out his errands in the market and no one comes to him (i.e. no one harms him).
His comrades put down strong men when lead out
   heroes and sons of fierce lions
A hero who, when hardship strikes, counts his property cheap
   a brave hero whose right hand distributes sustenance
He deserves the white turban of the martyrs(6)
   Famed Muḥammad in whom there is no doubt.

1 In the Arabian peninsula the small black 'Omāni camels were considered the best for speed. See DICKSON (1949) p.410.
2 al-'Āriḍh, the area of Central Najd south of Riyadh.
3 al-Ḥabl. This seemed to be a place name, but was not known to my informants.
4 Bani 'Amr, one of the branches of the Subai'.
5 In anger or excitement.
6 This may also refer to the ceremony of "whitening" performed in gratitude for a favour; GLUBB (1948) p.138.

TEXT 2

MUṬAIR

The Muṭair material consists of two stories recorded in Kuwait in 1977. The first was recorded at a Dīwāniyya, which is a social gathering of men for the purpose of exchanging news and with a strong bias towards older cultural forms such as poetry recitation, story telling and music. The second story was recorded in the tent of a Muṭair family encamped at Rauḍhatain, a well about half-way between Kuwait town and the Iraq border. Both of these appeared previously in "Zeitschrift für Arabische Linguistik", 2, 1979, although the transcription used there was slightly different. The dialect of the Muṭair as presented here shows the classic features of the Central Najdi type as outlined on p.87-94. Interjections of the audience are enclosed between brackets. The reader of the first text is Ḥāmid ibn Muḥammad al-Muṭairi.

TEXT 2(a) THE STORY OF TURKI IBN ḤUMAID

snitin min hā ssnīn, youm il 'ašāyir u youm ilbadāwah ṛukab tuṛki bin iḥmeid. hum 'alēhum wagt (1) u zimānhum wagt ma hū-b ṭayyib walḥalāl mihzil. u riċib tuṛki bin iḥmeid u mi'ih lih giṭ'at rabu' (minhu mizyad?) min i'tēba w ibin garmaḷah bin hādi (min hū-minh?) min g̣haṭān šex g̣haṭān ḥāċm innajd u miḥtimīh wa lā ḥadd yiṭubb najd alla bruxuṣtin (2) minh, min ibin garmaḷa. ṛikab tuṛki bin iḥmeid mi'ih lih giṭ'at rabu' u gōlin: "nabi nistarxaṣ imn ibin garmaḷa aġadīh (3) yasmaḥ-inna nimīl 'ala wad-arša. nimīl 'ala wad-

1 *wagt* "time". Here "bad times".
2 *birxuṣtin*: Cl. *biruxṣatin*.
3 *aġadīh* "perhaps he...". Compare Ḥarb *indīh* "perhaps" ḤĀZMI (1975) p.151; Negev *a'adīh* "I suppose" BLANC (1970) p.37.

-arša." wad-arša fīh sabi' alḥmuḏāt. i wumrabbi' wiybi (1) yarta'ūn fīh. rikib hu wujamā'tih u nawwuxaw 'ala bin garmaḷa. yōm agbaḷaw 'ala lmajlis wilyā hdūmih tiṭubb ilgā' 'alēh libs u 'alēh jūxah u 'alēh libs. ibin iḥmeid, tiṛki sallam 'ala bin garmaḷa u jalas ugāl: "ḥinna jāyīn zāyirīnik ya lamīr jāyīn zāyirīnik nabīk tarxuṣinna naba nimīl 'ala wadarša naba-rrabi' fīh u ḥalalna mihzil." gāl: "wēn ahaḷkum?" gāl: "ahaḷna xaḷḷeynāhum yamm aššifa." gāl: "wišḥaddaṛkum min dyarkum?" gāl: "ḥaddaṛna lwagt." gāl: "wara ma rićibtum min dīratkum illi intum fīha gabul u jītu tistarxṣūn?" gāl: "waḷḷa ḥinna taḥaddaṛna u youm jīna bmaṯnāt iṭṭurīź, ḥinna jīnāk gālṭīn." gāl: "mā nasmaḥ-ilkum alla tarja'ūn utiṛiddūn li-dyarkum wilā minkum ṯibattum bidyarkum tarkbūn u tistarxṣūn." hāḏa gōl ibin garmaḷa libin iḥmeid. gāl: "ma hī-b hi ya alamīr." gāl: "alla,(2) hi." baġaw minh, mā wāfag tišayyal ibin iḥmeid u gām mnalmajlis za'lān. u youm gām wlih hdūmih mā talḥag ila miṯāni sīźānih alli tasḥab gabul šālh-azza'al. 'ala mā miša u hi thāyag 'alēh m'azzibtih,(3) m'azbat ibin garmaḷa gālat: "yā bin garmaḷa lēh mā simaḥt libin iḥmeid yirabbi' fi najd?" gāl: " i'ugbi yā zuġba! anti šimtīlih." gālat: "ana mā šimtīlih lākin yā rajjāḷi šiftih waḷḷa yā rajjāḷi byirji'k(4) alġāra." gāl: "i'ugbi yā zuġba mā 'indić xabar." riji' ibin iḥmeid u youm jā jimā'tih u yiṛizz albērag. jima' 'atēba gāl: "ibin garmaḷa 'ayya yasmaḥ-inna wiš arrāy?" gālaw: "arrāy 'ala bin garmaḷa." u yajma' ġazwih u yṣabbiḥih ibin garmaḷa wiytilāgaṭōn hum wayyāhum u min ṭal'at iššams lēn garrab miġībaha. u halxeyl ytimāwah wiy'īnahum aḷḷa 'ala bin garmaḷa wyaksrūnih wiyšīl ibin garmaḷa min najd u min hāk alkasra mā šabb fīha nār tiwallawh 'tēbah u jala yamm wādi gḥaṭān u yamm ḥaṣāt gḥaṭān u hāk addīrah.

TEXT 2(b) EXTRACT FROM THE BANI HILĀL EPIC

bani hlāl jālihum dōrin wagt šwayya. šāfat bint ilamīr liha(5) barg šimāl u xāyiltih u xāyiltih u xāyiltih u xāyiltih balḥēl hāḏa lbarg. azzibda (6) innihum baġaw yḥīlūn yammih gālat: rawwiḥlik 'assās. rawwiḥlik 'assāsin

1 In many structures of this type the suffixes *-ūn*, *-īn*, *-in* are omitted from the first verb.
2 *alla* "yes" in reply to a negative question.
3 *m'azziba* "hostess", a common euphemism for "wife" in Najd
4 *biyirji'k* "He will bring back to you", from *arja'*.
5 For the length of vowel compare BLANC (1970), p.122.
6 *azzibda* "the cream", thereby "the result".

yi'issih albarg hād. u hu yirćib (1) hāk al'assās youm al'assās salf 'alēha u hi ṭhadun minh gālat: "yā nāšdin al'assās, lā yadkur annida, tara annida min ġeir ṣeid ihlāš (2) gāl: "ligeit šahhāb nahhāb lalwuṭa mūda' 'ala rūs iliḥzūm gšāš. yiṛidd 'alha (3) hāda ddōr. ḥālaw ligaw il'išib yamm iššay illi huwwa dbiḥa aw šismih azznāti nzạlaw 'ind azznāti u hu ṭaradhum min 'ala l'išib alla b'alya u gālaw: "'alya mā-yxālif nabi njawwizkiyyāha mēr xalna nar'a." u hu yijīhum uba zēd wiytill šārb azznāti wilyā hālsih wilyā tarkuḍ alxeil 'ala lxeil wiyṣalṭ (4) aḷḷa 'ala azznāti ujindih u bini hlāl tāli (5) addīra u tākil al'išib u taskin fi haddīra lli mā-lih mida. u salāmtik.

TEXT 2(a) (MUṬAIR) TRANSLATION

The Story of Turki ibn Ḥumaid

One of these years in the days of the tribes and the days of bedouin life Turki ibn Ḥumaid,(6) drought was upon them and their time was (a time of) drought. It was not good and the flocks were weakening. And Turki ibn Ḥumaid mounted up and with him (were) a small group of his companions (who was he Mizyad?). From 'Utaiba. The Shaikh of 'Utaiba. And Ibn Garmala ibn Hādi(7) (who from? (from which tribe)) from Ghaṭān, the Shaikh of Ghaṭān, the Ruler of Najd and reserving it and no one could enter Najd except with his permission, from Ibn Garmala. Turki ibn Ḥumaid set out and with him his small group of companions and said: "We will ask permission from Ibn Garmala, perhaps he will let us go over to Wādi al-Risha.(8) We will go to Wādi al-Risha." In Wādi al-Risha there were the seven *ḥamadhāt*.(9) Yes and it was in flower with spring vegetation and they wished to graze in

1 The causative pattern from *arkab* or *arćab*.
2 *hlāš* from *lā šay* .
3 Compare Dōsiri *'alina*, *'aliha* with the same stress pattern; see JOHNSTONE (1964), p.104.
4 *wiyṣalṭ*; compare Cl. *wa yuṣalliṭ*.
5 *tāli* for *tawli*. Initial weak verbs regularly show *ā* in these dialects: *yāgaf*"he stands", *yāṣal* "he arrives".
6 Ibn Ḥumaid: the leading family of the 'Utaiba. For their more recent history see GLUBB (1960) p.199-202 and passim.
7 Ibn Hādi: the leading family of Ghaṭān.
8 Wādi al-Risha: to the west of Riyadh, about Latitude 43°.
9 *ḥamadhāt*: saline plants on which camels graze.

it. He rode off with his companions and they couched their mounts at Ibn Garmala's camp. When he approached the *majlis* behold his clothes reached the ground. He was wearing robes, wearing a *jūkha*,(1) wearing robes. Ibn Ḥumaid, Turki greeted Ibn Garmala and sat down and said: "We have come to visit you Oh Emir, we have come to visit you. We wish you to give us permission. We wish to move to Wādi al-Risha. We wish to graze on the spring vegetation in it (for) our flocks are weakening." He said: "Where are your families?" He said: "We have left them near al-Shifa."(2) He said. "What made you come down from your *dīrah*?" He said: "Drought made us come down." He said: "Why didn't you set out from your *dīrah* where you were camped before and come and ask my permission?"(3) He said: "Well (lit. by God), we came down (anyway) and when we had reached half-way we rode over to visit you." He said: "We will not give you permission unless you go back and return to your *dīrah* and when you have settled in your *dīrah* ride over to ask my permission." These were the words of Ibn Garmala to Ibn Ḥumaid. He said: "It is not so (lit. it), Oh Prince!" He said: "Yes it (is)!" They asked him (again), (but) he didn't agree. Ibn Ḥumaid gathered himself up and left the *majlis*, in anger. And when he left behold his clothes did not reach halfway down his shins,(4) which were dragging (on the ground) before. Anger carried him off. When he left, she was watching him, his wife, the wife of Ibn Garmala. She said: "Oh Ibn Garmala, why didn't you give permission to Ibn Ḥumaid to graze on the spring vegetation in Najd?" He said: "Go away, O harlot! You felt sorry for him." She said: "By God, I didn't feel sorry for him but my husband, I thought by God, oh my husband, that he would return to attack you." He said: "Go away, you have no knowledge (of the matter)." Ibn Ḥumaid went back and when he reached his tribe he raised the war banner. He collected together 'Utaiba. He said:

1 *jūkha*: a heavy coat worn over the *bisht* or cloak; called *chōkha* in Iraq; see LANDBERG (1940) p.10.
2 al-Shifa: there are two localities of this name, one east of the Madina about latitude 41°, another northeast of Mecca about latitude 43°. This would seem to be the second which is southwest of Wādi al-Risha within the present 'Utaiba *dīrah* according to Cantineau's tribal map. It could also be taken to have its general meaning of "scarp", "cliff".
3 i.e. "Why didn't you come to ask permission before moving your families?"
4 i.e. because he left at speed.

"Ibn Garmala refused to give us permission. What is your (lit. the) opinion?" They said: "The opinion is (that we ride) against Ibn Garmala." He collected together his raiding party and attacked him at dawn, Ibn Garmala and they fought them. And from the sunrise till when its setting was near and the horses were galloping against each other. And God helped them against Ibn Garmala and they defeated him. And Ibn Garmala moved from Najd and from the time of that defeat he did not light a fire there (i.e. did not camp there). 'Utaiba drove him off and he camped near Wādi Ghaṭān and near Ḥaṣāt Ghaṭān(1) and that *dīrah*.

TEXT 2(b) (MUṬAIR) TRANSLATION

Extract from the Bani Hilāl Epic

Bani Hilāl, once there came to them a slight drought. The Emir's daughter saw (for herself) lightning(2) in the north, she watched it and watched it and watched it closely (lit. hard), that lightning. The result was that they wished to move over to it. She said: "Send for yourself a scout, send for yourself a scout to spy out that lightning." And he sent off that scout. When the scout came towards them and she approached him, she said: "Oh he who enquires of the scout, let him not mention the grass. For grass without game is useless." He said: "I found a charging rider, plunging down to the hollow, leaving husks(3) on the tops of the uplands." He answered her. This time they moved off and found grass near the thing which he had killed or what is his name, Zanāti.(4) They stopped near Zanāti and he turned them away from the grass except (if they would give him) 'Alya(5) and they said "'Alya doesn't matter, we will marry her to you; but let us graze." And (then) Abu Zaid came and he stirred them up and pulled the moustache of the Zanāti and behold he plucked it, and behold the horses charged against the horses and God assisted (them) against the Zanāti and his army. And Bani Hilāl took over the *dīrah* and fed on the grass and lived in this *dīra* which has no end. Your health!

1 Ḥaṣāt Ghaṭān: about lat.44°, long.23° in what is now the Ghaṭān *dīrah*. I was unable to locate Wādi Ghaṭān on any map.
2 The sign of rain in the desert, bringing grass.
3 In the context "husks" would seem to signify "carcasses", i.e. those of the animals Zanāti had killed in hunting.
4 Zanāti: the traditional opponent of Bani Hilāl associated often with the Zenāta Berbers of North Africa.
5 'Alya: the daughter of the Emir of the Bani Hilāl.
6 Abu Zaid: the hero of the Bani Hilāl.

TEXT 3

ḤARB: A CONVERSATIONAL MONOLOGUE
Relating to Modern Day Life Among the Ḥarb of Hijaz

The following text is a simulated conversation between two people performed by Ḥamza Muzaini, a member of the Bani Sālim branch of the Ḥarb, while he was a student at the School of Oriental and African Studies in London. He himself felt that it was not a faithful representation of the dialect, but in fact, on comparison with other Najdi texts shown, it seems to be structurally very accurate. It may however be that in terms of vocabulary it shows the influence of the dialect of his home town of Madina. The suffix */-in/* is conspicuously absent except in */killin/* "each one" and */ġaṣbin/* "by force", although in the speech of my other Ḥarb informant it occurred frequently. The dialect is best described as Central Najdi with Hijazi overlay. Features of this Hijazi stratum are pointed out in the text. The realisation of *jīm* is */ž/* and the fronted forms of *kāf* and *qāf* are palatalized but not affricated */ḱ/* and */ǵ/*, not */ć/* and */ź/* as in the other Najdi dialects.

TEXT 3

A *salām 'alēkum*
B *'alēkum issalām*
A *ḥāt al'ilūm ya mḥammad*
B *waḷḷah salāmatk žīna waḷḷah mn addīrah wu ḱān mi'na muṣlaḥ u 'abdaḷḷah wa nizalna lmdīnah u ḱān mi'na ba'ḏ̣ albḏ̣āyi' wa ba'ad mā tisawwagna fassūg u bi'na alli mi'na min 'awāyiz ligīna s'ūd wu 'izamna u ruḥna mi'ih ilbētih. waḷḷah mā gaṣṣar arrajjāl ḏibaḥlina u ġaddāna u tigahwina(1)*

1 *tigahwina* for *tigahwēna*. A similar shortening of the final radical vowel was noted for Dōsiri by JOHNSTONE (1964), p.91.

'indih waflaḥna waṣṣubḥ ba'ad ma bitna, waṣṣubḥ mišēna wištirēna ba'aḏ albḏāyi' alli ni'tāziha wa 'awwadna waḷḷah salāmatk, aḏā min nāḥyat inna nizalna / min hibaṭna lalmadīnah, lākinna 'aṭna xbār addīrah wij(1)-jāha min muṭar wij-jāha min xēr ba'ad almaxāyīl alli xayyalnāk.

A waḷḷah nzalat/nizal xēr imn-aḷḷah 'alēna, timallat arriyāḏ lāḱinn zey(2) mā t'arif aljimā'a māhum aljimā'a ll inta txabur, waljimā'a kull wāḥad ilih ṛāyih. kull wāḥad yibġā-lih šayy ilḥālih u žābaw iṭṭaraktarāt u ḥaṭṭaw iḥdūd u gaṭṭi'aw issyūl 'ala mizāri' ba'aḏhum. waḷḷah muškilah halḥīna gāyimah bēnahum lāḱinn almuṭar waḷḷah innih ḏufa 'alēhum wu timallat irriyāḏ killaha ġaṣbin 'alēhum ġaṣbin 'ala ba'aḏhum māhu bāġi yōm inh iygaṭṭi' ilḥidūd 'ala ba'aḏ jimā'tih. waḷḷah amma min nāḥyat almaškilah alli min bēn aljimā'ah tidaxxaḷ waḷḷah fīha 'bēd iṣṣirwāni wa 'abdaḷḷah ibin šaliyyah wa ḥallawha bēnahum lēlt al'īd. zeyy mā t'arif kānat bēnahum / ḏallat bēnahum almiškilah hāḏi ḥawāli xams sinīn u ba'dīn baġat tiži fīha rǵāb u baġat tiži fīha muṣāyib lāḱinna zayy ma t'arif almisilmīn māhum biygaṣṣirū/ (3) mā ygaṣṣirū lyā ḥḏaraw u ḥallaw almiškilah bēnahum wu tisāmiḥaw u tiṣāfaw u ti'āzimaw u tiḥābbaw alxšūm. bass zayy mā t'arif alglūb zayy algizāz lamm-innih tikassar mā yilliḥim. waḷḷah žāna xabar minhum. gālaw innih wāḥad minhum innih mā ruḏi 'an aṣṣulḥ alli bēnahum u gām iytanaggaḏ wuxzīh u sabbawh annās. killin yixzi 'alēh. killin yigūllih: "ant 'aṭeyt lizmatk want lāzm innak mā tnaggudha alḥīn." lakinn inšāḷḷa 'asaḷḷa yhadīh. tarāh māhu ba'īd lyā minnih ḥaṣṣal-lih wāḥad innih yiṛuddih. māhu ba'īd laḱinn zeyyma t'arif hāḏa mažnūn u lassā' žāhil waḷḷah māhu ygaṣṣir wlāhu ba'īd. bass innih zayy ma t'arif žāhil. walžāhil 'ala ṭurgat ma yži mnih wa 'asaḷḷah yhadīh. walḥīn gāmaw ḥatta xwānih yixzūn 'alēh. wiygūlūllih: "int muxṭi wint mā lak ḥagg baṭṭarīga-ḏi"(4) wa ammā min nāḥyat al'beydi, waḷḷah ruḥt lih gabil ḥawāli xams ayyām. tigahwēt 'indih mġarib wa filaḥt wa lā gaṣṣar waḷḷah. wu ligīt 'indih ba'ḏ aljimā'ah wa xarražtih 'ala lmiškilah alli bēn arrabu' wista'add waḷḷah. mā gaṣṣar ibn ilḥalāl. gāl innih biytuwažžah 'alēhum ṇāyif u muxlid u mi'tig u ṛaddit aḷḷah u yabōn yižōnahum. waḷḷah mā adri ... 'aṭāni mow'id mādri hu yamlāh walla mā yamlāh. laḱn inšaḷḷa ḥna 'ala gadd alamal fīh innih mā yxilfih. wamma ġeyṯ, waḷḷah štiṛālih siyyāra židīdah u gām ysāfirbaha 'ala rriyāḏ u lā huwwa biyxālif yižīblih filisbū' ṛaddēn ṯalāṯah ya'ni ražžāl mistirīḥ, ražžāl ḱirīm alli zayy ilḥuṣān illi mā žābh iḏharih akalih

1 *wij-jāha* < *wiš-jāha*
2 *zeyy* or *zey* "like, as" equivalent to Najdi *miṯil*.
3 *mā bi-*, a Central Najdi feature. See also p.94.
4 *-ḏa*, Central Najdi. See also p.92-3.

baṭnih. dāyim iḏḏibīḥa m'alligah u dāyim alnijir šaġġāl walmajlis malyān u 'asaḷḷah y'īnih ubu s'ūd. wa amma xūh 'awwād, waḷḷah innih mā adri 'anh innih yimkin mā yguḷḷ 'anh zayy mā t'arif annās yižūn min baṭin wāḥid u yixtalfūn. u 'asaḷḷah y'awwuḏ.

TEXT 3 (ḤARB) TRANSLATION

A Greetings.

B Greetings.

A Give me the news, Muḥammad.

B Well, may you be healthy. We came from the dīrah and we had with us some goods (to sell).(1) And with us were Muṣlaḥ and 'Abdallah and we came down to al-Madina and after we had bought provisions in the market and sold what goods we had, we met Su'ūd and he invited us and we went to his house. Well the man did not let us down (in hospitality). He killed a sheep for us and gave us lunch and we had coffee with him and we were satisfied and in the morning after we had spent the night there, and in the morning we set off and bought some (more) provisions which we needed and came back. Well may you be healthy (that is) if you want the news of our journey to al-Madina but give us the news of the dīra and what rain has fallen there and what good fortune(2) has come there after the clouds which we saw coming to you.

A Well good fortune did come to us from God and the hollows were filled with water but as you know the people are not as you would wish them to be, and each one has his own opinion and each one wishes something for himself and they brought tractors and put down boundaries and cut off the rain water from each other's fields. Well it is a problem standing between them but the rain came down upon them in abundance and the hollows were filled with water in spite of them, in spite of each other, each person not wishing (it) when he laid down boundaries in the way of other members of his tribe. But as regards the problem which exists among the tribesmen, 'Ubaid al-Ṣirwāni and 'Abdallah ibn Shaliyya interceded and solved the difficulty between them on the day before 'Īd. As you know the problem was between them / had remained between them for five years and afterwards calamities and rivalry were going to arise in it. But as you know the muslims do not forsake their friends (and they kept up their efforts) until the two sides came together and forgave each other and made up their differences and in-

1 Livestock or perhaps honey, which are the main products of the Ḥarb.

2 i.e. grazing.

vited each other to their homes and kissed each other. But as you know the hearts (of men) are like glass, once broken they cannot be mended. We had news from them that one of them did not agree to the peace that was made between them and began going back on his word and the people reviled him and insulted him. Everyone reviled him and said to him: "You gave your word and now you must not go back on it." And as for al-'Ubaidi, well I went to him about five days ago and had coffee with him in the evening and was satisfied and by God he did not let us down and I met with them some of the tribe and led him to the subject of the problem which is between the people and he made himself ready (to help) by God. He did not let us down, stout fellow. He said that Nāyif, Mukhlid and Mu'tig and Raddit Allah will confront them and come to them. Well I don't know he made an arrangement to come, but I don't know whether he will keep to the arrangement or not. But if God wills we have enough hope in the matter that he will not go back on it. And as for Ghaith, well he has bought himself a new car and begun travelling with it to Riyadh and he doesn't fail to get two or three journeys a week. He is a relaxed and generous man like the horse who eats whatever his back can carry. Always he has a slaughtered sheep hanging outside his house and always the coffee pestle is ringing and the majlis full of people and may God assist him Abu Su'ūd. And as for his brother 'Awwād, well I don't know about him, perhaps he is no less than him. As you know all men come from one womb but are all different. May God reward us.

TEXT 4

'ANIZA: A CONVERSATION BETWEEN TWO STUDENTS

The following is a conversation between two speakers, Sayyār Rāḍhi al-'Anizi and Lāfi ibn Sulaimān al-'Anizi, both of the Sba'a section of 'Aniza. Both were students of Kuwait University and enacted this conversation for me at the University in 1977. They themselves were bidialectal, speaking their own dialect when with their relatives and a modified form when in the University. Both had relatives who lived the nomadic life in Kuwait and Saudi Arabia, but lived themselves in al-Jahra. The Sba'a are in the main a tribe of the northern Euphrates, while Sayyār's particular clan, the Muwāhīb, are also found in the Western Najd. Their original homeland is the Ḥarrat 'Uwairiḍh or Ḥarrat al-Muwāhīb west of Madāin Ṣāliḥ,(1) but in recent years many have come to Kuwait. The text is a fairly faithful rendering of the dialect and portrays quite well the position of the younger generation of educated bedouin in the Gulf countries who live mainly in the towns but retain close links with their fellow tribesmen and often marry within the tribe. In general, also, considerable contact is maintained between the 'Aniza of Syria and those of Saudi Arabia. Nowadays Syrian members of the tribe bring their livestock to sell in Saudi Arabia in early summer. Traditionally the northern 'Aniza used to return to Central Najd in certain years for the foaling season.(2)

TEXT 4

A *ṣabbaḥk aḷḷa balxēr.*
B *yā hala ṣabāḥ alxēr. šlōnak?*

1 See DOUGHTY (1964) p.444-5 and Ch.XIV generally.
2 RASWAN (1935) p.243.

A *aḷḷa ysallimk.*

B *'asāk ṭayyib. keif hālak?*

A *waḷḷa bxēr aḥamdillāh.(1) yā walad marreit 'aleikum hāssbū' alli ṭāfat. mā ligeitkum ibbeitkum.*

B *yōm alxamīs. ēh. ṭala'na lalbarr.*

A *ṭala'tu lalbarr?*

B *ēwaḷḷah ṭala'na hnāka la'māmi. ībil!(2)*

A *šlōna.*

B *waḷḷa raḥna lalġanam hnāk u byūt aššā'ar hnāk. mšōṭḥīnin yā walad hnāk waḷḷa. ībil! u raḥna lyammahum addụhur. wuṣanna 'indahum addụhur. ībil! u min halliban yā walad. širibna liban. u yōm širibna liban u naṭla' hnāk išwayya ntifassaḥ u šifna ṭṭilyān u 'ugub jalasna šwayya hnāk.*

A *tigahwētu?*

B *ī jalasna. 'awad gāl-lina guṣīdah, guṣīdtin 'ajibatni.*

A *t'arif minha šay.*

B *ībil. kitabtiha yōm innih gālha liyya. tabīni agūlha laḳ.(3)*

A *gilha!*

B *ygūl:*

yā l'ēn lić balhawa laftah
mānti 'ala dīn alixwāni.
balāć min wāḥdin(4) šiftih
'ūdhin mnazzēn rawyāni
alkiḥil bal'ēn sāyiftih
aswad tigil rīš ġirbāni
wassils battōb ḥāyiftih
tigil masāḥīb dībāni.

A *māšaḷḷa. wa šlōna aljuww ihnāk?*

B *waḷḷa tamām xūš.(5)*

A *hā 'ām ribī'.*

B *al'išib waḷḷah.*

A *lā, 'ām ribī'.*

B *waḷḷa hassana mi(6) mitl al'ām.*

1 *aḥamdillāh* < *alḥamdillāh.*
2 *ībil* < *ībillah* "Yes, by God!"
3 *laḳ.* Both in Shammar and 'Aniza dialects the *ḳ* is emphasized. LANDBERG (1940) writes this as *lakk*, p.71.
4 *wāḥdin* for *wāḥditin.*
5 *juww, xūš* for *jaww* and *xōš*. See also BLANC (1970) for neutralization of *ū* and *ō*, p.118.
6 *mi* for *mā-hi.*

A *mā fīh xuḏratin halḥēl.*
B *aṭṭili yašba'. mā dām aṭṭili yašba' albduwi mā 'alēh šay.*
A *lā waḷḷa, hi bass winsatha waḷḷa taswa. ṭal'at halxiyām ya'ni taswa ćiṯīr.*
B *u yōm intaha aṭṭal'at laha wjīt inta hnayya.*
A *jīna hnayya w dāwamna biljām'a w axaḏna muḥāḏirāt.*
B *ayyihin aḥsan? aḥsan ṭal'atk lalbarr walla jayyatk hnayya.*
A *waḷḷa stānasna balbarr hnāk ćiṯīr 'ind harrabu'. u hāššībān, harrubāba.*
B *mā li'abt 'arrubāba?*
A *lā waḷḷah ana mā a'arf al'ab. 'indi uxulli (1) hnāk yijirr 'alēha. lah jarrāt.*
B *waḷḷah wuddina 'indina rubāba nasma'k.*

TEXT 4 ('ANIZA) TRANSLATION

A Good morning.
B Welcome. Good morning to you. How are you?
A God keep you.
B I hope you are well. How are you?
A Well, I am well, praise be to God. I came to see you last week, but did not find you at your house.
B On Thursday. Yes. We went out to the desert.
A You went out to the desert?
B Yes, we went out to my father's relatives. Yes!
A How was it?
B Well we went to the sheep there and the tents. Yes, we went to them at noon. We reached them at noon. Yes, and there was liban.(2) We drank liban. And when we had drunk the liban and went out to walk about there a while, we saw the young lambs and afterwards we sat for a while there.
A Did you have coffee?(3)
B Yes, we sat for a while. 'Awaḍh told us a gaṣīda, a gaṣīda which pleased me.
A Do you know anything of it?
B Yes. I wrote it down when he recited it to me. Do you want me to say it for you?
A Say it!
B He says:

1 *uxulli* < *uxwin-li.*
2 liban: yoghurt mixed with water. The first drink offered to a guest if there is no fresh milk.
3 Coffee is served as an honour to the guest. However a poor family may serve only tea or milk.

Oh my eye you have turned your attention towards love.
  You are no longer of the religion of my brothers.
Your trouble is from one whom you have seen
  Whose branches have drunk up beauty.(1)
She had marked her eyes with antimony
  So that they were black as the feathers of a crow.
And she had sewn a border on to her dress
  So that you would say it was the tracks of a snake
    in the sand.

A Wonderful. And how was the weather there?

B It was perfect.

A Ha, then this year there is spring grass.

B Yes, by God, there is grass.

A No, it is a year of spring grass.

B Well, this year is not like the last.

A There is not that much grass.

B There is enough to satisfy the young lambs.(2) So long as the young lamb is satisfied, the bedouin has no trouble.

A No, by God. And it is just that the outing there is worthwhile. Going out to those tents is worth much.

B And when your journey there had finished you came back here.

A We came here and went back to work at the university and took up our lectures.

B Which of them is best? Is it best to go out to the desert or to come here?

A Well we enjoyed ourselves a lot there in the desert among the tribesmen and the old men and the viol.

B Did you play on the viol?

A No, by God, I do not know how to play on it. I have a brother there who plays. He has skill in playing.

B By God, I wish we had a viol here and could hear you.

1 The girl is compared to a supple young tree.

2 The phrase "the young lamb is satisfied" is traditionally expressive of the minimum possible amount of grass for comfortable existence. This understatement of the quality of grass and weather is customary among bedouins. See GLUBB (1960) p.236 for other criteria for the quality of pasture.

TEXT 5

'AWĀZIM: A CONVERSATION WITH THE POET SĀLIM AL-DAWWĀY

This is the text of an interview with the poet Sālim ibn Twaim al-Dawwāy (Abu Jum'ān) at his home in Kuwait. The poet was speaking in the beginning on the history of the 'Awāzim in Kuwait, and the first, second and last passages address this issue and are traditional poems of the 'Awāzim. The rest are Ibn Twaim's own verses and page references are given to the Dīwān al-Shā'ir Sālim al-Dawwāy. Verse is alternated with the explanations of the poet. The dialect is basically Central Najdi, showing however */-ik/* rather than */-k/* (2nd m.s.) and */-ah/* rather than */-ih/* (3rd m.s.), which links it with the Gulf dialects (see pages
The Rashāyida informants seemed to have basically the same type of dialect, as is shown in this text. The text also shows */-am/* for */-aw/* in a number of cases, i.e. */ṣāram/* "they have become", which is again shared with the Rashāyida. My thanks are due to Abdallah Dōsiri of Kuwait for help in the translation of parts of these poems.

TEXT 5

miḥtimīn addār min yōm bindagna fitīl
jannbūha ji'il tafdūnha 'iyyī-bha
ćam ṣubiyyin fi naḥāna 'ala rāsah nimīl
yi'ṭi lbindag u hu gabul mā yaṣxī-bha
fal'awāyid naḏbaḥ aššēx walgibba laṣīl
lēn xallēna ljanāyiz ykayyif ḏībha

iššiʼir hāḏa bēnna wbēn, maṣādim al'ašāyir bēnātna. gabul kān min hannō' hāḏa miṯil gibīlah tḥādd gibīlah 'ind ḥidūdha. u hāḏa yōm aljahal gabul. walyōm ṣāram bḥamdillāh killahum ša'ab wāḥid u killahum nafs wāḥda. lākin hāḏa min ḏ̣imin mā ygūl ša'arā gibīlat al'awāzim wilbindig ilfitīl kānat gabul. gabul halašya hāḏi mnawwal bindig fitīl yḥuṭṭūn-bih raṣāṣ u bārūd, raṣāṣa wiḥda u šayy īh bārūd, hāḏa hu. waddār ya'ni hi alli sikanna, wuṭanna alli ḥinna fīh miṯil likweit. mū hu kill al'ašāyir yḥamdūn halašya al'ālim hu haššikil. wiygūl ba'ad:

yaḷḷah inni dāxilik 'an maḥāḏīf alguṣa
lā twarrīna nnakāyir wḥinna misilmīn
ćān ni'ṭi min ṭarafha wnanwi baṣṣaxa
u nikirmah ilmiskīn ḥaddita ġubr assnīn.

ya'ni lo jāna wāḥid maḏkūka alli ḥaddita ġubr assnīn ni'ṭīh min halāyilna. hāḏa min nō' mā ygūl. falyōm aššī'ir muhūb iššī'r ilawwal. gām ytaġayyar alwaḏi' wal'ašāyir illi gabul ṣāram killahum wāḥid. kill dōla bša'bha miṯil mā taḏkir fa hāḏa lli ntimanna mnaḷḷa. wagūl fi wāḥdin mnal'iyāl:

yabūk waḷḷah ġāyt algalb wimnāh
tiṣīr sam'atkum ma' annās zēnah
walla tara mā kān ḥayyin ibdinyāh
y'īš lēn al'umur tagḏi isnīnah
albārḥa zirna mḥammad u šifnāh
lah wagt dūn imwājhi ḥajrīnah
min 'ugub ḏīk alfaxfaxa walm'āyāh
miṯil ilg'ūd alli halah 'āsfīnah
yabūk ixiḏ min wāldik 'ilim wouṣāh
wṣāt min waṣṣa siwāti(1) jinīnah
tara lwalad mā yiḏihrah ġēr yimnāh
'azmin u jazmin tiṣīr ćabdah mitīnah
yā(2) waffigah jazl al'aṭaya w maššāh
nāl al'ila fi himmitah min yimīnah
waṣṣidg bēn annās mā lih mlādah
wiykammil arrajjāl yā(2) ṭāb dīnah
tšūf kill alli ḥawālēh tadrāh
ḥišmah u taqdīrin u rabbih y'īnah u salāmtik

wagūl ba'ad fi uxūlli(3) mitwaffi u lik ṭūlt al'umur.

źizat 'ēni wḥārabt arrgādi
u malleit almajālis walga'ādi
a'addi min ṭuwīlah fi ṭuwīlah
wahabbibha lyā habb albarādi
wafaḏḏi xāṭrin mā dallahanna
'an alli yimtini kiṯr adduwādi
ašūf almargad albārid wa'īfah
mnalli ṣār fi jōf alfwādi

1 *siwāt* compare *hassuwa*.
2 *yā* "if", *hassuwa* "thus".
3 *uxūlli* < *uxwin-li* "a brother of mine".

'aleik aḷḷah wakbar yā zimāni
ja'al fi ḏ̣āmri miṯl aććidādi
ćidād aṣṣulb yā ḥamyat simūmah
w'an 'irźah tara lġidrān ġādi
bidat fīh aššhūbah ćinn rūsah
maxārīzin mnalmaḥdad ḥidādi
'al-alli mā ḥaṣal-li rufgatillah
uhu šafyi u hu ġāyat mrādi
rifīź aṭṭīb maḥmūd assijāya
ṭuwīl albāl fi sā'at i'nādi
ilyā min ḏ̣āg bāli zān bālah
uyirḏ̣īni bharjah barrakādi
wilyā min zall ġēḏ̣i ṭi't šōrah
tiba'tah miṯil muṭwā'in ygādi
lajal 'indi xabar fi māgufillah
ilyā ćallat maḥāfīr ijtihādi
ilyā minni šikēt alḥimil šālah
u gaṭṭ albadd 'anni wišdādi

ilyā 'ajizt 'anh ya'ni yarfa' aḏ̣ḏ̣ēm 'anni

yiji lalḥimil wasmin fi mtūnah
wana amraḥ ma' garāhīd alḥimādi
'ala ḥaggin i'yūni lo bićanna
isnādi kill mā gāl istinādi
yiḥillinn al'abāyir min nuḏ̣īri
walo fīhin mida laddam' zādi
ygūlūn al'arab gabli u 'ugbi
tawārīxin 'atīźātin ijdādi
fa la tabći ddumū' alla lināfi'
ḥagīgah gāṣd inneišān ṣādi

ya'ni mā tabći lla 'ala lli yanfa'ik. alli yḏ̣urrik mā tabći alēh.

asāl aḷḷah ywaffig kill ṭayyib
mnahl albarr walli filblādi
lajal fi kill ṭayyib nō' šīmah
ḥayan falwajh u ć'āmin m'ādi
wafaḏ̣ḏ̣il min nuṣūḥin binnaṣīḥa
ilyā šīwir y'allim bilwkādi
wa lō hu mā yḥibb imšāwrīnah
yijīlah 'an ḏ̣unūn issū' ḥādi
yiḥiddinnah š'ūrin fi ḏ̣imīrah
u yiršid ḥadd jihdah barrašādi

ya'ni lo istašartni yā stād wana mā aḥibbik, axāf imnaḷḷah a'allmik baṣṣaḥīḥ. 'adil? lo inni mā aḥibbik a'allmik baṣṣaḥīḥ. ḏ̣imīri y'allmik. lajal min šāwarik daxal fi ḏimmitik. min istišārik, gāl: "wištigūl yā flān?" wa lōk mā tḥibbah, yājab t'allmah. gult: "wa afaḍḍil min niṣūḥin binnaṣīḥa". ya'ni illi yaxluṣ u yanṣiḥ, ilyā šīwir y'allim bilwukādi, biṣṣaḥīḥ. ya'ni mā yigdar yaćḏib lajal aḏḏamīr jayyid miṯil alḥākim al'adil walḥākim alli yimīl. waḥḥad waḥḥad. fīh ġāḏi yimīl u yijhif ufīh ġāḏi 'adil. annās māhum bwāḥid. 'adil? wišinhu(1) lḥādi? alḥādi alli tḥuṭṭ lilḥḏāra walla lizzari' lā yākilh addibaš. īh salāmtik.

yā rāćbin min fōg sittin hamīmāt
nijāybin sibḥān xāliź iṣwarha
idgāg miźdim wimgaffa jilīlat
manḥūft aḏḏir'ān fijjin naharha
fīhin imnarrīma ḥalāyā wšibhāt
allin(2) wiḥdathin tiḥadib ḍaharha.

hāḏōli ljeiš ilhijin. alibil(3) fīha nāgah. ufīha mwaṣṣaṭa w fīha ḏilūl. aḏḏilūl halli 'aliha halwaṣfāt: ḥurrah, i'māniyya u baṭniyya waṣāyif miṯil tawṣīf assayyārāt kadlak u šafar u byūk. hāh miṯil hannō'.

migdimna dgāg u mwaxxarha jabal

miṯil mā tigūl 'alya min bini hlāl:

aba zēd dawwir faššta samir'iyya
u falgēḍ dawwir mnikbār aṯṯimāyil
ġazāliyt almigdim jamāliyt algufa
'aleikum - ibha yā rāćbīn arraḥāyil

wtigūl ba'ad:

abāzēd low inn annisa tarkab anniḏa
lifētik 'ala wajnin mnalhijin ḥayil
laćinn ṣirīx alkōr ḥadri u fōgha
ṣirīx alguṭa min maḥkumāt ilguwāyil

gāyilha ṭyūr tiṣir(4) mnaḍḍuma.

1 *wišinhu.* This may be the effect of Kuwaiti. In general, bedouin dialects show the particle *wiš-* for "what". See p.87 . However the dialect of the 'Awāzim is, as stated earlier, closer to the Gulf type than are the other bedouin dialects of the area.
2 *allin* < *alla in* "except that".
3 Note *alibil* not *albil* as in Central Najd.
4 *tiṣir* < *tiṣirr*.

yaḷḷah yalli dibirt annās bīdēh
mā ġērk aḥdin nirtijīh u nisālah
jazl al'aṭa lli mā yxīb imtarajjīh
'allāmin barraḥma 'aḏ̣īmin jalālah
ji'il likweit mbaććir alwasm yisgīh
fi ḥisibt alxamsīn miźdim liyālah
dārin rubēna fīh wamwātna fīh
alla wlā narġab blādin bidālah
dārin lyā jāha lfaġīr imtannaṣīh

ya'ni lḥālah ḏ̣a'īf

yā lētni fi ḥafilt al'īd mā jīt
u ṣaddēt 'an nazlat haḏōḷa wa ḏōḷāk(1)

(ya'ni hnāk firīg u hināk firīg. killihum kān jannabt. mu aḥsan-li? lajil yōm rāḥ ilhaḏōḷa, z'alam 'alēh haḏōḷāk. win rāḥ ilhaḏōḷāk z'alam haḏōḷa. walḥibb ma'haḏōḷa alḥibb..)

walla ba'ad mā fīk lal'ēn laddeit
ṣaddēt 'an yimmat yumūmik u mamšāk
māni bnāsin waguftik bayman albeit
youm int tarfa'li salāmin byimnāk.
wiš fiyy yā sīd arra'ābīb sawweit
aḷḷah lā minni balaḥsān yajzāk
yalli 'alašānik 'an il'irs 'ayyeit.

(ya'ni mā abġ atizawwaj aḥad all ant.)

arji jilīlin mink waṣbir ibrajwāk
yā šift zōlik dūn ġērik tahanneit,
il'ēn ti'jibha maṯāyil ḥalāyak.
zid bah lyā jīt ibḥadam wista'addeit
waradt ṭarād alhawa hōḏ̣ aladrāk
yā šiftni finnazil yā gbalt wagfeit
mā li tara ḥāja wġurḏ̣ān lou lāk
anwīk baljayya wilyā gbalt ṣaddeit
min xōftin ba'ḏ̣ almaxālīź tašnāk
wagti ḥadāni 'ank mā 'ank sajjeit
willa 'ala wirdik ḏ̣awāmi hallāk.
-----
dārin lina fīha mḥallin u minzāl
min yōmha sīfin xaḷa min yirūdah?

(ya'ni min hum alli yrūdūnha min hum ahalha ya'ni inćānkum tafhamūn kalāmi...)

1 *haḏōḷa*, the *ḷ* is characteristic of the 'Aniza also; see also CANTINEAU (1936) p.107.

yā mā ća'amna dūnha kill min 'āl,
yā xān xaṭw im'āhdin min 'hūdah.
yā mā hafa fīha min alxēl wa rijāl,
rāḥat ḏaḥāya lilikweit wiḥdūdah.
rā' alwaṭan mā ġērah kill 'aḏḏāl
algalb mā yraxxiṣ masākin jidūdah.
giltah wana gabli min annās min gāl,
killin yiji ḥabbah 'ala baḏir 'ūdah.

TEXT 5 ('AWĀZIM) TRANSLATION

We have protected the homeland from the time of the matchlock rifle.
Defend it and may you be sacrificed for it, the land which has been fought for [so long].
How many young men in the face of our charge against them
Have surrendered their rifles, although previously they were not so generous.
And it is our custom to kill the shaikh [of the enemy] and the pure bred stallion
So as to leave healthy corpses to satisfy the wolves.(1)

This poem is between us and ... in the battles of the tribes between us. Previously it was like this; it is as when one tribe borders on another, on their borders. And this was in the days of ignorance previously; and now they have become one people, thanks be to God, and as one soul. But this is something of what the poets of the 'Awāzim tribe have said. And the matchlock gun was in the former times, before these things that we know now. Previously there was the matchlock in which they put powder and shot, one shot and something. Yes, powder! That is it. And the homeland means this which we are living in; our homeland which we are in, I mean Kuwait. For in fact all the tribes praise these things. The world is like this. And he says also:

Oh God I seek refuge with you from the evils of hardship
Do not show us the course of wretchedness, for we are muslims
We should give of the best we have and be of generous intent
And be kind to the unfortunate man whom evil times have restricted.

1 Part of the poem of Mubārak al-Hīm on the occasion of the battle of Muraikh between the 'Awāzim and the 'Ajmān at the beginning of the century. 'UBAYYID (1971) p.59, 131.

This means that if someone comes to us who is in hardship and whom evil times have put in a difficult position, we will give him of what we have. This is the sort of thing which [the poets] say. And today is not like the early poetry. The situation has begun to change, and the former tribes have all become one, every nation with its people as you mention and this is what we wish from God. And I have said [the following poem] for one of my children.(1)

Oh my son,(2) by God, the ambition and wish of my heart
  is that your reputation will be good among the people
For whatever creature is alive in his world
  lives until his life completes its span of years
Last night we visited Muḥammad and saw him
  For some time they have kept him from my sight(3)
After his past pride and stubbornness
  he has become like a young camel whose people have bridled him
Oh my son take from your father knowledge and advice
  the advice of one who advised his son like me
For nothing supports a young man except his right hand
  [he should be] strong and resolute with a strong heart
If the Benevolent One makes him fortunate and moves him forward,
  still he acquires greatness in his endeavours by his own hand
And truthfulness has no substitute among men
  and makes a man complete if he is of good faith
And you see that all around him treat him well,
  with respect and consideration and God assists him.

And I have also said [the following] about one of my brothers who died; may you live long!

My eye remained awake and I avoided sleep,(4)
  nor could I find comfort if I rose from bed,
Walking from hill to hill,
  walking briskly when the wind blew cold.

1 This poem, which is given in full in AL-DAWWĀY (1976) p. 75, is of the type known as *naṣīḥa* or "advice" to the young.
2 *yābūk*. Such expressions are common; also by the mother to her son or daughter *yumma*. See YASSIN (1977).
3 The poet brings in the example of a relative or friend who has suffered a fall from grace for some reason.
4 AL-DAWWĀY (1976) p.94-96.

And I tried to pour out my thoughts
  which they could not distract.
I see the cold bed and forsake it,
  because of the pain which lies in the depth of my being.
May God save me from you, Oh my fate
  which has left in my soul something like a thorn(1)
A hard thorn, such as when the Simūm wind has become hot
  and the moist soil of the rain pools is far from its roots
And greyness has appeared in it as though its tips
  were needles(2) made of hard iron, and sharp
Because of the one whose companionship I cannot retain
  although he was my comfort and most beloved friend
The good friend of praiseworthy qualities
  patient when I was stubborn
When I was in ill humour, he was of good cheer
  and slowly made me content with his words
And when my anger ceased, I followed his advice
  I followed him like a trained camel being led
Because I knew of his attitude towards me
  when my store of energy was exhausted;
When I complained of a burden, he took it from me
  and threw off the saddle and the ... (3)

When I became tired of it, he took the oppression from me.

He came to the burden, with the brand of the ropes in his shoulder
  while I rested with the gazelles of the steppe
If my eyes weep for him, they have the right,
  my support whenever I needed help.
The tears flow from my eyes
  and if there is a limit to crying, they exceed it.
The Arabs before and after me have said it
  and it is recorded of old and in recent times
Tears do not fall except for those who bring support
  a truth which aims at the mark and strikes it.

I mean you do not cry except for one who helps you. You do not cry for the one who harms you.

1 *ćdād* or *ćtād* a thorny bush of the area.
2 *mixrāz*, the large needle used for sewing leather.
3 Similies comparing man's burdens to that of a camel are common. Compare the stanza: *xaṭw alwalad mit̲l ilblēhi ilā t̲ār; zoudin 'ala ḥimlih yšīl ḥiml ilīfih*, "And some young men are like the Bulaihi (pack camel) when it stands up; and lifts the burden of its companion as well as its own". The word *badd* was not known to my informants.

I ask God to give success to all good men;
those of the desert and those in the cities.
Because in all good men there is a type of honour
a modesty in the face, and resistance to the enemy.
And I prefer as a counsellor
he who, if he is consulted, gives true counsel.
Even though he does not like those who ask his advice
a barrier comes between him and evil thoughts;
The feelings of his conscience stop him;
and he guides correctly to the extent of his ability.

I mean if you ask my advice *ustād*, and I do not like you, I fear God and tell you the truth. Correct? Even if I do not like you, I tell you the truth. My conscience speaks to you. Because he who asks your advice, enters into your protection. Whoever asks your advice and says: "What do you think?" even if you do not like him, you must tell him. I said: I prefer as a counsellor he who, if he is consulted, gives true counsil." I mean the one who is sincere and gives advice. I mean he cannot lie because his conscience is good, like the good judge and the judge who veers from the truth. They are each different. There is the judge who veers from the truth and acts wrongly, and there is the honest judge. People are not all the same. Correct? And what is the *ḥādi*? It is the thing which you put around fish traps or fields so that the flocks will not eat them. Yes. Your health!

Oh they(1) who ride on six hastening steeds,
well-bred camels, how beautifully God has created them
Slim in the forequarters and broad along the back
slim in the forelegs and broad in the chest
With some of the qualities of the gazelle
except that each one of them has a humped back.

These are the war camels, the thoroughbred camels. Camels include racing camels, ordinary camels and leading camels. The leading camel is the one which is of the following types: Ḥurrah (freeborn), 'Omāniyya and Bāṭiniyya(2) types, like different types of car, Cadillac, Chevrolet and Buick. Hah of this type.

1 This is taking *rā́cbin* as poetic license; singular for plural. However, perhaps more accurately, "Oh rider in a troup of six hastening camels". AL-DAWWĀY (1976) p.155-6.
2 See DICKSON (1949) p.412. The Ḥurra is from the northern tribes, 'Omāniyya from the Trucial Coast, and Bāṭiniyya from the Bāṭin coast of 'Oman.

Slim in the forequarters and like a mountain behind

Or, in the words of 'Alya of the Bani Hilāl:

Abu Zaid, find in winter a slim camel,
and in summer find one of the largest around the wells
Like a gazelle in front and like a camel behind,
they are for you, oh riders of the swift mounts.

And she said also:

Abu Zaid, if women were to ride the swift camels,
I would come to you on a dappled pure bred, riding fast
As though the creaking of the saddle under me and above it
were the cry of bird in the heat of the afternoon.

He compares it to the screeching of birds.

Oh God, who has the deliberations of man in his hands,(1)
there is no one but you from whom we hope for success
and pray to.
The generous one who does not disappoint his supplicants
of familiar mercy and great glory.
May Kuwait have an early spring rain to water it,
of fifty days duration beginning some evening soon.
The home land in which we grew up and in which we die,
and to which we would prefer no other land
The land to which, if a poor man comes in refuge

I mean someone who is in a poor situation

I wish that I had never come to the 'Īd celebration(2)
and had refrained from visiting these and those people.

I mean here there is one group and here another. I should have avoided both of them. Wouldn't it have been better for me? Because when he went to these, those others were angry with him, and if he went to those, the first group were angry and his love for these was like his love ...

I was troubled by seeing you
and turned away from where you were and where you
walked.
I have not forgotten you standing to the right of the
house,
when you lifted up a greeting to me with your right
hand.

1 AL-DAWWĀY (1976) p.83.
2 Ibid., p.142-3.

What have you done to me, Oh best of the slim-waisted girls?
The one for whose sake I have renounced marriage.

I mean I do not want to marry any one but you.

I wait for a favour from you, and am patient in waiting
If I see your figure in the distance in place of some other I am happy
The eye is pleased by such as your beauty
Let me see you more and if I come to a place and wait
I came to the well ... unclear ...
If you see me in the camp, if I approach then go away,
You know that I have no need or ambition except you.
I hope to come to you, but when I approach, I turn away
in fear of some people who may be angry with you.
My fate has kept me from you, I did not avoid you,
while in fact my thirst to approach you is killing me.

A homeland in which we have a place and a settlement.(1)
From the time when it was an empty coastline, who used to protect it?(2)

I mean who were they that used to protect it, who were its people. I mean, if you understand my words...

How often have we repelled all who came to attack us,
when they betrayed us in some treaty.
How many men and horses have died in it,
gone as martyrs to Kuwait and its borders.
He is the leader of the homeland; there is no other defender.
The heart does not count cheap the dwellings of the ancestors.
I say it and many before me have said the same:
Each person's flower blooms on the pattern of the seed of his line.

1 Al-DAWWĀY (1976) p.35, a poem in praise of the Amīr 'Abdallah al-Sālim al-Ṣubāḥ.
2 The 'Awāzim claim to be the oldest of the present bedouin groups in the Kuwait region.

TEXT 6

SHAMMAR: THE STORY OF THE SHILGĀN RAID

This text was given to me by my main Shammari informant 'Uraifij al-Shilāźi, one of the attendants of the Amīr Muḥammad al-Sudairi on his estate near the Wādi Turmus. His home was the settlement of Shu'aibāt (Shu'aibāy) north-east of Hail on the edge of the Nafūd. This was settled fifty years ago after the fall of the Rashīd dynasty and was an entirely Shammar village and served as a camp for the Sinjāra during the summer months. North of Shu'aibāt was al-Bag'a, another Shammar settlement of a similar type, and to the southwest al-Ajfar. Informants felt that all the Najd Shammar, whether settled or nomadic, spoke a very similar dialect with the exception of the 'Abda who spoke a dialect similar to the Ḍhafīr, their neighbours to the east. I had, however, no opportunity to confirm this.

TEXT 6

haḏōḷa ṭāl 'umrak iššilgān faḏōḷa ġazwin 'ala hwēṭāy u ba'ad ma xaḏaw albil nhajaw ilhwēṭāṭ 'ala xeil u xaḏōham. xaḏōham ya'ni 'ugub ma'raktin ṭuwīlih. u yōm inn hum xaḏōhum yā ṭuwīl il'umur u fassuxaw ḥitta hdūmaham. mā xallaw 'aleham hidūm. hāḏa xawiyyam bin axīham jīd arrubū' iksumōh ilḥwēṭāy iksumōh mi' rij^əlu mi' fax^əḏu u gāl: "yā xawāli rūḥu ana rajjālin abamūt wintam rūḥu lahalkam." rāḥaw 'ala 'yūnu wattigoublaham(1) ḥazim. ygūl 'ād: "hāh lā waḷḷah rāḥaw, rāḥaw xallōnan lā waḷḷa rāḥaw." u yirźib hu rij^əlu hu mintaṯrih ya'ni ḏ̣āmah rja'aw 'alēh u gālaw: "ibšir bummak ibšir bummak" jaw ya'ni miṯil, miṯil slimi albil 'alēh, ya'ni

1 For this particle peculiar to the Shammar dialect *-bla-* signifying -l-, see also CANTINEAU (1937) p.209. He also gives *'andelu* < *'and+lu*.

mġīrīn 'alēh ġāreih" "yā hanuwwak bummak yā hanuwwak brab'ak." u zuxxūh(1) yā ṭuwīl al'umur u ḥaṭṭaw na'aš miṯil na'aš ilmeit luh u mwišaw ya'ni gīmat xamsat 'ašar lēlih aw sab'at 'ašar lēlih u ham / ham allēl wannahār yamšūn. ma'ham hdēb aššām abaćli alli hu 'aźīdaham, abaćli bin fāliḥ aššilāźi. abaćli yā minnaham gayyilaw xaḏāw ṭāl 'umrak 'ugbitēn yšīlu ṭāl 'umrak 'ugbitēn ya'ni sammōh bi'ugbitēn miṯil yā yšīlūnu hāḏōli jimī', hu yā minnaham istarāḥaw ja u xaḏa rrajjāl 'ugbitin ṯānyih ya'ni rāḥ, ēh, marritēn yšīlu u ham ṣġār ya'ni ham gīmat i'māraham ya'ni ṣġār bhalwagt haḏāk mā haw kbār. killaham jid'ān. yā innu ṭāl 'umrak yaḏharin maḥāšm u yaḏharin źibālaham. u ydill yḏafḏuf rūḥu w mā yabi ham yšūfūnu balḥēl mā 'alēham hdūm, killaham mā 'alēham u yḥibbu aḥadēham yḥibb xuṣyānu ydill yištakk yōm ygūl "xūy, yā / wiš ismu / yā mjeida' yā xūy ḥinna miṯᵊlak šuf xuṣyānna killaham maṣālīx, ya'ni mā 'alēna šay . lā tistiḥi!" ṯmurta innaham rāḥaw ṭāl 'umrak u yōm innaham instahlikaw mātaw mnal'aṭš ṭabbōblaham nigrat(2) u gayyilaw ya'ni bhaššijrat(3) moutā(4) yabūn ymūtūn mnal'aṭš. ġrayyib dilīlah ġrayyib ibin 'ayźih rāḥ minham yōm innaham šāfaham nāmaw u hu yrūḥ lixabran yxabr innahu / yōm inn. ya'ni gabul yōm ilmaġāzi. u yōm ja lxabra yamma hi malyānih u yōm innu ṭabb 'ala lxabra. w yṭubb ma'u lu šinag bargan 'alyah u šāf alma u yarja' ma' iṯaru naks. mā ḏāgah lillah abad! u yōm ja nimar 'ala ga'datham gāl: "ibširu barri!" u ham yfūḥūn faraḥ: "wēni?" gāl: "īh, bhāḏa(5) grayyib." u ham yamšūn yšiddūn nfūsaham u yanglūn xawiyyaham alli hu / ilyā mā jaw alxabra, lamman jaw alxabra gāl: "uṣbru šufu ṯari, lā tḥasbūnni ya'ni inni raḥt 'āyifkam, ilyā mni(6) širibt u tifaṭṭant likam šufu iṯari. hāḏa ṯari tar inni mā ḏigtah šufu iṯari!" bi'dēn yōm innaham ḏibaḥham aljū', mā min / iddyār xluww. mā bah aḥad. aldyār gṭū' mā ba aḥad mnannās. ṣādōlaham jarbū' u šuwōh walkill y'ayyīh innu mā yji aḥad mā yji ya'ni lugmwitin balfum. dallaw yta'ādōn walkill: "uxḏu yā flān." ham yi'ṭūnu wġeidin ma'ham yigāl-lu(7) ṭāl 'umrak, yigāl-lu šaḥḥād ibin mxeimir. šaḥḥād ibin mxeimir laffuh birīmu abad hu aṣġarᵊham laffu bbirīmu. 'ugub mā jaw ahalham wistirāhaw 'ād-/ya'ni wzāru ya'ni birīm ya'ni mwiḥzam miṯil iḥzām/, hāh laffu balḥizām lamman jaw ahalham

1 Narrative imperative.
2 *-at*. For retention of the *-t* see p.70.
3 Ditto.
4 *moutā*. In Arabian dialects the masculine plural of some adjectives has the ending *-ā*, *noumā* "asleep".
5 *bhāḏa* "here", see p.98-9.
6 *mni* North Najdi, more normally *minni*.
7 *yigāl* internal passive, see p.41.

gāl: "yā šilgān lā tḥasbōnni. kaleit aljarbū' illi antam 'aṭeitūni lu mwiddat 'ašart ayyām hāḏa ljarbū' ill antam / yōm 'ād jaw ahalham wistarāḥaw / hāḏa ljarbū' il antam txabrūn mā ḏigtu." šufu šīmat arrijāl u šḥāmiyyatham u ygūlūn ṭāl 'umrak innaham ġazaw 'ala jeiš marratin ṯānyih innaham ygayyilūn 'ala maźīlaham wiyġaddūn 'ala mġaddāham u y'aššūn 'ala m'aššāham hijratᵊna falgā' ygūlūn ya'ni mā gad yinwiṣil almamšah mašya hāk alwagt haḏāk. ya'ni hāḏa giṣṣat iššilgān u hi ṯmurtah ṭāl 'umrak gaṣīdtah bass mā 'arif.

TEXT 6 (SHAMMAR) TRANSLATION

There were, God give you long life, the Shilgān(1) and they were a raiding party against the Ḥuwaiṭāt.(2) And after they had captured the camels, the Ḥuwaiṭāt attacked them on horses (3) and captured them after a long battle. And when they captured them, O long of life, they stripped them even of their clothes, they didn't leave clothes on them. This was their companion, their cousin Jīd al-Rubū', the Ḥuwaiṭāt maimed him, in his leg, in his thigh and he said: "Oh my uncles,(4) go! I am a man who is going to die so you all go to your families." They went from his sight and were hidden by a hill and he said: "Hah, no by God, they've gone and left me. No, by God, they've gone." And he bound up his leg, it was broken, I mean the bone of it. They returned to him and said: "Rejoice for your mother. Rejoice for your mother." They came like a herd of camels to him, I mean running to him at the gallop (saying): "Rejoice for your mother, rejoice for your companions." And they picked him up, O long of life, and brought a stretcher, like the bier of a corpse, for him and they walked about fifteen nights or seventeen nights and they were walking night and day. With them was Hudaib al-Shām 'Abaćli. He was their leader, 'Abaćli ibn Fāliḥ the Shilāźi.(5) 'Abaćli, when they had rested in the afternoon, carried him, O long of life, two turns, he carried him for two turns, I mean, they call it two turns, for instance when they had carried him, all of them (once), he, after they had rested, came and took the man a second turn. I mean, he went, yes and carried him twice. And they

1 The Shilgān, a branch of the Sinjāra Shammar.
2 Huwaiṭāt, a tribe of southern Jordan.
3 Long range raiding was by camel, but the raided camp could counterattack after the raid on horses, which were faster over a short distance.
4 Relatives on the mother's side, in general.
5 Of the Shilgān; see also PHILBY (1922) p.257 vol.I, who mentions him although he gives the name as Abaqili.

were young, I mean they were about, I mean, young, at that time. They were not old. They were all youths and when, God give you life, their loins were exposed and he began trying to cover himself he didn't want them to see him at all, they had no clothes on them. All of them had no clothes and he covered his loins, covered his nakedness and was embarrassed. And he said, "Oh my brother / O / what was his name / O Mujaida', O my brother, we are like you, look at our nakedness. All of them were naked. "I mean we have nothing on, do not be shy!" The result of it was that they went and, God give you long life, when they were dying of thirst, perishing of thirst, they came to a well and rested in the afternoon at this tree, dying on the point of death from thirst. Ghrayyib, the guide, Ghrayyib ibn 'Aiźah, went from them, when he saw that they had gone to sleep he went to a hollow that he knew of / when he I mean before the time of the raid. And when he came to the hollow, near it, it was full and when he came in to the hollow and he came to it, there was a slope with fine sand on it and he saw the water and went back on his tracks returning. He didn't taste it, by God, at all! And when he came and burst on to the place where they were sitting, he said: "Rejoice in the quenching of thirst!" and they leapt in joy. "Where is it?" He said: "Yes, here quite near." And they walked, pushing themselves on and carrying their companion who/when they came to the hollow, he said: "Wait, see my tracks, do not think that I went, leaving you and when I had drunk, I remembered you. See my tracks. There are my tracks. You see that I didn't taste it. See my tracks!" Afterwards when hunger had almost killed them, there were no / the lands were deserted, there was no one there. The lands were deserted, there was no one there, no people. They caught a jerboa for themselves and roasted it and all of them refused it, no one came. There wasn't a morsel for the mouth. They began competing with one another: "Take it O *fulān*." They gave it to a young boy with them who was called, May you live long, who was called Shaḥḥād ibn Mukhaimir. Shaḥḥād ibn Mukhaimir hid it in his loincloth. Not at all, he was the smallest of them. He hid it in his loincloth. When they had got to their families and rested, then / I mean his loincloth, I mean his belt, like a belt/ Hah, he hid it in his belt and when they came to their families, he said "Oh Shilgān do not think that I ate the jerboa, which you gave me, ten days ago. This is the jerboa which you / they when they came to their families and rested / this is the jerboa which you know of, I haven't tasted it." See the honour and pride of the men. And they say, May your life be long, that they went off on another raid by camels a second time. And they rested where they rested, and had lunch where they had lunch and dined where they dined.(1) Our journey by foot, they say that that journey is not possible, the journey of that time. I mean this is the story of the Shilgān and the point of it is the gaṣīda, Long life to you, but I do not remember it.

1 The meaning of this is unclear. It seems to mean that they left immediately.

TEXT 7

RUFAI': POEMS AND SENTENCES ABOUT NOMAD LIFE

The first part of this text was recorded, the rest dictated. It was obtained from an encampment of the Rufai' at the Hollandi Canal, northeast of Nāṣiriyya. The Rufai' had just come in from the desert after the end of spring and were encamped in groups of four or five tents at a number of places in the vicinity. This particular group were encamped near a village of Sūdān marsh dwellers where they had the use of a well for their camels, which also grazed on the ḥamaḏhāt in the vicinity. The dialect of the Rufai' showed features of the North Arabian type but also some of the characteristics of the periphery area. This was consistent with their position as bedouins of original Najdi origin with a long history of contact with Iraq and Shi'ite in religion. The text shows a great similarity to the dialect of the Ahl al-Shimāl (Text 9) with the important exception that it shows the characteristic North Arabian form of the feminine suffix /*-ih*/, while the Ahl al-Shimāl text shows /*-ah*/. The form /*-ih*/ is consistent with the tribe's Shammari connections. Shammari informants regarded the Rufai' and the related Ḥumaid, Sā'da and Bu'aij tribes as members of the Ṣāyiḥ group, Shammar tribes who had gone over to Iraq in the past and taken the Shi'ite faith (*tišayyi'aw*).

TEXT 7

abārḥa(1) činna 'ala yāl mallih
abāṣir binafsi čēf attadābīr
'arrār birru sābiji fi maḥallah
birru sūsa yā 'ašīr almasāyīr

1 *abārḥa* < *albārḥa*.

dann aḏḏilūl u muṣ'ab azzamil xallah
uḥuṭṭ arrisan bissifīfa čima ṭṭēr
ḏōd alma'ādi lāzim nišillah
nišdi 'an maghōra u nigfuḏ ibyillah
u kill mā dabbar abāri(1) gilna xēr.

yā bint yā ṣāyim 'alīč aḷḷa lannič tijīfīn
lamman nigūl ibniyyat alxēr rūḥi
'aḏrōbha ilhalha lyiḏbaḥūn alba'ārīn
ilnijrin tawāli lliel ḥissu ḏibūḥi
amma linhēdi miṯil ṭal'a lbasātīn
walla tafāfīḥin 'ala yāl mūhi.(2)

Sentences to do with nomadic life:

1 *almuṭar muṭar iššimāl, wilfi'l fi'l iryāl, walšēl šēl iymāl.*

2 *iddinya ṣāḥi walā bah ġēm, wilṣār iġbār nsammīh 'ayy.*

3 *sraḥat alabā'ir, lo ġyāb iššamis rawwiḥat. lo ṣār inšarat, iṣṣubuḥ.*

4 *iṭla'aw lilbarr irja'aw liddīrih. baššita niḏhar. wāḥid yrawwid 'išəb yiṭla' arrawwād. lo ṣār mā liga yiḏul. (3) iddinya maḥal u gaḥaṭ mā-buh ši. iddīrih miḥīlih.*

5 *rabbu'at iddinya. nirwi māy ġadīr. māy šurba. nwarrid. "šīlu rabī' ibširu balxēr."*

6 *"ibširu balxēr. ibširu barrabī' u šīlu wintaklu."*

7 *"abašširkum bah xēr u bah 'išbin lā yṭūl."*

8 *irja'aw liddīrih. ḥaddaraw šaṭṭ ilfarāt. inzalaw halna banaw ilbyūt. "ibnan ibsā' giṭa'na ljū' nrīd ačil u čāy."(4) iydigg ighawih wiyyūn almasāyīr yišurbūn ighawih "ḥayyuh, ḥayyuhum! aḷḷa balxēr antum!"*

TEXT 7 (RUFAI') TRANSLATION

Last night I was on a hill of trouble,(5)
Thinking to myself what plans to make.
'Arrār,(6) feed my mare where she stands
Feed Sūsa(7) O friend of the wayfarer.
Bring forth the swift riding camel and leave the untrained difficult camels,

1 *abāri* < *albāri*
2 Compare *timūh* "it flows".
3 *yiḏul* < *yiḏull*
4 Mesopotamian; *šāhi* in Najd.
5 *mallih* literally "burning heat".
6 'Arrār, a man's name.
7 Sūsa, the name of the horse.

And put on the head-stall with the tassels resembling
[the feathers of] a bird.
We must carry off the herds of the enemy
We leave the small camels and take the best
And whatever the Lord brings we accept.

O pious girl, why by God do you wait?
When we say with good intention, go!
Her only failing(1) is her family who slaughter camels [for the guest]
And the coffee pestle which rings late at night.
As for her breasts they are like the buds of a garden,
Or like apples on a well-watered hillside.

Sentences to do with nomadic life:

1 The rain is the rain of the north,(2) the deed the deed of men and the carrying, the carrying of camels.(3)

2 The weather is clear and there is no cloud. If there is dust we call it *'ayy*.

3 The camels have gone out to pasture. If it is in the evening, we say *rawwiḥat*,(4) if we say *nšarat*(4) that is in the morning.

4 They have gone out to the desert. In the winter we go out. One person goes out to scout for pasture. He, the scout, goes out. If it happens that he finds nothing, he stays [until he does find something]. The land is dry and in drought, there is nothing there. The *dīra* is in drought.

5 The land is covered in grass. We drink water from the pools, drinking water. We bring the flock down to drink. "Move camp! It is spring, rejoice in the good fortune."

6 "Rejoice in the spring. Rejoice in the good fortune. Move camp and trust [in God]!"

7 "I bring you good news. There is good fortune and there is grass which is not far off."(5)

8 They have come back to the camping ground. They have come down to the river Euphrates. Our families have dismounted and pitched the tents. "Pitch the tents quickly (O women!) Hunger has broken us. We want food and tea!" He pounds coffee and the wayfarers come in and drink coffee. "Greeting to him! Greeting to them.(6) God keep you well."

1 *'aḏrōb* "a failing" here used ironically to mean virtue, as the poet then lists various signs of generosity.
2 The best rain is thought to be brought by the north wind.
3 Carrying of the camp equipment which is loaded on camels.
4 Different verbs denoting movement of flocks.
5 Or perhaps "which will not last long".
6 In greetings formulae the person addressed is often referred to in the third person. See also INGHAM (1976) p.75.

SHAMMAR (MAS'ŪD): GAṢĪDA FROM THE BANI HILĀL EPIC

The following gaṣīda was recorded from Shaikh Aḥmad al-'Allāwi of the Mas'ūd. The Mas'ūd are descended from the Aslam branch of Shammar settled around Karbala. The gaṣīda is part of the Bani Hilāl epic, but shows the main features of the dialect, namely the Shammari suffixes of the third person singular /*-uh*/(m.), /*-ah*/(f.). Elsewhere on the tape the suffix /*-an*/ for /*-ni*/ (1st s.) occurs. However the other main North Arabian characteristics did not occur in this dialect. It constitutes a form similar to that of the other Euphrates bedouin, but more clearly assimilated to the Mesopotamian type. My thanks are due to Ṣāḥib 'Ali of Ḥilla for obtaining this tape for me.

TEXT 8

gāl:

ijēna 'ala rās ilwa'ad ḥinna wḥimyar.
ḥinna t̲alāt̲īn mā nzūd zōd zāyid.
u humma t̲alat̲miyya kāmlīn ili'dādi
u'aširtin min rab'i ṭalligaw rūs xēlahum (širdaw)
u 'aširtin min rab'i hāfḏ̣īn iššahāyid.

(wugfaw 'al ḥiyād d̲ōla)

u 'aširtin min rab'i xallaw izzān biṣdūr il'ida
čahašīm ilwujāyid.
wuhgin ṭa'anni wana mšīḥ ilġēruh
u xalla ddiri' fjambi bijāyid.
xayyāl ḥimyar u bismu lāni 'ārfuh
yinxūn wēn wuhig wēnu bil'awāyid.
wuhgin ṭa'anni wana mšīḥ ilġēruh
u gāmat ilxaḏ̣ra tijūlib b'idditah 'alayy.

(ilxaḏ̣ra frusuh)

u xallatni čašann 'ajūzin 'ala lgā' bāyid.

(aššann ajjirba l'atīga)

fazzēt wilyā xayyālin yinḥa lxēl 'anni.
yinḥāh čima sēlin tinḥāh innifāyid.
'afya bin ixiyyin ṯana 'ind xāluh
aṯāri mirṯa gāydin ibn gāyid.

(sūr ibin gāyid hāḏa min bini hlāl)

TEXT 8 (SHAMMAR MAS'ŪD) TRANSLATION

He said:

We came to the appointed place, ourselves and Ḥimyar.(1)
We were thirty men or not many more.
And they were three hundred or not less.
Ten of my companions had loosed the reins of their horses.

(they had fled)

And ten of my companions had held their council

(they stood aside, in neutrality)

And ten of my companions left their lances in the breasts of the enemy [which shattered] with the brittleness of burnt twigs [as on a fire].
One called Wuhig struck me while I was engaged with another,
and left my coat of mail ripped in shreds on my side.
[He was] a horseman of Ḥimyar whom I did not know by name.
While the enemy called out "Where is Wuhig, where is the hero!"(2)
Wuhig struck me while I was engaged with another.
And Khaḏ̣hra was tumbled over on me with her trappings.

(Khaḏ̣hra was his mare)

1 The ancient tribe of southern Arabia, the enemies of the Bani Hilāl before their exodus to North Africa.
2 The custom was to call out the name of a hero in a battle as a rallying cry *naxwa*, hence *yinxūn; 'awāyid* "heroic qualities".

And left me like an old woman's water skin deserted on
the ground.

(a "shann" is an old water skin)

When I recovered, lo! a horseman was turning the horses
away from me,
Turning them away as a sand dune separates a flood.
Bravo for a nephew of mine who turned back to save his
uncle.
I saw that it was a descendant of Gāyid son of Gāyid.(1)

(that is Sūr ibn Gāyid of the Bani Hilāl)

1 Gāyid ibn Fāyid ibn 'Āmir, the grandfather of Abu Zaid, MUKHLIṢ (1964) p.141.

TEXT 9

AHL AL-SHIMĀL: THE STORY OF IBN JASH'AM AND IBN 'ARAI'IR

This text was recorded from a family of bedouin encamped at Umm al-'Aish, a well to the north of Kuwait town. They would not tell us what tribe they were from but only that that were Ahl al-Shimāl "people of the north". Their speech identified them as nomads of the southern Euphrates area and was very similar to the idalect of the Ḥumaid and Rufai' interviewed later in the area of Nāṣiriyya in Iraq (Text 7). In the same area were also families of Shammar and Bani Khālid, altogether about twenty tents in all. These were all sheep herders. One Najdi informant from Midhnab in Qaṣīm, on hearing this text, said it was the speech of *shūyān* "sheep herders" from the north. However the Ḍhafīri informant regarded them as *mintifij* "bedouin" of the north. This is illustrative of the vague nature of the designation "bedouin" as applicable to these northern nomads.

TEXT 9

yubu ġānim, yigullak ibin imhēd lu indu luh'abd wal'abd timallak ibxaḏ̣ra u tūnis huwwa ššēx ṣār bxaḏ̣ra wal'abd wakkiluh btūnis u youm innihum wakkiluh yā ṭuwīl al'umur, istašḥal aššēx ugām yāxiḏ ḏibīḥa w minīḥa. wastašyaxa šēx. ibin i'rē'ir yā ṭuwīl il'umur, hāk aljaš'am yinṭīh xaryiyya (1) kill sinah min āl jaš'am. youm in rāḥ-lu yā ṭuwīl il'umur aṯāri yinṭīh 'isrīn lēra, ibin imhēd kill sanah.(2) u yannab(3) ibin imhēd iššēx u rāḥ lil'abd u sayyar 'alal 'abd u liga l'abd šaġlitu muxriṭa nās tiḏbaḥ, nās tiṭbax,

1 *xaryiyya* for *xarjiyya*.
2 *sanah* "year". Three lines above the form is *sinah*, this is variation between North and Central Arabian forms, compare Shammar *sinah*, Ḍhafīri *sanah*, Shammar *šinag*, Sudair *šanag* "side".
3 *yannab* for *jannab*.

nās tinfax u 'aṭīt-allah. xaḏa ṯalaṯt ayyām yā ṭuwīl al'umur, akrumu hāl 'abd. akrumu lxamsīn lērah u čisāh u hallā-bu u rāḥ ilhalu. marr 'ala ššēx 'amm al-'abd. youm inn yarrah(1) hā ṣṣaḥan, ṣaḥan ibin i'rē'ir yā ṭuwīl al'umur u galaṭ addīra u gliṭaw ham(2) ma'zūmīn, galaṭ aljaš'am hu wiyyāhum. u gāl luh ibn i'rē'ir: "yā bin jaš'am ham šift wāḥid akram minni?" gāl "Ībillah lā tilḥag lā ṯiliṯ wa lā rub' min 'abdak." gāl: "minu hnā ?"(3) lā waḷḷa ḥāḏrīn il'abīd. gāl "ṭiggūh balḥadīd?" baljaš'am, arbuṭaw ajjaš'am, ḥaṭṭōh balmuḏīf. ēh! gāl: "ḥinna yo inn xaryiyyak(4) mrabba' 'alēna, alxaryiyya yo(5) nwaxxir rāsak." irkubaw ḥirwitah ṯamānīn xayyāl. al'abd ilā nigal iddalla mā yinṭīha balyisār, alfinyāl, alla balyamīn. u youm inn yā ṭuwīl al'umur ḥawwalaw 'indu, lā waḷḷah sawālf aljaš'ami killhin wkād. hāḏa ibin i'rē'ir saḥab assēf yabi/yirīd(6) yiḏbaḥ hāl'abd. jā'id wara ddlāl. nās tidigg u nās tiḏbaḥ u nās tinfax. hāḏa yā ṭuwīl al'umur isḥab assēf u ḥuṭṭu jiddāmak, (7) wa ddīwān jā'din 'indu. gāl yā ṭuwīl al 'umur "ana arīd minnak gaṣīdtēn, u rāsi 'alēk ḥalāl." 'indu walad ismu klēb. mā sammāh ġēr ḏāk al yōm u hu rajjāl. gāl: "yā klēb yā wlidi. 'aṭni rrubbāba!" inṭāh arrubbāba yā ṭuwīl al'umur u gām yašḥaṭ-bah al'abd. gāl:

"naṭṭēt rās imgayyir u šift azzuwāl u jilīb šēx sayyār.
miyat hala baššēx hu walmasāyīr
albunn yiṭbax walbalašt imhayyal
waṣṣīx yir'af iḏnu balgarājīr
lu šāwrin(8) bah čīs mā hu m'ayyar
maydū' jiddām annišāma ta'āmīr
ana lo 'ayyirōni b'amāmi māni m'ayyar
li xawāl u li ydūd mašāhīr.

šiddak ra'ani warāk(9) mā gilit(10) ya klēb
u lā gilit šubb annār yā mūjid addalla

1 *yarrah* for *jarrah*.
2 *ham* "also" Mesopotamian.
3 *hnā* Mesopotamian.
4 *xaryiyyak* < *xaryiyyatk*. One would expect *xaryiytak*. This may be the influence of neighbouring Central Najd dialects.
5 *yo* "either ... or". The normal Mesopotamian is *lo*, Arabian *yā*. This represents a synthesis.
6 *yirīd/yabi* "he wants". Here first the Mesopotamian then the Arabian lexemes are used.
7 *isḥab assēf u ḥuṭṭu jiddāmak* "draw the sword and put it in front of you!" Narrative imperative.
8 *šāwrin* nunation.
9 *wara* used in negative questions for "why".
10 *gilit* < *gilt*. The Mesopotamian anaptyctic vowel. See p.60-1.

yā m'ayyiš alyitmān hum walmaḥādīd
yā walad min ṣār al'aṣa ṯālṯillah
tičfi maḥālīb u tij'id maḥālīb
u čabdin tyabbisah u čabdin tibillah
māni nihētak yā jilīl il'aḏārīb
lo tistiḥi mānt ḥāwi aṭṭīb killah"

'āf 'innuh u akrumu hāddīrah. tislam u ti'īš yubu ġānim.

TEXT 9 (AHL AL-SHIMĀL) TRANSLATION

Oh Abu Ghānim(1) he says to you(2) that Ibn Muhaid(3) had a slave and the slave... He [Ibn Muhaid] took possession of Khaḍra(4) and Tūnis. He became the Shaikh at Khaḍra and he entrusted the slave with Tūnis. And when he entrusted him with it, Oh long of life, the Shaikh [i.e. the slave] became powerful and began taking Dhabīḥa and Manīḥa.(5) Ibn 'Arai'ir...,(6) Oh long of life, the Jash'ami [Ibn Muhaid] used to give him a stipend every year from the Āl Jash'am. (7) You see he used to give him twenty liras, that is Ibn Muhaid, every year. He [Ibn 'Arai'ir] avoided Ibn Muhaid,

1 The story was addressed to a member of the audience.
2 "He says to you" a conventional way of beginning a narrative or story.
3 Ibn Muhaid is cast here as the Shaikh of the Jash'am (Qash'am) see p. 20. The clan of Ibn Muhaid are however shaikhs of the Fad'ān of 'Aniza. See GLUBB (1978) p.155 for a further story of Ibn Muhaid. Hereafter the name is dropped in the narrative.
4 Khaḍra and Tūnis. The narrator uses these as purely mythical names. In fact Khaḍra is an epithet of Tūnis, Tūnis al-Khaḍra, "Tūnis the fertile". He has imported these names from the Bani Hilāl stories and uses them to symbolize the great extent of the power of the Jash'am.
5 Dhabīḥa and Manīḥa, a system of tribute in kind and hospitality exacted by powerful shaikhs of the Euphrates area; see DICKSON (1949) p.443-4.
6 Ibn 'Arai'ir, the shaikhly house of the Bani Khālid, previous rulers of Kuwait and al-Hasa; see also p.65f above for the dialect of the Bani Khālid.
7 Al Jash'am (Qash'am), an important confederation of the middle Euphrates comprising the tribes Qash'am, Ḥumaid, Rufai', Bu'aij and Sā'da and sometimes referred to as the Ghizya. In the 18th century they controlled the grazing lands west of the Euphrates between Hit and Samāwa. Later in the 19th century under pressure from the Shammar and later the 'Aniza they moved south and the Ḥumaid and Rufai' joined the Muntafiq. OPPENHEIM (1952) 1-2,p.408-13; AZZĀWI (1956) IV, p.52.

the shaikh, and went to the slave and he called on the slave. He found the slave enjoying himself. Some people were slaughtering [sheep] and others cooking and others pounding [coffee beans] and the gift of God!(1) he took [stayed] three days. He took three days, O long of life, and the slave gave him a gift of fifty liras and gave him a gift of clothing and made him welcome and he went back to his family. [On the way] he visited the Shaikh the uncle [i.e. master] of the slave. And when he took it away, the food, the food of Ibn 'Arai'ir(2) [i.e. after eating] and they went in to the town ... and they also went in as his guests - the Jash'am went in with him - Ibn 'Arai'ir said to him "Oh Ibn Jash'am, and have you seen anyone more generous than me?" He said, "Yes, by God, you do not reach a third or even a quarter [in generosity] of your slave". He said "Who is here?" No, by God, the slaves were all present. He said "Chain him up, the Jash'ami". They chained the Jash'ami and imprisoned him in the guest-house. Yes. He said "Either we will multiply your stipend four-fold, or we will remove your head." They mounted up, approximately, eighty riders. The slave, when he takes round the coffee-pot, doesn't pour coffee from the people on the left, but starts from the people on the right. (3) And when they came up to them, No, by God, [they saw that] the story of the Jash'ami was all true. Ibn 'Arai'ir drew his sword wishing to kill the slave. He was sitting by the coffee-pots and people were pounding coffee and others cooking and others blowing on the fire. He, O long of life, drew the sword and put it in front of him, and all the dīwān were sitting in front of him. He [the slave] said, O long of life, "I want from you [to let me recite] two gaṣīdahs, and then my head is lawful for you [if you still want to remove it]." He had a son named Kulaib, whom he had not called [in public] other than on that day, although he was a man. He said "O Kulaib, my son, give me the Rabāba [viol]!" He gave him the Rabāba, O long of life, and the slave began to play on it. He recited:

"I came over the hill at Mugayyir and saw the figures in the distance and the well of Shaikh Sayyār.
A hundred welcomes to the Shaikh, him and the guests.

1 An expression of wonder at generosity or plentifulness.
2 At this point the narrator corrects the names of the characters in the story. It is Ibn 'Arai'ir, not Ibn Muhaid, who is the owner of the slave and Ibn Jash'am the dependent.
3 The correct way to pour coffee is starting with the guests on the left of the host. The significance of it here is not plain.

The coffee beans are roasting and the coffee pot has been prepared with cardamon.
And the edge of the roasting iron rings against the hearth-stones(1)
He has a tobacco box(2) with a tobacco pouch in endless supply
Thrown down in front of the heroes for them to replenish their pipes.
If anyone insults me by my forebears, I am not insulted.
I have marriage-relatives and ancestors of great renown.

Bear up, why didn't you tell me O Kulaib,
Why didn't you say to light the fire, O bringer of the coffee-pot.
Oh he who provides for orphans and prisoners,
O son of he for whom his staff is a third(3)
You knock over one milk bowl and set up another(4)
And you make the heart(5) of one man dry and moisten the next.
I did not forbid you, O blameless one.
If you are shy, you will not attain all virtue." [generosity]

He [Ibn 'Arai'ir] forgave him and gave him that whole country as a gift. Live in health, O Abu Ghānim.

1 The word *garājīr* was not known to my informants, but the sense seemed to be as above.
2 Tobacco and coffee were in the old days the great luxuries of the desert and always in short supply.
3 The meaning is obscure. One suggestion was that he had only one son and that he, the son and his staff were three.
4 A sign of generosity.
5 Literally "liver". The phrase signifies taking care of the needs of guests.

TEXT 10

KAWĀWILA (AHWAZ): EXTRACT FROM THE BANI HILĀL EPIC

This text was recorded in 1972 from the Mulla Thāni Kawāwila (Gypsies) of Ahwaz. Two similar texts were also recorded in Ahwaz and at Chawādir just outside Basra (in 1969 and 1974 respectively). All of these were of substantially the same dialect type, namely South Mesopotamian of a highly nomadic type as regards syllabication. This is exemplified by the forms */sma'at/* "she heard", */ṭfurat/* "she jumped", */ndiha/* "he awoke him" in this text. The texts were all stories from the Bani Hilāl epic except for one which was about local tribal affairs. The text was delivered at great speed and interspersed by sections of music on the rabāba or viol. This may explain the occasional confusion of the names of the characters in the story. However the main course of the action remains clear nonetheless. At certain points also although the words are clear the implications of the actions of the characters are not. It may be that in these cases the stories are so well known in the society that a degree of vagueness is acceptable. The translation given here is based on work done with an informant in this country, Mrs. Sājda Ḥasan of Ba'gūba in Iraq. Ethnographically the text is an interesting example of an old orally transmitted tradition (perhaps in some places now re-interpreted) with occasional introductions of aspects of modern life.

TEXT 10

tubba' 'ajīdhum šibīb. lamīr ḥasan u šibīb ittubba' hāḏōla bilgabul 'adāw. šibīb kital ubu bāzied gāmaw 'alie uḥaṭṭaw bjisir ḥāṣarōhum. min ba'dan alān maṯal waṣṣa wṣiyya 'ala maṯalan gāl ihlāli yṭubb u yiṣ'ad fōg ilyisir. ḥaṭṭla arba'īn faras. hāḏōl nuwāṭīr yṣi'dūn 'alie l'adāw, miṯil marrat zilma yṣīḥ "lihlāli halakum tardūnha!" aku jisir.

il'alya, ixt bāzied 'āšiktih, šibīb. 'āšikt šibīb il'alya u middahna wyā u ḏōla ṣār-ilhum dōm. ši māṭi(1) 'ala ši. 'adāw. min ba'dan šibīb, 'idhum yawwāl ḥāša lḥuḏūr tuwaffa lyawwāl ḏall 'inda ḥurma ḥilu maḥsūn. galla: "ḥabīb xūy!" šibīb galla, "hāḏi lieš mā tāxiḏha hāy umm ilifrūx, ham 'ēnha šab'ānih(2) u ham 'idha ḥalāl wāyid w inta 'alie u rāyiḥ." galla "mu middāynin 'aliena šlōn iyṣīr," galla, "īh mā yxālif ixiḏhi!" gām 'alieha wxaḏāha 'arras 'aliehi, (3) xaḏāha. sma'at il'alya bi'ann šibīb m'arris. gālat "waḷḷah aṭlub rayyit ṭilmiṣān." ta'annat ilamīr ḥasan. gāl: "labbieč!" gātla: "tara ilak inta ibin 'ammi." gālha: "tfaḏḏli, ahlan wa sahlan!" gām 'alieha u 'arras 'alieha. yābōha lḥama w zaffōha. gallōla gāltla "ta'āl agillak inta lyōm šiex w inta b'iris / winta mā yṣīr t'arris 'alayya bhalliela hāḏi wizzilim mdawwīn u hāy" gātla "... bilginīṣ nirūḥ wyāk lilbarr." šaddaw xēl huwwa wyāha 'algā'. 'attilāl u bilbarr. gālha: "yā bit 'ammi. halyōm ba'ad māku aḥad bieni w bienič." gātla "lā yamīr ḥasan. ilyōm inta šiex. winta lyōm malik. winta minnā w minnā w mā yṣīr iḥna n'arris bhaččōl wḥina 'aṭšānīn. kūn n'arris ibšaṭṭ izzaḥāmi." gālilha: "ta'āy agillič. ilyōm šaṭṭ izzaḥāmi manṭūr. wiḥna w ḏōla ittubba', wmā yṣīr iḥna." gātla "bkiefak" galla "ča bkiefič. ana bxidimtič. ana kūn arūḥ liššaṭṭ liyissamma, ḥāṭṭīn bī 'abid nāṭūr. sārḥa ttiṭīḥ yāxiḏ minha nāga. wsārḥa ttiṭla', yāxiḏ minha nāga." gātla: "lā, lā yāba yā šibīb, lā tbūg ilmāy bōga. kūn tāxḏa bissief." miṯil ma yšūf innūgi kāttāt, gātla: "ḏāk irrā'i". gāl: "ard aḏibb ibsalāma 'ala hāḏa imiḏī' ilmuṭmis balkit aḷḷa huwwa šijā'." lamman kattilha lfaras 'alie, liga l'abid nāyim. gāl "ni'mat ubūy wiydādi!" gāl: "mā a'arif. mā akitlanna, illa atnāda wayyā, wāxiḏ ilmāy minna bissief." ndiha. tubāraz wyā lamīr ḥasan. tubāraz wyā ḏibaḥ il'abid. bḥīn mā ḏibaḥ il'abid, aġma 'aliehum. kattatan ilarbāš čayytat biššaṭṭ, hiyya mālt 'alya, tuwannisaw. u tammumaw bḏāk iššaṭṭ u hāy. gālha: "yā rūḥi, bit 'ammi, ta'āl ihnā n'arris!" gātla "lā ta'āl agillak, ilyōm šibīb inta maṭlūb-ilhum w-axāf yōmiyya yfugdūn iššaṭṭ. iḥna agillak ykūn il'iris 'idd ahalna." šibīb ḥalmān buṭṭēf. ḥilim. wilḥilim a'āda 'ala xūh. galla: "xūya ana mā agdarla. irkab iḥṣānak iṭṭayyār winrūḥ liššaṭṭ. halbat tilgālak rā'i min bani hlāl, huwwa yfassir ḥilāmak ḥattan nṣīr 'iyāl"

1 More normally *nāṭi* or *minṭi* from *niṭa* "to give".
2 *-ih* as a feminine suffix resembling the N.Arabian type.
3 *-hi* for *-ha* occurs occasionally in this text. This also occurs in the dialect of the Negev bedouin; BLANC (1970) p.124.

"ana ḥalmān, ana ḥalmān buṭṭēf čān gāṣid ibsiefi,
wana ḥalmān yā 'ammi čān šārib min bīr dammi.
wana ḥalmān čann nār iltihab min(1) ḥayammak lie ḥayammi."

tigill:
"čannak ḥalmān, čān gāṣid ibsiefak.
hāḏa 'abdak čitil ibšaṭṭ izzaḥāmi
waridd:
čannak ḥalmān čān šārib min bīr dammak.
hāḏa zād ilyitāma 'aliek ḥarām wiṯim ḥarāmi.
waridd:
čannak ḥalmān nār iltihab min ḥayammak lieḥayammi
gōmi 'ala gōmak miṯil hadm il...
yā šibīb ilkital 'abdi u gaḷḷal haybiti
(2)lajazzi iḥalāl ma' ilḥarāmi."(3)

galla:
"kitanna 'abdak u nilḥag sayyda
u rawwa' iddinya lḥarub hāy."

čaffat iṭṭayyār 'aliehum. gāl: "ta'ā agillkum" gallatla hiyya: "lābis hdūmak jāy!?" huwwa lābis čōxa ḥamra. gallatla: "lo ṭlubak inta, inta ttalāga wyā. alā ṭlubak wyāna, ntalāga wyā wguḏēna." galla: "aṭlub minkum fad wāḥid atlāga wyā, wāḥid wāḥid. intum nafarēn wana wāḥid." galla: "gūl!" galla: "aṭlub ḏāk ubu ččōxt(4) ilḥamra." gātla: "ba'ad minnak wayyāh." galla: "inṣub!" šibīb ygilla. galla: "yahu minkum? inta lo ani!" galla: "bkēfak." niṣab šibīb, šibīb tubba' inṣab u hāḏa yāba yna''im 'alie. lamma at'aba killiš, dās birrumuḥ u čāka ṯāni. irrumuḥ fāt bḏahr issayyid hāḏa wiltāf ḥadir baṭn ilfaras winšičax birričāb. galla: "yaḷḷa inta inṣub innōb 'alamīr ḥasan!" niṣab 'alamīr ḥasan šibīb, u ḏāk yna''im 'alie, iṭṭayyār u hāḏa nāṣibla. gabul ma yṭīḥ, ṭufar. širad minna. širad jiddāma. mā ḥāša. gām iyyība minnā wiyḥuṭṭa minnā. gām yḥill u yšīlhum. hiyya rāčba kumurṭān, bitt ilxara. huwwa rākib iṭṭayyār. ilkumurṭān kūn yṣīr akrab min liḥṣān iṭṭayyār. ibn xaryān lamman fakkatta(5) iddiri', ṭāḥ 'an nhiedātha, hālkubur. "'alya ma' alasaf, wič inti lihnā jieti!" gām 'alieha minnā w minnā yrīd ykuḏḏha, mā yliḥga iliḥṣān.

1 *ḥayammak* for *yammak*. The introduction of the syllable *ḥa-* is common as evocative of grief or emotion.
2 *la-*, the jurative *la-* used in oaths.
3 *ḥarāmi* for *ḥarām* for the rhyme.
4 Note the retention of the *-t* of the feminine suffix.
5 *-atta* doubling of the *-t* of the feminine *-at* in positions before a vowel initial suffix is common to the Shaṭṭ al-'Arab area.

ṣadīxtih(1) gallatla: "xāyib yā lamīr ḥasan yahaw lšāf marta ykuḏḏūn bīha wiyġādun bīha jiddāmak winta xāyif?" čanna huwwa aṣlaḥ huwwa intiṣab irrumuḥ id'a(2) rrumuḥ bī ṯlaṯ aṣābi'. birrumuḥ ṣāba. tiṣawwab u 'ād lāf 'aliḥṣān. bḥīn ma 'ād lāf, iya lie'ind iṭṭāyfa: "mṣawwab hāḏa lamīr ḥasan yah "(3) yā lie'ind iṭṭāyfa:"yā hali.

lāgāni šibīb yā 'ammi. lāgāni šibīb bkubr ilbaḥar wakbar.
talaggieta miṯil šaṭṭ izzaḥāmi.
lāgāni šibīb bkubr ilyibal wakbar
talaggieta miṯil ibn izzaḥāmi.
lāgāni šibīb bkubr ilbalad wakbar
talaggieta miṯil farx iligṭāy.
čān ṭayyib u bwidda ṭayyib
yjazzīni lḥalāl ma' ilḥarāmi.
riḥīl yā halna rḥīl
wlā tubga 'alazzarga mugām."

talaggata l'alya tigilla:
"yā amīrna wamīr gōmna
'idna laṭāmi w 'idhum laṭāmi."(4)

bāzied nāyim mgaffaṣ yiṭla' barra. xaḏa brīj u taxalla wṣalla wyā. ḥaṭṭ librīj 'algā' u šāl čākieta wi'gāla wḥaṭṭhin 'alie. galla: "ahlan wsahlan!" gāl: "mnien yietak?" galla: "waḷḷa yieti min dīrat tubba'" gāl: "xōš, tubba' šinu aškālha? š'idhum axbār a'lām ġēr?" gāl: "waḷḷa mā agillak aḷḷa killši axbār mā 'idhum. fuḏal bass šibīb mṣawwab. talāga hu walamīr ḥasan u ṣāraw majāfi. u ydawwir bass iṭṭabīb." galla: "ča fi amāllā nsallim 'aliek." u ḥaṭṭ īdie wšaddaw ... u marr ba'dien bjindal(5) māl giṣab ḥimašla ġabba minha. gaṣṣaṣ sīm yḥuṭṭ bīha šrār u ġēr u hāy ṣār ṭabīb. ṭabb sūg yūnis. tirasla šanṭat rummān u niemu lyadd ijjihāl. hāḏa gabul mā yōṣal lijjisir/ kāḏḏīn ijjisir / lifrūx šabhaw, yard yṣīḥūn: "la'ad hāḏa hlāli!" gabul ma yard yṣīḥūn, ḏabb lirmāna whalniemu jiddāma. lifrūx čallaw 'ala iššay hāḏi. gām yimurr min bien rūshum. lwaḥda ydigg ijjisir. larba'īn killhum giṭa'hum u dās 'ajjisir. ṣāḥ: "hlāli, hlāli hāḏa! māku yamma ḥad!" ṭabb iddīra, ṣāḥ: "ṭabīb, ṭabīb, ṭabīb!" illi ṭāyfa(6)

1 *ṣadīxtih* for *ṣadīqtih*.
2 *id'a*, only used in the imperative. Here the narrative imperative. Also occurs in the dialect of Sudair, *da'ih* "leave him, it!"
3 *yah*, an exclamation of surprise.
4 *laṭāmi* "breast beating, bereavement".
5 *jindal* from Persian *jangal* "wood jungle".
6 *ṭāyif + a* "passing him" not *ṭāyfa* "tribe".

wyistaxbur ilšibīb limṣawwab, yrūḥ yiṭṭi lxabar liššiex, yinṭīhum an'ām. iššiex mtaččilla wiyhiffūn 'alie zilim, šibīb. galla: "yā 'ammi, hāḏa ṭabīb." gāl: "jību!" ja lšibīb mfarra', liga fad aswad ṭuwīl mṣabbuġ rūḥa, mġayyir nafsa. galla: "hā šinu hāḏa?" "waḷḷa ṭabīb ana 'ammi." galla: "yaḷḷa yaḷḷa imši! 'idna šibīb mṣawwab widdāwī!" galla: "'ammi, aḷḷa yṭawwil 'umrak ana fad faġīr, ṣāḥb ifrēxāt ṣāḥb i'yāl. ana wēni u mwaddīni li'id(1) šibīb. hāḏa bass yšūfni ygūl: "hāḏa bāzied!" u yāxiḏ rāsi." gāl: "lā ana ajībak. šlōn hāḏa? lieš? iḥna mā 'idna min iṣwāb?" galla: "imši, imši!" galla: "'ammi! hāḏa bass yšūfni ygūl "hāḏa bāzied." intum šitsawwūn bī? walaw ana ṭabīb ba'ad. huwwa mwadda' fīna. huwwa mtaččal iššiex." ba'dien sallam 'aliehum. gāl: "ahlan. ahlan!" 'ala bāb ilxēma gāl: "ha! mā gittilkum 'ammi?" galla: "ta'āl jāy. tfaḏḏal. ta'āl ig'id yammi!" šibīb ygilla. gāl: "hā mā gittilkum!? šinu hāy msōdan hāḏa bāzied." gāl: "hāḏa ṭabīb?! šiftu intum? hāḏa raḥ yimḥīni." galla: "yahū!(2) inta msōdan inta mibtili biṣwābak." gāl: "wilkum! bāzied! ana mitlāji wiyyā wšaḥči? nōba nōbtien sawwa 'alayya tara ḥīla." gām 'ala ṣṣīwān ḥaṭṭō. ṭaggat čiela 'ind iṭṭāyfa rād minhum. 'ālaj minhum. gāl: "xāybīn. na'al iššieṭān. wilkum! bāzied!" tara hāḏa jāy 'ala būzi u ba'ad sā'a yāxiḏ rāsi!" mā riḏaw bjawāba. galhum: "tara yā jamā'a asallim 'aliekum. agilkum ana ḥisbūni mū šilčān(3) ba'ad." šālō ḥaṭṭō bilxēma w dašš 'alie. galla: "ta'āl ana mintīk tubba' sab' isnīn, ma'āk ilak. wayyāk tāxiḏ rāsi." ygilla: "'īf 'anni!" galla: "rayyāl ṭayyib!" galla: "wilak inta bāzied mā a'urfannak(4) ana?!

> *dibči(5) yā rūḥi dibči*
> *dibči 'ala rūḥi yibči!*
> *lo ḥallaftak bilkitbi mānta bāzied?" šibīb ygūl.*
> *"lā tiḏlam baxtak winta ṣbayy.*
> *ana ṭabīb iššām ilḥilbi*
> *ana lāni ṭabīb yā 'ammi*
> *wa lā šibīb yṭīb*
> *ana mit'anni 'ala rāsak yā šbīb."*

1 *lie'ind > li'id.*
2 *yahū* an exclamation of surprise and disbelief; not *yahu* "who?"
3 *mū ši il čān* "not a thing which ever existed".
4 *a'urfann-.* For the suffix *-an(n)*, see p.83.
5 The prefix *d(i)-* is an emphatic particle often occuring with imperatives in the Mesopotamian type. It does not however normally occur in the South Mesopotamian area, and is here a feature of the poem.

dašš 'alie wḏibaḥa wgām 'ala baṭna wšaggha. u ṭalla' iddiri' u ḥaṭṭa bṣaḥan u yāba liṭṭāyfa wgām 'alie u laflafa wxallā. lamman šāf iṣṣaḥan bī wuṣla mniddiri' ṭagg ilhalāhil. gāl: "ta'āl agilkum ilyōm šibīb ġāyba rūḥa wlā trūḥūn 'alie hassa! xallū šwayya wyaḷḷa trūḥūn 'alie!" galla: "'ammi ḥabīb. likrāw 'indi fad ḥurma gālatli anṭēta dū wtinṭīni ḥibūbi. wxallaw ġadāy lamma arūḥ hnā waṣalli." gāl: "hā! ča šlōn? ygūlūn hāḏa bāzied." ḥabīb ygūl. 'inda biet, biet naxal. ḥissat raḥḥa, ḥāṭṭīnha brās ijjisir duwwēna. makīna tsawwi ṭaḥīna. hāḏa ḥīn ma y'ūd digri:(1) "luwēn?" gāl: "hā 'ammi bwaḥdak?" gāl: "iṭla'!" gāl: "waḷḷa 'indi hāḏa / hāḏanni i'dūl aṭ'ām widdaššišliyyāhin." u hāḏa gā'idla bḥalg ilbāb. hāḏa bḥīn ma iyaw, ligaw šibīb rāsa mafṣūṣa wbaṭna mašgūga. willa(2) ṣāḥat iṣṣuwāyiḥ: "yābahātkum ilxēr xērkum tara šibīb ġidir."(3) ḥabīb ibgufa ṭṭayyār u ligaf irrumuḥ bīda, yā lilyisir ṭufra!(4) lie'idd ilyūni: "lyūni!" gāl: "hā 'ammi?" gāl: "wilak mā ma'āk zilim?" galla: "yā 'ammi ba'ad 'ēni. marr 'alayya zilma ḏāk huwwa mā adri šiysawwi lḥūs. galla: "šlōn?" galla: "hāḏa 'ammi š'inda mā 'inda mā adri šbāyig." gāl: "wilak kiss ummak ta'āl, ta'āl!" gāl: "hā! ta'āl 'aliḥṣān!" galla: "'ammi axāf min liḥṣān. axāf yi'uḏḏni." galla: "man'ūl(5) ilwāldien (ḥāša lḥuḏūr) ta'āl kuḏḏa!" galla: "ča šu mā huwwa šinsawwi?" gāl: "wilak kital šibīb hāḏa." bḥīn mā dašš ḥabīb u hāḏa ṭala' māku bīda ṭaḥīn u biliḥṣān kaḏḏ 'alie galla: "ḥabīb!" galla: "hā!" galla: "tara ani bāzied tfaḏḏal hāḏa rāskum wana mxallīk šihīda lil'arab." galla: "'aliek il'āfya, 'awāfi" (bgalba). galla: "ana māxiḏ minna šūr." galla: "ča sallim 'aliek! ma' issalāma." bāzied liga l'arab gāṣīha ilamīr ḥasan u mā mxalli biet mā māxiḏ il'arab bissier wissirīd u čān bass yaḥya wmaryam awlād ixta. gālilhum: "tānūni!" humma w 'ummhum wyāhum. lamma ygūla: "hā xāḷi." gāl: "waḷḷa mtānīk xāḷi wilamīr ḥasan ilyōm xaḏa l'ār winkisar wiḥna bass tānīnak." mišaw biṭṭurīg 'ṭišaw. gāl: "waḷḷa xāḷi čanna 'ṭašna wmā 'idna māy wilmāy ingiṭa' 'aliena." galla: "xāḷi andall fad bīr yingālla bīr zaru min zamān masḥi u maḥḥad šārib minna.

1 *digri* "straight away, straight ahead". This is unusual. The normal local form is *gubal* or, on the Shaṭṭ al-'Arab, *sīda*.
2 *willa* "behold, lo!", equivalent to classical *wa iḏā bi-*.
3 *ġidir* internal passive of *ġidar* "to deceive"
4 *ṭufra* "jump it" imperative for past action in narrative.
5 *man'ūl* for *mal'ūn* is common in the whole area.

lamman yiena ilbīr zarwa min xilif 'ašwa
masḥi u madri min isnīn il'adāmi.
wēn ilyirwīna wyirwi rčābna
wiyxalli lmāy fōg min ilbīr ḥāmi."

ṭufar mir'i lilbīr mā yṭubba ġēra
"larwīkum.(1) warwi rčābkum
waxalli lmāy fōg imnilbīr ḥāmi
mir'i lfāyitāt iḍḍawāmi."

galla: "yā xāḷi ḥadir 'aliek wilfōr 'alayy." bḥīn ma nazzal irriša wdašš mir'i, ḥass aku irbīd bilbīr. awwal mā dašš, ingiṭaf gām yākil bī min ḥadir ilirbīd u hāda yizlig. lamma ṭāf ilmāy 'aliehum wiygūl bāzied: "yā xāḷi, asma' ḥiss ixtibāṭāt, la'allak yā xāḷi mnilbīr sāmi'." galla: sāmi' u lāni sālim. ḏirabni wid'a rriša mnīdi w xaḏā-mni."(2)galla: yā xāḷi iṭwi rriša wta'āl liyya wjawwi 'azmak yā jilīl il'azāmi." galla: "ḥalfān larwīkum warwi rčābkum warwi ġazāl bilbarr ḥāmi. lākin yā xāḷi ūṣīk tawṣiyya, ḥuṭṭ gabri fōg naxla ṭuwīl halbat yimurrūn 'iyāl lihlāli wyiṭwūn 'alayya 'alāmi." ṭfurat umma gātla: "yā mir'i hāḏa bāzied ilmā rāfja rifīj u radda sālim." za'al 'alieha yaḥya wḏirabha ṭabra wlāḏat fi ḏirr ilhadāmi. gāmaw 'alie lamma ṭala' imnilbīr tuwaffa gburō wḥaṭṭō birrišān(3) 'āli w tammumaw u hāḏi w mišaw u ḥidaw 'al'arab māxḏīnhum bissīr wissirīd 'alamīr ḥasan. wirtāḥat il'arab. wilḥagg 'aliehum u ḥaṭṭathum wit'īš inta sālim.

TEXT 10 (KAWĀWILA) TRANSLATION

Tubba', their leader was Shabīb.(4) Amīr Ḥasan and Shabīb the Tubba' they were, in previous times, enemies. Shabīb had killed the father of Bāzaid. They rose against him and encamped at a bridge, they surrounded them. Afterwards, now, for instance, he gave orders [that] if for instance

1 *la-arwīkum.* The jurative particle *la-* used with the first person singular in oaths.
2 *xaḏā-mni* reminiscent of the Shammari type of structure *mni* "from me", *mnak* "from you", *mnu* "from him". This does not occur elsewhere in the texts. Here it serves to fit the rhyme. Similarly the verb *id'a* "take!" occurs in these texts but is not a common Mesopotamian lexical item.
3 Perhaps *rōšan* "alcove, window".
4 Shabīb al-Tubba', the king of Damascus in the legend. He is said to have been the ruler of the area of Ma'ān in Jordan in fact. MUKHLIṢ (1964) p.170.

anyone said "The Hilāli [is coming]!" he should go in and mount the bridge. He put there in waiting for him forty horses. These were watchmen, which the enemy could come on to the bridge upon. For instance if a man passed by, he would call "The Hilāli, up and at him!" There was a bridge. (1) Al'Alya, the sister of Bāzaid, was in love with him, in love with Shabīb, Al'Alya, and was having an affair with him, and they had been like this for a long time. One thing had led to another. They were enemies. Afterwards Shabīb / they had a herdsman. May it be far from you!(2) The herdsman died and there remained his wife who was a beautiful woman. He said to him: "Ḥabīb, my brother," Shabīb said to him, "why don't you marry her, the mother of the children? She is a contented woman and also she has much property [i.e. flocks] and you will be in a good position." He said "But aren't we at war with them. How could it be possible?" He said, "Yes, but it doesn't matter. Marry her!" So he married her. Al'Alya heard that Shabīb had got married. She said "Well I will ask the opinion of an oracle." She went to Amīr Ḥasan. He said "I am at your service." She said to him "I am yours my cousin." He said "And welcome!" He rose and married her. The men of the family brought her in the bridal procession. They said to him / she said to him: "Come I tell you. Today you are a sheikh and you / in the wedding / and it is impossible for you to consummate our marriage with me on this night, while the men are celebrating and everything." She said to him: "...(3) on the hunt, I will go with you to the desert." They saddled up their horses, he with her, and left across country, on the hills, in the desert. He said to her: "Oh my cousin, today there is no longer anyone. It is between me and you." She said to him: "No, Amīr Ḥasan. Today you are a shaikh, and today you are a king and you have business here and there and we cannot consummate our marriage here in this wasteland, in a state of thirst. We must marry at Shaṭṭ al-Zaḥāmi." He said: "Come, let me tell you. Today Shaṭṭ al-Zaḥāmi is under guard, and we and those people the Tubba' [are at war] and it is impossible for us..." She said to him: "It is up to you." He said "No, it is up to you. I am at your service. I must go to river [Shaṭṭ] which you have mentioned [lit. which is named], they have put a slave there on guard. From every herdswoman who goes down to the river, he takes a camel and from every herdswoman who comes

1 The exact course of the action of this part of the text is rather obscure. However in general the burden of the story is that a trap is laid for Bāzaid at a bridge.
2 An expression used when mentioning a lowly occupation such as herdsman.
3 The tape is unclear at this point.

up he also takes a camel." She said to him: "No, no O Shabīb, do not take the river by stealth. You must take it with the sword." When he saw the camels crowding together, she said to him "That herdsman [is the one]." He said: "I am going to go and give my greeting to that accursed fellow, perhaps he will prove to be a brave man." When he charged the horse up to him he found the slave asleep. He said "By the luck of my father and ancestors, I do not know, but I will not kill him except in fair fight and take the river from him by the sword." He woke him up and fought with him. Amīr Ḥasan fought with him and killed the slave. When he overcame the slave. They [the companions of the slave] fainted in fear. Suddenly the men charged the river, those followers of 'Alya. Then they enjoyed themselves and finished everything at the river. He said to her: "Come on, my cousin, here we will be wed." She said: "No, come let me tell you. Today Shabīb, you are wanted by them and I am afraid that every day they will search the river. We must have our wedding with our people." Shabīb had had a dream and he related the dream to his brother. He [the brother] said to him: "My brother I cannot interpret it. Mount your flying horse and we will go to the river. Perhaps you will find for yourself a shepherd from the Bani Hilāl, who will explain your dream so that we may remain friends."

[sung by Shabīb]
"I had a dream, I had a dream that he attacked with my sword,
and I dreamt, O my uncle, that he drunk from the well of my blood.
And I dreamt, it was as though a fire had flared up from me to you."

She said to him [interpreting the dream]:
"It seems that you dreamt that he attacked with your sword.
This is your slave who was killed at Shaṭṭ al-Zaḥāmi.
And I repeat:
It seems that you dreamt that he drunk from the well of your blood.
This is the food of the orphans which is forbidden to you
And I repeat:
It seems that you dreamt that a fire flared up from me to you.
[this means]
My people against your people like a great destruction.

O Shabīb,(1) you who killed my slave and humiliated me,

1 The personalities are somewhat confused at this point,

I will repay the lawful with the forbidden."

He said to him:
"We killed your slave and we will pursue his master.
And the world will be astounded by this war."

He charged up to them on the flying horse. He said "Come let me tell you." She said to him: "I see that you have come wearing your wedding clothes!?" He was wearing a red cloak. With them it was the custom that a bridegroom wore a red cloak. She said to him: "If he challenges you along with us, we will fight with him and finish him off." He said to him: "I challenge one of you to come out and fight one to one. There are two of you and I am only one." He said to him: "Say [which one you want]!" He said: "I challenge that one with the red cloak." She said: "Now it is up to you." He said "Attack!", Shabīb said to him. He said to him: "Which one of you, you or me?" He said: "As you wish." Shabīb attacked, Shabīb of Tubba', and the other, O my father, began to flail at him. When he had tired him out, he thrust with the lance. The lance came out of the back of the man, turned once under the stomach of the horse and stuck into the saddle. He said to him: "Go on, you attack this time against Amīr Ḥasan." Shabīb charged Amīr Ḥasan and the other began striking at the flying horse while he was attacking. Before he [the horse] fell, he jumped clear and ran, ran off in front of him. He did not catch him. He began to attack from this side and that. It became a rout.(1) She was riding a rhinoceros, the clever one.(2) He was riding a flying horse. A rhinoceros is of course more terrible than a flying horse. The blaggard, when she opened her coat of chain mail, it fell away revealing her breasts(3) which were this big. [He said]: "'Alya I regret that you have been brought so low." He began grabbing at her from this side and that side, but the horse would not reach her. His friend said to him: "Oh you wretch Amīr Ḥasan who would stand by and watch his wife being chased and harassed here and there in front of him and remain afraid?" At this it was as though he took heart. He took up the three-pronged

but it becomes obvious that it was in fact Amir Hasan who killed the slave of Shabib, and Shabib who had the dream.

1 Lit. "He began untying them and carrying them off" (like a man carrying off loot or plunder).

2 Lit. "daughter of excrement".

3 Reminiscent of the custom of Arab girls baring their breasts and loosing their hair in order to encourage their men in battle. In this case however it seems that she did it to distract her enemy.

lance and struck him with the lance. He was wounded and wheeled around and retreated on horseback. When he retreated he came up to the tribe. [The cry went up] "Amīr Ḥasan is wounded." He came to the tribe [and said]: "Oh my tribe

Shabīb met me in battle even greater than the sea
  I drove him off like the River of Zaḥāmi
Shabīb met me in battle even greater than the mountains
  I drove him off like the son of Zaḥāmi
Shabīb met me in battle even greater than the land
  I drove him off as though he was a young partridge
He was a good man and desired the good
  and repaid the lawful with the forbidden
Away my people away!
  There is no more staying for us at the blue water."

'Alya met him and said:
"Oh our prince and prince of our people
We have lost men and they have also lost men in battle."

Bāzaid was lying in a crouching position. He stretched then took up his sword and the water pitcher and set out. He took the pitcher and washed and prayed and came. He put the pitcher on the ground and took off his headrope and put them on top of it.(1) [A passer-by came up] he said to him: "God keep you, fellow. Where are you going, O wayfarer?" He answered: "Welcome!" He said: "Where are you coming from?" He said: "Well I am coming from the dīra of Tubba'." He said: "Good, and how is their situation, what news is there of them?" He said: "Well I cannot tell you anything good, there is no good news. All that there is, is that Shabīb is wounded. He met in battle with Amīr Ḥasan and they retreated and now they are looking everywhere for a doctor." He said "Goodbye, we greet you" and set his hands to the horse and they sped away... And after that he passed by a clump of reeds and pulled out a handful of them. He then cut some wire and put on it metal pieces etc. and became like a doctor.(2) He entered the village of Sūg Yūnis and

1 Perhaps in order to make a dummy to act as his companion so that he would not be taken as a lone traveller. As elsewhere in these stories Bāzaid is attributed magical powers. This section of the story was, however, not clear to my informants.

2 I.e. he fashioned a stethoscope from these components. As elsewhere in these stories the narrator introduces aspects of modern life to the legend, whether through ignorance or for my benefit, I do not know.

filled a bag with pomegranates and limes for the children on the way. Before he reached the bridge (as you know they had captured the bridge) the children recognised him. They wanted to call out: "Then this is the Hilāli." But before they could call out, he threw the pomegranates and limes before him. The children leapt forward to gather them up, and he began passing between their heads [while they were scrabbling on the ground]. On his own he struck the bridge. All forty of the guards he cut down and stepped onto the bridge, calling out: "I am the Hilāli, the Hilāli and there is no one with me!" He entered the village and called out: "[I am] a doctor, a doctor!" Whoever passed by, he asked about the wounded Shabīb and he in turn would go and give the news to the Shaikh [of the village] who would give him a reward [for the news]. He was a client of the Shaikh with men protecting him, Shabīb that is. He said to him "My uncle, there is a doctor!" He said: "Bring him!" He came to Shabīb(1) with his head bare [wearing no head cloth], and they saw a big tall black man as he had dyed himself and was in disguise. He said: "Hah, what is this?" "Well, my uncle, I am a doctor." [He said] "Quickly, let's go! Shabīb is lying wounded with us and you must treat him!" He said "Uncle, God give you long life, I am a poor man and have a family and children, what have I got to do with Shabīb? As soon as he sees me he will say, 'This is Bazaid!' and will have my head off." He said: "No, I will take you. How could this be? Why do you not think that we have any honour?" He said to him: "Let's go, let's go!" He said to him: "Uncle. As soon as he sees me, he will say: 'This is Bāzaid.' What will you be able to do with him? Although I am really a doctor. He is an honoured guest among us, a client of the Shaikh." They he [Bāzaid] greeted them and said: "Greetings, greetings!" at the door of the tent. He [Shabīb] said: "Didn't I tell you, uncle?" He said: "Come over here. Sit beside me, please!" Shabīb said to him: "Didn't I tell you?! What is this? Are you mad? This is Bāzaid. Is this a doctor!? Can't you see? He will annihilate me." He [the Shaikh] said to him: "You are mad! You are raving because of your wound." He said: "Look. He is Bāzaid. I have met him before, so what shall I say? Once or twice before he has played tricks on me." He got up and went to the tent and they laid him down. [It was as though] a shot had been fired among the tribe [i.e. the news broke suddenly]. He pleaded with them, begged with them, "Wretches, he has come for my life and in a moment he will take off my head!" They did not believe him. He said: "O people, I bid you farewell. I am telling you, consider me already gone." They took him off and laid him in the tent

1 In fact to the Shaikh, not Shabīb.

and he came in to him. He said: "Come. I will give you the [leadership of the] tribe of Tubba' for seven years, yours to be with you, but woe on you if you take my head." He said: "Leave me alone!" He [the Shaikh] said: "He is a good man." [Shabīb] said "But this is Bāzaid, don't I know him?!

Cry O my soul, cry
  Cry for my soul who cries!
If I adjure you by the Holy Book, are you not Bāzaid?"

said Shabīb. [Bāzaid]:

"Do not destroy your fortune while you are still young
  I am the Syrian doctor from Aleppo
I am no doctor
  and nor will Shabīb recover.
I have come for your head O Shabīb."

He came in and killed him, then he cut open his stomach. He took out his heart(1) and put it on a plate and brought it to the tribe and wrapped it up and left it. When he [the sheikh perhaps] saw the piece of the heart on the plate the crying broke out [in the tribe]. He said: "Come I will tell you. Today Shabīb is unconscious, so don't go to him now! Leave him for a while and then go to see him!" He said to him: "Uncle, Ḥabīb,I have a woman patient whom I gave medicine to and who told me to give her some more pills. So leave my lunch for me until I go there, then pray [and then return]." He said: "How can that be? They say this is Bāzaid," that is Ḥabīb said this [the brother of Shabīb]. He had a house built of palm trunks [from which came] the noise of a mill-stone, which they had put at the head of the bridge grinding away, a machine, that is, which makes flour. When he returned directly [he said]: "Where to?" The other answered: "What, uncle are you alone?" He said "Come out!" He said: "Well I've got this/these baskets of food so please take them in for me." The other man was sitting there at the doorway. As soon as they came they found Shabīb with his head split open and his stomach cut open and then the cry went up: "O people you remain fortunate, but Shabīb has been betrayed." Ḥabīb was immediately on the flying horse and snatched up his lance and came to the bridge and leapt

1 This seems to be the intention of the speaker, although the word *diri'* in fact signifies originally "a coat of chain mail". It may be that the narrator in transmitting this text has re-interpreted it as "heart" since "chain mail" is no longer a live concept, while the act of cutting out the heart or liver of an enemy is not unknown in traditional stories.

straight across it to Al-Yūni(1) [and called]: "Al-Yūni!" "What?" he answered. "Is there anyone with you?" "Well uncle" [said Al-Yūni] "there was a man who passed by here, that odd fellow but I don't know what he was doing." He said: "How so?" He said: "That one, uncle, I don't know what he has with him, or what mischief he's up to." He said: "Come on! Come on! Jump onto the horse!" He said: "Uncle, I'm afraid of the horse, it might bite me." He said: "O man of accursed parentage (may the mention of it be far from you) come and take it!" He said to him: "But what is it, what are we going to do?" He said: "That man killed Shabīb." When Ḥabīb went in [to the house] and the other one came out and had no flour in his hands and he caught hold of him on the horse and said "Ḥabīb". He said "Yes." He said "You see now that I am Bāzaid. Here you are, this is the head of your leader, and I have leaving you as a witness to the arabs." He said to him: "Good health to you". (Secretly in his heart) he said to him: "I seek advice from you." He said "Greetings, I bid you farewell." Bāzaid found that the Amīr Ḥasan had gone through the length and breadth of all the arabs and had not left a single tent in which the story had not run through them like wildfire. There were only Yaḥya and Maryam his cousins. He said to them and their mother "Wait for me!" When they arrived [he said]: "Yes, uncle!" He [Yaḥya] said: "We are waiting for you, uncle. Today Amīr Ḥasan has taken away the shame from us and he [Shabīb] has been defeated and we were only waiting for you." They set off. On the way they became thirsty. He said: "Well uncle, it seems that we are becoming thirsty and we haven't got any water and we have no access to water." He said to him: "Uncle, I know of a well, called Bīr Zarw(2) which has been blocked up for a long time and no one has drunk from it. [sung]

When we came to the well of Zarwa, in the late evening
It was blocked and long forgotten since years immemorial
Who will quench our thirst and that of our mounts
and bring the water pouring out over the lip of the well."

1 Al-Yūni, this character is not mentioned elsewhere or in other versions. There is, however, Mūnis ibn Yaḥya, leader of the Bani Hilāl invasions of North Africa, MUKHLIṢ (1964) p.182.
2 In the western version of the legend the name of the well is bīr naġwa. Zarw is reminiscent of Bilād Sarw wa 'Ubāda, the home of the Bani Hilāl in the south of Arabia, MUKHLIṢ (1964) p.363.

Mur'i leapt down into the well, no one but him would enter it [saying]:

"I will quench your thirst and that of your mounts
  and bring the water pouring out over the lip of the well
[I am] Mur'i whose days are numbered."

He Bāzaid said to him: "Oh my uncle the going down is your job, and the filling of the cistern [above] is mine." When he let down the rope and Mur'i entered [the well] he felt that there was a great serpent in the well. As soon as he entered, he was caught and the serpent began eating him up from below, while he was gradually slipping down until the water came up and flowed around them.(1) Bāzaid called: "Oh my uncle, I hear sounds of movement in the well, perhaps you also can hear them." He answered: "I hear and I am mortally wounded and it [the serpent] has struck me and snatched the rope from my hand and taken it." He said: "Oh my uncle throw up the rope and come up to me and strengthen your resolve, Oh man of high ambitions." He answered: "I have sworn to quench your thirst and quench the thirst of your mounts and that of the gazelle bounding in the desert. But, my uncle, I make one dying request. Put my grave high up in a palm tree, so that perchance the companions of the Hilāli come past and tie marks upon my tomb.(2) His mother leapt forward and said to him: "Oh Mur'i this is Bāzaid whose companions never return alive."(3) Yaḥya became enraged against her and hit her a blow and she fell senseless. They went to his aid and when he came up out of the well he died. They buried him and put him on a ledge high up. They then completed everything and set off and sung the song of these deeds to the arabs and the story of Amīr Ḥasan took them like wildfire. After this the arabs became calm and this news made them calmer and the right of the matter was against them [sic]. May you live in health.

1 Perhaps a mistake for "him", i.e. Mur'i down in the well.
2 Reminiscent of the Shi'a practice of tying strips of material to the metal grille of a saint's tomb.
3 Bāzaid, although possessed of magical qualities, often brought ill luck to his companions.

'AMĀRA: THE STORY OF MUGHDĀD

The following is the text of a story recorded from an Ālbu Muḥammad informant in Basra in 1971. His dialect, however, is not completely typical of the 'Amāra area. It can be classed as rural southern Mesopotamian and is quite similar to the dialect of the Kūt Sayyid 'Anāya informant. It contains some examples of the nomadic syllabication type, i.e. */glubō/*, */tubāṛaz/*, */taḥārab/*, */gaḷab/*, etc., also */xalla/* rather than */xallī/* for "let him!" The text shows hesitation between */y/* and */j/* as the reflex of */jīm/* although one would expect */ž/*. The occurrence of */yahu/* "who", */ča/* "what!" and */dašš/* "to enter" mark it as "southern" as defined in this study. The story is an example of a fairly widespread type of narrative common both in Iran and Iraq among both Persians and Arabs and contains reference to various legendary figures including Amīr Ḥamza, Aswad al-Kindi, Ḍhaḥḥāk, and Kisra (Khosrow) the Emperor of Achaemenid Iran. These stories, which are common to urban and rural populations, are often told by wandering storytellers and Derwishes, and are also available in book form. They represent a stage of removal from the sphere of nomadic existence into the more general Middle Eastern sedentary society. The narrative however ends with the theme common also in the Bani Hilāl stories, */ṭaššaw bukānhum u mišaw ġēr mukān/* "They spread over that land and moved on to another place," harking back to the nomadic way of life.

TEXT 11

sālfa ya'ni māl ilmuġdād waswad ilkindi 'ala mūd bitta / hassa aḥči? / aku fad wāḥid isma jābir iḏ̣ḏ̣ahhāk jābir iḏ̣ḏ̣aḥḥāk 'inda bnayya ḥasna, bilḥisin kāmila tamām. lākin ḏōli maḥḥad yizzawwajha. illi yizzawajha illi yiġlubha bilḥarub yaḷḷa tḥārub hiyya wyā. alā ġalabha hiyya tizzawwija. ba'dien tiji 'alieha l'ālam min b'īd min ilajānib min kill bukān ijūn 'alieha illi yġulbūnha. millieš? hiyya ḥasna ḥasna killiš. alā iyyi 'alieha hāy ilmlieḥa lli yḥārba witkaššif wujihha, min ḥisinha iyṭīh. yiṭīḥ iddišš 'alie wiyṭīḥ hiyya dġulba. ḏall aku 'idhum ibin 'amha isma ilmuġdād. ilmuġdād huwwa rā'i bilġanam yisraḥ iybāwi' iyšūf il'ālam hāya. yahu lyiji 'alieha dġulba. ba'dien rāḥ lamma galha "ā yumma ana arīdič tiṭṭīni fard iḥṣān arūḥ aḥārib bitt 'ammi ilmayāsa walla arūḥ āxiḏha liyya mara azzawwajha." gātla umma. "inta wēnak u wēnha? hāy idġulbak wiṭṭurḥak witkitlak." galha: "lā inti mā 'alieč. ana aġlubha." rāḥ lubūha. galla: "yā jābir arīd bittak ana aḥārubha. walā aġlubha ana āxiḏha." galla: "rūḥ!" 'alma rāḥ 'alie wuṭṭāraḥ wiyyāha wil'ālam itfarraj 'aliehum minnā wminnā bil-ālāf bissugūf yitfarrajūn hāḏa ġalabha. min ġalabha, nabb abūha hāḏa jābir. gāl: "ana mā aṭṭīkiyyaha." "yāba iššabab māṭṭīnīha? lieš mū ana ġlabitha?" gāl: "ana mā aṭṭīkiyyāha alla tyībilha ṣadāġ. ṣadāġ idyībilha."(1) "yāba šinu ṣadāġha?" galla: "arīd arba'īn / arba' miyt nāga. arba' miyt jimal mmlaswad. arba' miyt jimal mnil abyaḏ. warīd mḥammilāt kilha min ṣnāyi' muṣir, tḥammilhin. warīd ittāj māl čisra." gāl: "mā yxālif ana ajībhin." hāy wēn iyḥaṣṣilhin? b'īd iddarub 'alie. galla: "bass tāḏinni furṣa, middat šahrēn ana ajībhin." hāḏa rāḥ, liga hāḏanni innūg 'id fad wāḥid, ya'ni fāris kāmil / ēh / wism ilfāris 'ali ilfāris iṯṯāni ilwayyāh isma lḥamza. galhum: "xallu hāy illaḏi 'idkum wilju barwāḥkum lā tmūtūn. amawwitkum!" gālōla: "inta tmawwitna?" gāmaw gālaw: "šlōn itmawwitna-nta? wilak(2) iḥna nmawwitak." galhum: "lā māku, ča ana wyākum ilḥarub." taḥārab wiyyāhum. min taḥārab uyāhum, ba'dien huwwa ġlubō / ġulbō.(3) tāli gālaw: "inta minu waddāk 'aliena?" gāl: "waḷḷa ana maḥḥad mwaddīni 'aliekum lākin ana jiet 'ala mūd(4) ṣadāġ ilbint 'ammi ilmayāsa. walġalbatni ...." gālaw: "'āyš imn iyyīlak, xiḏhin!" axaḏhin ba'dien yirūḥ yiji 'al ittāj. yrūḥ iyyīb ittāj māl kisra wiyji 'alie. yimši yōm yōmēn ṯlaṯ ayyām mā wuṣal. biddarub liga fad wāḥid u isma abu lxamsa, mčattifa fad wāḥid štāf(5) u bitta yamma. yrīd yikitla wyāxid bitta. hāḏa ija 'alie, galla: "inta lieš imčattif hāḏa witrīd tāxiḏ bitta wtikitla?" gāl: "inta yā māltak bī? ana ard akitla wāxiḏ bitta." taḥārab

1 *tyībilha-dyībilha* again hesitation between sedentary and nomadic types, the sedentary type *dyībilha* shows assimilation of the prefix *t-* to the following *y*.
2 *wilak, wilič*, etc. exclamatory particle.
3 Hesitation between nomadic and sedentary types; see p.51-3.
4 *'ala mūd* "because of", a Mesopotamian characteristic.
5 *štāf* for *čtāf*.

huwwa wyāh. tubāraz huwwa wyāh bilbarāz. qutil(1) /ēh/ qutil ḏāk. fakk hāḏa mnilḥadīd. galla: "yaḷḷa, xiḏ bittak inta wrūḥ!" galla: "bass inta wēn rāyiḥ?" galla: "ana rāyiḥ ajīb ittāj māl kisra." rāḥ wuṣal ilwlāya māl kisra. galla: "šinu inta trīd." galla: "arīd ittāj." galla: "inta mā aṭṭīk ittāj. inta bwaḥdak aṭṭīk ittāj lō wiyyāk 'askar?" galla: "lā bass ana! ana wyākum ilḥarub." jarraw 'alie 'asākir. yahaw liywaddūn 'alie ykitla: "yāba iṭṭūh ittāj!" aṭṭōh ittāj, aṭṭōh-ilha. min yāb ittāj wija, aku 'idhum sabi' maḥbūs bḥadīqa. issabi' hāḏa min yxallū 'alie, ykitla. nabb 'alie lwazīr. galla: "issabi', lieš mā thaddi ssabi' 'alie wkitala? lo hāddīn 'alie ssabi' wkātla aḥsan willā ttīh ittāj." gāl: "hiddū ssabi'!" haddaw issabi' 'alie. tiba'a ssabi' tubāraz wiyā ssabi' uṭubra(2) bissief. māt issabi'. ēh mawwata. galla: "ta'āl!" galla: "hāh?" galla: "inta mawwatt issabi!?" galla: "ēh!" galla: "hāḏa iṣṣūč mū mnissabi'. iṣṣūč min ilwazīr." gāl: "hallu 'alie balkit itkitla!" jāb hāy wija 'ala bitt 'amma. liga bitt 'amma mzawwijha abūha lġēr wāḥid. galla: "yāba inta šlōn zawwajitha lġēr wāḥid? mū inta gilit jībilha ṣadāġ u xiḏha!" galla: "ēh inta buṭēt u mā jiet u zawwajitha lġēr wāḥid." iyyi ḏāka ba'adha mā m'arsa. ēh. mzawwija lākin ba'ad mā m'arsa. ba'ad fad yōmēn t'arris. gallōla: "wiyyāk ilharub. yalla ntīkiyyaha." tahārab wiyya abūha kital abūha. ēh. 'arras 'alieha. ṣārat marata xallaf minha jhāl iṯnien. uba'dien hāḏōla ṭaššaw bukānhum u mišaw lġēr mukān.

TEXT 11 ('AMĀRA) TRANSLATION

A story, I mean of Mughdād and Aswad al-Kindi(3) about his daughter / shall I speak now? There was once a man called Jābir al-Ḍaḥḥāk(4) who had a beautiful daughter, perfect in beauty. But nobody could marry her. Only he who could defeat her in battle could marry her. If he fought with her and if he beat her, she would marry him. Then all the world came from afar, from other nations, from everywhere, they came for her, those who sought to defeat her... Why? Because she was beautiful. Very beautiful. Whoever faced her, this beautiful one and wished to fight her, she just uncovered her face, and he would fall unconscious from her

1 *qutil*, Classical borrowing.
2 Imperative for narrative past.
3 Aswad al-Kindi, who does not in fact appear in the story. Kinda was an Arab kingdom of Central Najd before the time of Muhammad.
4 Jābir al-Ḍaḥḥāk is borrowed from the Persian pre-Islamic legends. Zahhāk Mārdūsh (serpent-backed) was one of the enemies of Rustahm. The name Mughdād is also Old Persian signifying "Given by the Magi".

beauty. He would fall and she would come in and conquer him. There remained only her cousin, whose name was Mughdād. Mughdād was a shepherd working with the sheep. He watched and saw all this multitude of people, whoever came was conquered. Then he went to his mother and said: "Mother, I want you to give me a horse, so that I can fight my cousin Mayāsa, and I will take her as my wife and marry her." His mother said to him: "Who are you to think of your cousin. She will overcome you and throw you down and kill you." He said to her, "No, do not concern yourself. I will beat her." He went to her father and said to him: "Oh Jābir, I want [to marry] your daughter. I will fight her and if I beat her I will marry her." He said: "Go then!" When he went to her and wrestled with her, with the crowds watching in their thousands here and there and on the roofs of the houses, he beat her. When he beat her, her father Jābir jumped up and said: "I will not let you marry her." "Why [exclaimed Mughdād] Haven't I beaten her?!" He said: "I will not give her to you unless you bring her a dowry." "Well what is her dowry?" He said: "I want forty, no four hundred female camels of the black, four hundred white and all of them carrying goods of Egyptian manufacture. And also I want the crown of Kisra." He said: "All right, I will bring them." Where was he going to find these things? The road was far, but he said: "Just give me two months time, and I will bring them." He went and found these female camels with a man who was an experienced and valiant warrior. Yes, whose name was 'Ali.(1) And the name of the second warrior who was with him was al-Ḥamza.(2) He said to them: "Leave those things which are with you and look to yourselves unless you die, for I will kill you!" They said to him: "You will kill us!?" They rose and said: "How will you kill us? We will kill you." He said to them: "No, this will not happen, now let us fight." He fought with them. When he fought with them, they beat him. Then they said: "Who sent you against us?" He said: "Well, no one sent me against you. But I came for the dowry of my cousin Mayāsa. And ... ."(3) They said "Long live whoever meets you, here take them!" He took them and then went to get the crown. He went to bring the crown of Kisra and come to him. He travelled for one day, two days, three days. Still he did not arrive.

1 'Ali the son-in-law and nephew of the Prophet and Ḥamza his uncle were champions of the faith in the early days of Islam and were later adopted into the mythology of the Iranian people under Arab domination. This later became part of the folklore of the Shi'a populations of Iran and Iraq.
2 See fn.1 above.
3 The tape is unclear at this point.

On the way he met a man called Abu l-Khamsa, who had been tied up by another man and whose daughter was beside him. The other man was going to kill him and carry off his daughter. He said to him: "Why have you tied up this man and why do you wish to kill him and carry off his daughter?" He said: "What has it got to do with you. I am going to kill him and carry off his daughter." He said: "Leave him and come and fight with me!" He fought with him. He fought a duel with him. He was killed. Yes. That other one was killed. He untied the chains of the captured man and said: "Go on. Take your daughter and go!" He said: "But where are you going?" He said: "I'm going to get the crown of Kisra." He went and reached the land of Kisra. He said to him: "What do you want?" He said: "I want the crown." He said: "I won't give it to you. Should I give it to you while you are on your own or if you had an army with you?!" He said: "No, there is just me alone! And there is war between us." They brought their soldiers against him, but whoever they brought against him, he killed. The King said: "Quickly give him the crown!" They gave him the crown. They gave it to him and he came away. There was a lion kept captive in a garden. This lion killed anyone he was set on to. The wazir(1) jumped up and said: "The lion! Why don't you set the lion on to him so that he kills him." Is it better if you set the lion on him and he kills him or that you give him the crown." He said: "Loose the lion!"(2) They loosed the lion on to him. The lion followed him and he fought with the lion and dealt him a blow with the sword. The lion died. Yes, he killed him. He [the King] said to him: "Come!" He said: "Ha, what?" He said: "Did you kill the lion?" He said: "Yes!" He said: "The fault is not with the lion, but with the wazir." He said: "Go to him and perchance you will kill him." He brought this one [the King] with him and came back to his cousin. He found that his uncle had married his cousin to another. He said to him: "How did you marry her to another. Didn't you say, 'Bring for her a dowry and take her!'" He said: "Yes, but you were away a long time and didn't come so I married her to another." That other one [the groom] came and [they found that] she was married, but the wedding was not yet consummated. They were to marry in two days time. They said to him: "Come and fight and then we will give her to you." He fought with her father and killed him. Yes! He married her. She became his wife and he had two sons by her. And afterwards those people spread all over that country and then moved on to another place.

1 Notice the character of the wazir or "minister", completely absent in the bedouin texts and in the Kawāwila story.
2 lit. "Loose him, the lion!"

TEXT 12

KŪT SAYYID 'ANĀYA: LIFE IN KŪT SAYYID 'ANĀYA

This text was part of a taped conversation with a young boy called Sa'dūn who worked at the University of Jundi Shāpūr in Ahwaz. His home village was near Kūt Sayyid 'Anāya above Ahwaz on the Kārūn. He was from the Zuhairiyya, the majority of whom live near Nāṣiriyya and are counted as part of the Budūr. His dialect and that of his elder brother was typical of the northern areas of Khuzistan and resembled that of the Bani Ṭuruf informants. This is shown in the text by the occurrence of */a/* rather than */i/* in open syllables in such forms as */ištaġal/*, */xaḏa/*, */banēna/*, */garēt/* rather than */ištiġal/*, */xiḏa/*, */binēna/*, */girēt/*. The occurrence of */j/* rather than */g/* in */tij'id/* "you stay", */jirīb/* "near" is also characteristic of the northern area and contrasts with the dialect of the Shaṭṭ al-'Arab. The North Najdi type of second masculine plural forms */intam, -kam/* also occurred elsewhere in this dialect. A high degree of Persian vocabulary is used in connection with government institutions. Interesting in connection with the Ahwaz-Nāṣiriyya link is the following poetic fragment:

ṭila', ṭūla ḥilu rāhi hawāzi
gitla "mnien" gāl: "hawāzi"
gitla: "laṣil mnien". gāl: "mninnāṣiriyya".

"He came forward, a man of good appearance and height with the look of an Ahwāzi. I asked him: 'Where from?' He answered, 'an Ahwāzi'. I asked him: 'Where are your roots?' He said, 'In Nāṣiriyya.'" This was given to me by my Muṭūr informant (see Text 16) who did not however know its origin.

TEXT 12

lifa maktūb šawwašni
lifa maktūb šawwašni min ahlāy
garēta w ṣabb dama' 'ēni
yā diny-anti lḥaramtīni min ahlāy
ana ġarīb u sāčn ilġurba

ana twuladit ibkūt sayyid 'anāya. ana čint farax 'idd(1) uxūy. uxūy akbar min 'iddi. uxūy iya hnā štaġal biddānišgāh(2) štaġal ija lilahwāz, ištaġal ihnā biddānišgāh. ilḥāṣil galli: "wākūn tiyi 'iddi." hu čān 'idda mara ba'ad hu mū m'arris iya bilhawāz.(3) gāl: "wākūn tij'id tigra daris." agilla: "mā ayi", u hāy u ḏallēt abči. čint iṣġīr ilḥāṣil mā ridit ayi innōb bzūr,(4) bzūr yābni. yābni lahwāz u ḥaṭṭni bilmidirsa u hāy millikläṣ(5) ilawwal. u garēt ḥatta kaḏḏēt šīšum.(6) kaḏḏēt šīšum ṣirt ġabūl(7) kaḏḏēt tiṣdīġ ṭala'it min ilmidirsa. min ṭala'it ištaġlēt hinā biddānišgāh. ištaġlēt. čān hinā yomiyti sittīn iġrān hassa. iddīra jirīb. ṯilṯ firsixāt fōg milhawāz. iššuġul, šuġulhum zirā'a ḥunṭa š'īr rajji lūḅa, xōb naxal la! hōš 'idhum. 'idhum ġanam 'idhum ṣxūl. ḥāṣilhum ḥilu. dīra zhīriyya(8) u xōb ham issina iya xaḏāna zzōd u hāy. ṭāyiḥ ibyūthum. ēh min izzōd činna ḥāṭṭīn 'ala ššaṭṭ. mā ṭaggna zzōd ḥīšanna ṭāḥan. ṭāḥan šinna minnāk. šinna xōb iddoula sawwa kumak(9) u hāy. šinna ḥaṭṭēna 'aṣṣafāt hassina ḥaṭṭēna 'aṣṣafāt hassa banēna bġēr makān. šinna. īh jirīb liššaṭṭ 'iddi ummi wuxūy 'iddi ṯilṯ xuwāt u 'iddi ham uxūy ḏall ihnāka bil'arab.

1 *'idd* < *'ind*
2 *dānišgāh.* Persian *dānešgāh* "university".
3 *hawāz* dialect form for *ahwāz*, which also occurs.
4 *bzūr.* Persian *bezūr* "by force".
5 Persian *kelās* "class".
6 Persian *šīšum* "sixth grade".
7 Persian *ġabūl šudam* "I passed (was accepted)".
8 Note the incidence of *ī* for *ē* in *zhīriyya.* Common in N.Khuzistan and 'Amāra; see also p.80.
9 Persian *kumak* "help".

A letter arrived which troubled me.
  A letter arrived which troubled me, from my family.
I read it and the tears flowed from my eyes.
  O my world, you who have separated me from my people.
I am a stranger dwelling among strange people.

I was born at Kūt Sayyid 'Anāya. I was a child there with my brother, my brother who is older than me. My brother came here and worked at the University. Anyway in the end he said to me: "You must come to stay with me." He was married [although] when he came to Ahwaz he was not married. He said: "You must stay and study." I said: "I am not coming" and all that and I kept crying. I was only a child. In the end I didn't want to come, then he brought me by force. He brought me to Ahwaz and sent me to school from the 1st grade and I studied until I got to the 6th grade and passed and got my certificate. I left the school. When I left I began to work here at the University. My pay here was sixty Qrāns a day.

The village [that I came from] is quite close. Three farsangs above Ahwaz. The work, their work there is the growing of wheat and barley, watermelon. Date palms? No, there are none. They have flocks; they have sheep and goats. Their harvest is good. It is a village of the Zuhairiyya, and well this year the flood came and our houses(1) collapsed. Yes, because of the flood. We were encamped near the river and when the flood came our houses collapsed. They collapsed and we moved away from there. We moved away and well we encamped on the open ground. This year we have encamped on the open ground. Now we have built houses in another place. We moved off. Yes, near to the river. My mother and my father are now with me and three sisters, but I have also a brother who has stayed with the arabs [i.e. out in the country].

1 Probably reed-huts, which are easier to rebuild.

GACHSĀRĀN: A CONVERSATION WITH AN OLD SAYYID

This is the text of an interview with a lone Sayyid in a hamlet in the hills above Gachsārān. The inhabitants of neighbouring villages were Qashqāi Turks and Lurs and so he was living outside the Arabic language area, although Bani Ṭuruf buffalo herders were also in the vicinity up-country from the main centres of their area. The Sayyid illustrated the story of his life with the words of a popular song. The use of the form /*hāna*/ "here" is characteristic of bādiya speech in Khuzistan, contrasting with /*hnā*/, the form of the Riverine Arabs. The text shows a number of examples of /*ī*/ for /*ē*/ as in Texts 12 and 14.

TEXT 13

lā mā a'rif hāḏa ll anta tgūlha iḥna ngūl a'riḏ̣ ibxidimtak. ngūl ništiġil nigḏ̣i nizra' š'īr. inta šissawwi? ē na'am anta tištaġal bijjām'a. ana 'ayšti šuġli azra', akrub, aḥṣid, alimm ḥunṭa, aḥišš bardi. aḏarri aḥišš giṣab abī' ayīb aštiri awaddi ayīb. ēh tigzar.(1) mālti ana tigzar. hāḏa šuġli ana. winnōba a'riḏ̣ ibxadimtak ygūl:

> *"yā mkawwira(2) wēn itrīd*
> *ṭarrat nazinna*
> *lirrīda mā yinṭūn*
> *kuffār ahanna."*

1 *tigzar* Persian *gozar* "to pass".
2 cf. *kwār* "pad used by women when carrying loads on the head". The pad, made of palm fibre, is put on the head then the load is carried above it. Therefore *mkawwira* signifies a woman with the *kwār* on her head.

tiftahim? hāḏa farid wāḥid 'āšig, 'āšig farid mara. yāt u ba'ad lā huwwa yrūḥ u lā hiyya tiyi. ṭarrat, iyat ṭarrat bilfirīj. ya'ni iḥna ngūl firīj. 'ajami ygūl ābādi walo ammā 'arabi ygūl firīj yāt ṭarrat bilfirīj. ṣāḥibha šāfha šadd 'alīha bīt. gāl: "imkawwira wēn trīd ṭarrat nazilna lirrīda mā yinṭūn kuffār hanna" tisma'? ēh. "u bieni la bien ihwāy itwahhamiet u yiet šiyriddni rdūd." ya'ni 'ūd min ilmaḥal ṭala'it. ṭala'it u yiet. riḥit yiet bilfariḏ hāna. tuwahhamit u mā agdar ariddan. mā agdar aridd ana warūḥan lihali. hāna ba'ad balašit. balašit wa ba'ad mā biya urūḥan. tuwahhamit mā biyya aridd rdūd warūḥ lihali.

Interviewer: *u māku 'arab ġērak ihnā?*

lā bass ana. ana farid mara 'indi māl / -ham kirdiyya 'ijmiyya ana ahli māl zietān māl amīr almu'minīn yāy zāyir millāġažāriyya u yiet hāna mara xaḏēt min ahil išṭīt. ahalhum hāna čānaw bkumbul. yiet hāna. ba'ad balašit hāna. ba'ad mā riḥit. ḏallēt. īh ḏallēt fard uwkāt iššūf arūḥan ihnāk amurran 'alilahal ayi hāna.

TEXT 13 (GACHSĀRĀN) TRANSLATION

No, I do not know this thing which you are saying. We say, I submit to you, we say that we work. We pass the time, sow seeds, barley. What do you do? Ah, yes, you work in the University. Myself, my work and life is that I sow seeds, hoe the ground, reap the harvest, collect the corn, cut rushes, winnow the corn, cut reeds. I sell, bring, buy, carry, take. Yes, it passes. My life passes. This is my life. And then I say to you, he [the poet] says:

> "O girl carrying a load on your head, where are you going?
> She passes through our settlement.
> The girl I want, they will not give to me,
> because my family are unbelievers."(1)

Do you understand? There was a man who was in love, in love with a woman. She came away and then he wouldn't go [to see her] and she wouldn't come [to see him]. She passed by, she came, she passed through the village. I mean we say "*firīj*" [village]. The Persians say "*ābādi*" [village], but as for the arab he says "*firīj*". Her lover saw her and composed a

1 "Unbelievers" perhaps signifies Kawāwila (gypsies), with whom the Arabs will not intermarry.

verse for her. He said:

"O girl carrying a load on your head, where are you going?
She passed through our village.
The girl I want they will not give to me
Because my family are unbelievers."

Do you hear? Yes.

"And between me and my love
I have got involved and come away and what can take me back?"

I mean, you see, from the place, I have come away and come [here]. I went and came for instance here. I became involved and cannot return. I cannot return and go to my family. Here then I have become involved. I cannot go back.

Interviewer: "Aren't there any other Arabs except you here?"

No, just me. I have got a wife from / Kurdish, Persian. My family are from Zaitān, belonging to the Commander of the Faithful.(1) I came as a visitor from Āghājāri and came here and took a wife from the people of Shuṭaiṭ.(2) The people were here at Kumbul. I came here and got involved here. After that I didn't go. I stayed. Yes, I stayed. Sometimes, you see, I go there and drop in on the family and come back here.

1 Signifying Sayyid ancestry, or perhaps "from Māl Amīr (al-Mu'minīn)" which is often used to mean the area of Zaitān, the eastern part of the former Ka'b realm. STOCQUELER (1832) p.91.
2 Shuṭaiṭ, a tributary of the Kārūn in the northeast.

TEXT 14

BANI ṬURUF: AN ACCOUNT OF THE TRIBES, DIALECTS AND OCCUPATIONS OF THE REGION OF ḤUWAIZA

This text was recorded in 'Abbādān in 1969. The main speaker, Ya'gūb Ṭurufi (YT), is a Shaikh of the Bait-Ṣayyāḥ of the Bani Ṭuruf, of the region of Khafāyiyya, now renamed Sūsangard. He was in 'Abbādān as the guest of another Ṭurufi (T2) at whose house the recording was made. Also there was Ṭāhir Fāḏhili (TF) of the Bāwiya. The speech of these informants was regarded as 'arab, i.e. "nomadic type" by my ḥaḏhar informant, although the only feature apparent as the text is transcribed is the use of /*ġād*/ "over there" which is markedly "rural". In the final section Ya'gūb Ṭurufi imitates Mi'dān speech with some success, the main distinguishing feature being the use of the negative particle /*'ēb*/. As befits his shaikhly status, Ya'gūb uses a number of classicisms in his speech, namely /*allaḏi*/ "which" and /*ḏālik*/ "that" in place of the more colloquial /*illi*/ and /*ḏāk*/; also /*minḥēṯ*/ "because" alongside the more normal /*min ṭaraf*/. My own promptings have for the most part been omitted since the text makes perfectly good sense without them.

TEXT 14

YT ismi ya'gūb ana min bani ṭuruf. bani ṭuruf issina zara'hum killiš zien u ya'ni zirā'athum 'āyd issina killiš 'āyid kāfi. maḥṣūlhum? la'! ḥunṭa wši'īr u šilib. lākin issina ḥēṯ kiṯar ilmāy 'alīhum čiṯīr ṣār, ṣār zira'hum šilib ya'ni timman. min ḥēṯ ṭuġyān ilmāy mā ṣār ḥunṭa wši'īr 'idhum faqaṭ timman ṣār. yzir'ūna biliḥwēza isimha. gabul isimha lxafājiyya lākin hassa sammōha sūsangard. ī na'am 'ala šṭūṭ, šaṭṭ u aku nahrān iqasmūn minna 'ala l'arāḏi. hiyya tinṭi l'arāḏi māy. u ba'ad ḏālik iḏā qall ilmāy ysiddūn hāḏa ššaṭṭ mā yxallūn māy yrūḥ lilhōr. ysiddūna wiyxallūna 'ala ššilib yisgi iššilib. lākin ibqillat ilmāy. iḏā lmāy qalīl ysawwūn ḥunṭa wši'īr. hāḏa 'ala makāyin. ī na'am iddawla nṭathum makāyin. ilhōr wāqi' bēn il-/ bilḥidūd ṣāyir bien il'arāq wa īrān. iššaṭṭ hiya ṭāyiḥ bilhōr šṭūṭ īrān bilhōr ṣāyrāt wišṭūṭ il'arāq ham bilhōr. ibṭarafēn ṣāyrāt hāḏa waḏa'iyyat zirā'at bini ṭuruf. wa ammā zirā'at xazray w ičnāna ḏōlāk ġād bijjibāl ḏīč iṣṣafḥa hāḏōl mā 'idhum šilib faqaṭ ḥunṭa wši'īr yzir'ūn. ġād aku jabal ġād min nahr ilkarxa. lākin zara'hum ḥunṭa wši'īr šilib mā 'idhum. iššilib bass 'idna iḥna. fi daštmīšān wili'māra. 'ašāyir ili'māra ilimḥāddidīn ilhōr ham fi'lan killa šilib zār'in. lākin iḥna ni'matna zāyda xuṣūṣan bini ṭuruf ni'matna wāyid zāyda min ṭaraf iddawla wāyid sā'datna wāyid anṭatna, makāyin anṭatna. wšilibna utimmanna 'idna wši'īr wāyid ya'ni ilmann sitta twāmin ilmann iṯmānya warba'īn čīlu bisitta twāmin. iḏā trūḥ hināk arāwīkiyyā. ilmilla tištiri ddawla tištiri itbā'(1) išši tbī' 'ala ši. tijjār yištirūna wiyxiznūna wba'ad ḏālik iyyībūn iybī'ūna. īna'am anābīr.(2) yāxḏūn ilawādim kilman 'inda ybī' u tāli nōba yqasmūna ybī'ūna wēn mā yrīdūn. madāris wāyid 'idna xuṣūṣan hnāka ya'ni iddihāt(3) illaḏi aṣlan čānat ilmadāris mā y'arfūnilha kill dīra bīha madrasa. kill dihāt bīha farid madāris iṯnien imxallīha bīha ddawla m'allmīn ham mxallīha waṣāyil wāyid mrattiba. sipāh dāniš(4) mxallīha sipāh tarwīj(5) ham aku hnāk. maṯalan jinābak iḏā šarrafit ruḥit ildaštmīšān tšūf awwal nrāwīk sūsangard min ba'ad bustān min ba'ad issuwāri hāy laṭrāf allaḏi hiyya bdaštmīšān ...

T2 nḥāčīk 'an bini ṭuruf 'an illaḏi nidri bšaṭṭna hnāk. wa illā iḥna hnā šuwāġīl. šuwāġīl iḥna biššarika. šēx ya'gūb w ana ya'ni illaḏi ṭāhir fāḏili yixuṣṣna kāmilan u ṣadīgna hāḏa tagrīban xamsa w'išrīn sina u ṯlāṯīn sina kāmilan laḏi yxuṣṣna

YT lākin bzaman šēx xaz'al. ta'rif jinābak šēx xaz'al gām ylagguṭ wēn mā zēnīn. min kill 'ašīra ylagguṭhum wēn mā 'ašīra bīha wāḥid zēn ya'ni šijā' ufāhim. šēx xaz'al yčaṯṯirha binni'ma wiyjirrha ila. hāḏōl iyjurrhum min 'idna šēx xaz'al u axaḏhum bilma'rūf. u ṣāraw mn ahl ihnā hassa. lākin mnēn, iḥna lli ba'ad 'irfaw 'amāmhum hāḏi siyāsathum alinglīz hāy. wammā llisān kamā 'idna, bani ṭuruf hāḏōl

1 *tbā'* perhaps the Class passive *tubā'*. This is the only example of the internal passive recorded and may be a classicism.
2 Persian *anbār* "store house".
3 Persian *dehāt* "villages".
4 Persian *sepāhe dāneš* "Education core".
5 Persian *sepāhe tarvīj* "Progress core".

ilfōg ygūlūn "yība". d̲ōlāk illad̲i brāyg ilhōr ygūlūn "žība". kamā xazray u čināna ygūlūn "yība". yxallīha šwayy. suwāri uḥayādir u sawā'id hād̲ōli māl Īrān hād̲ōli sākint ilhōr hād̲ōli ygūlūn "žība" bilhōr 'idhum duwāb

T2 ta'āl ij'id ibbukāni!

TF ya'gūb inta hnāk bilhōr šinu jjini māla iḥči m'ēdi killiš!

YT jinīna duwāb. duwāb nijla'. duwāb 'idna niḥlibhin wiḥna m'īšatna 'alīhin(1) lākin issina bḥēt̲ it̲ṭala mālhin 'ēb(2) yiṭla' minnā w minnā miḥtiṣrāt bilibyūt 'indi taġrīban xamis šīš(3) žāmūsāt(4) waḥiššilhin ḥašīš mnilhōr u'ēb yṭil'an barra. bīhin willid t̲alāt̲a wilbājiāt šuwwal 'ēb bīhin īdām min kat̲rat il'alaf mā yṭil'an barra. mā 'idhin d̲illa yrūḥan winḥiššilhin ḥašīš mnilhōr nyībilhin algōr šaḥaf lākin 'ēb ysirḥan. ġēr ilḥašīš mā ilhin 'ilāj māku bass hād̲a lḥašīš. kill wakit marbūṭāt bilbiet.

TF mā thiddūnhin

YT lā 'ēb nhiddhin

TF lā mā yigdar ykammilha m'ēdi tamām lā.

TEXT 14 (BANI ṬURUF) TRANSLATION

YT My name is Ya'gūb, from the Bani Ṭuruf. This year the harvest of the Bani Ṭuruf was very good, I mean the crop this year was good and sufficient.

Interviewer: Do you have date palms there?

YT Their crop? No! Wheat and barley and rice. But this year because there was too much water, it became too much, their crop was rice, I mean rice.(5) Because of the floods, there was no wheat or barley among them, only rice. They sow it at al-Ḥuwaiza (Dasht Mīshān). That is Sūsangard, its name is al-Khafājiyya. Before its name was Khafājiyya, but now they have named it Sūsangard. Yes, along the rivers, a river. And there are irrigation channels by which they distribute [water] from it to the land plots. They bring water to the land. And then if the water is not enough, they dam up the river and do not let water go to the Haur. They dam it up and let the water go to the rice fields to irrigate the rice fields. But with the scarcity of water, if there is not much water they make wheat and barley. That is by use of agricultural machines. The government has given them machines. The Haur is

1 *'alīhin* for *'aliehin* characteristic of 'Amāra and N. Khuzistan.
2 *'ēb* negative particle used in Mi'dān speech.
3 Persian *šīš* "six".
4 *žāmūsāt* "buffaloes"; note the use of *ž* for *y*.
5 *šilib* "the rice plant", *timman* "rice as a foodstuff"

situated between -/ on the borders between Iraq and Iran.(1) The river flows into the Haur. The rivers of Iran flow into the Haur and the rivers of Iraq are also into the Haur. They are on both sides. This is the state of the Bani Turuf's agriculture. But as regards the agriculture of the Khazraj and Chināna,(2) they are over there in the mountains, on that side. They have no rice just wheat and barley. Over there there are mountains on the other side of the river Karkha. But their crop is wheat and barley; they have no rice. The rice is only here at Daht Mīshān and al-'Amāra. The tribes of al-'Amāra who border on the Haur, they also of course all sow rice. But here our luck is good. Especially the Bani Ṭuruf, our luck is very good because the government has helped us a lot and given us much. It has given us machines. And we have our rice and much barley, I mean at six toumans to the mann.(3) The mann is forty-eight kilos, at six toumans. If you go there I will show you. People buy it, the government buys it. It is sold. One thing is sold for another. Merchants buy it and store it and after that they bring it and sell it. Yes [in] store houses. People bring it. Whoever has some sells it and then they divide it up and sell it, whenever they like. We have many schools, especially there, I mean, villages which did not even know what a school was, every village has a school. Every village has one or two schools which the government has put there, and have also put teachers and very good facilities. They have sent the Education core and also there, there is the Development core. For instance if you went to Dasht Mīshān you would first see / we would show you Sūsangard and then Bustān and then al-Suwāri, there outlying areas around. Dasht Mīshān...

T2 We are telling you about the Bani Ṭuruf about what we know of our river there. But otherwise we here are employees, employees of the [oil] company. Myself and Shaikh Ya'gūb I mean, whom Ṭāhir Fāḏhili looks after very well. He is our friend and has been looking after us for twenty-five or thirty years.

YT But in the time of Shaikh Khaz'al. Do you know Shaikh Khaz'al? He began picking out people wherever there were good men. From every tribe he took them, wherever there was someone good, I mean a brave or intelligent man. He would load them with gifts and pull them over to him. These people Shaikh Khaz'al took from us and counted them as his own. And now they have become part of the people of

1 Haur al-Ḥuwaiza.
2 Tribes to the north of the Bani Ṭuruf beyond the Karkha River.
3 *mann*, a Persian unit of weight measurement for agricultural produce.

this region. But, from where? We are the people who know who their ancestors are. This is their policy, the English. (1) But as to the language as we have it, the Bani Ṭuruf those who are up-country say "*yība*" [bring it!]. Those who are on the edge of the Haur say "*žība*!" As also Khazraj and Chināna say "*yība*!" They draw it out a little. Suwāri and Ḥayādir and Sawā'id, those who belong to Iran and live in the Haur, they say "*žība*". In the Haur, possessing buffalos.

T2 Come and sit over here in my place! [to a guest arriving].

TF Ya'gūb, you [when you are there] in the Haur, what is the livelihood there? Talk like a Mi'aidi completely!

YT Our livelihood is buffaloes. We graze buffaloes. We have buffaloes, we get milk from them and our livelihood depends on them. But this year because of their thala [a disease of livestock] they do not go out here and there. They stay at home confined in the reed houses and I cut fodder for them from the Haur and they do not go out. There are among them three bearing young and the rest... They have no ..., because there is so much fodder they do not go out. There is no sheltered place for them to go to so we cut fodder for them from the Haur and bring it for them on boats in bales, but they do not go out and graze. There is no cure for it except grass. They are tied up all the time in the house.

TF You don't let them loose?

YT No., we do not let them loose.

TF No, he can't do it completely [to speak] Mi'aidi completely, no!

1 This remark was a humourous attack on the Muḥaisin league of Khorramshahr, a confederation of mixed tribal elements. Their leader Shaikh Khaz'al was an ally of the British at the turn of the century. The Bani Ṭuruf harried him unsubdued from the north. Part of the humour was, of course, directed against me as an Englishman. See WILSON (1911) passim.

TEXT 15

KA'B: THE HISTORY OF THE KA'B IN KHUZISTAN

The following is part of a long recording of a meeting with a number of the Ka'b shaikhs at the Muḍhīf of Shaikh Muḥi of the Āl Bu Ghubaish section in Shādigān in 1969. The main speaker (B) is Shaikh Muḥi himself, who gives a spirited account of the history of the Bani Ka'b and their arrival in Iran. Speaker (C) is the author. The dialect is basically of the Shaṭṭ al-'Arab type, differing slightly however from the dialect of the Muṭūr informant in a higher incidence of */g/* rather than */q/* or */ġ/* as a reflex of */qāf/* in elevated vocabulary, i.e. */'irāg* or *'arāg/* "Iraq", */gaḍiyya/* "matter", */yifriq/* "it is different", */tagrīban/* "approximately". The tape reveals a considerable amount of Persian vocabulary within the larger Arabic macrostructure and makes interesting allusions to the relationship of the Ka'b with the Persian nomadic tribes to the north. Shādigān is the new Persian name for Fallāḥiyya, the traditional capital of the Ka'b, before they were eclipsed by the Muḥaisin under Shaikh Khaz'al.

TEXT 15

A na'am yiji min jarrāḥi, killa ṣār makāyin karxānāt(1) killman hamma yāxiḏ haqqa 'abāra(2) min ilmayy bilkarxāna mālta wgā'-iyzir'ūn killa zirāyi' makāyin. lā xēr hassa hi māku. māku sidūd. ēh min ḥēṯ ilmayy qalīl hassa. hāḏa ilšaṭṭ iljayy min jarrāḥi mittiṣil minnāk yāy, min ṣafiḥtēn min ṭarafēn aku makāyin pampāt māy...

B walla ddawla niṭāna halmakāyin wkillha lā zir'a warāhin wa lā ši ġēr aṭṭalāyib waṣṣēḥa. lā 'amal warāhin

1 *karxāna* Persian "factory, machine".
2 *'abāra* "approximately", also used in Kuwaiti.

wa lā yṣīr 'amal... ḏabuṭ ṣōt?(1) ya'ni yiḏbuṭ ṣōtna? iḥna niḥči killši 'anna. ana iḏā čān aḏḏāyig min haḏḏabuṭ ṣōt... yā ḥayātak! amman n'īd 'ala lmas'ala. tīmsār X. min yšūfni min b'īd ayi, iḏā šāf iššyūx yṯūr min ihnāk. min kilumitrēn yṯūr 'ala ššyūx. amma hāḏa, mā la xilig. xalli ykuḏḏa! lā kuḏḏa, xāyif?! šmālkum(2) txāfūn. walḷa ana gāyil ibrūḥa X. wġēra, amma lmuwāmīr likbār, ašrāf. killhum awādim. Alā tta''ibna! lā hiyya mū gaḏiyat šisma, hāḏa yāy yit'allam billuġa. il'umda 'ala lluġa, 'ala llahya wmin jimlat hāḏa si'al 'arrufāha...

B iḥna lḥukūma rāḏīn minha. lā rāḏīn u fidāyīn dowlatna kulliš sarbāz,(3) amma ḏāk abulfarax linsān ilxayyir, la!

C hāḏa farid ši kitabha wāḥid min zumalā'i 'ala lluġa blībya... ayībha maṯalan...

B inta mšān-ēš šāyil hadduwal il'arabiyya 'alēna? iḥna wēn n'arif hāḏa lḥači?! ēh hāḏa:

"mā tinfa' al'adab bil'ilm walhija
wa ṣāḥibuhā 'inda lkamāl yamūtu?"

iḥna wēn n'arif hāḏa lḥači?

C ṭab'an illuġa walwaṭaniyya yifruġ.

B ēh hāḏa llisān hāḏa maḥalli wa illā milliyatna iḥna īrāniyya. hāḏi luġatna-ḥna, 'idna luġa xāṣṣa. wiliḥwēza luġatha ġēr luġatna-ḥna. bāwiya luġatha ġēr luġatna-ḥna. al'ān maṯalan xurramšahr wilimḥēsin kulliš laha luġa xāṣṣa. iḥna walxanāfra yifrug. 'asākira jiddan yifrug. haššikil! 'ala llahja, la'ad yig'ad 'idna mudda, 'indak mudda wāyid yit'allam. ḥatta min ilxanāfira yit'allam wmin hāḏōli lbarhān. walla hassa wakit balābil iṣṣyām ṣāḥla: "hō, ṭiggha ṭāḥat ihnāka wukḏa!"(4) hāy luġatna-ḥna.

A lā wāḏiḥ halḥači ḥuṭṭa! min jumlat zien u šien.

B lō yrūḥ wiyyāhum lilbarr yitwannas, nisma' ṣēḥathum. hāḏa hi. hassa bīrān hassa, iḥna hāḏa luġatna... lākin hāḏōla llur mā y'arfūn luġa. farid marra ana wiyya lmarḥūm šēx mašāyix ibṭahrān. 'inda amīr hu min bīrjird yōm min ayyām il'ašāyir ilbaxtyāriyya. čān yindall bičānhum u hāḏōla 'araft-ilhum. gāl: "aṇa aḥibban(5) hāḏa llibās whāḏa lmizwiya," wšāyif ana waḥči, waḥibb aḥči ana lurri wiyya hāḏōli lli čānaw yjūn. hāḏa mā y'arif. hāḏa lur, hassa hu mā y'arif luga sawā'an an mā y'arif 'arabi. hassa 'idna hēči ubkill mukān hēči. lākin iḥna īrāniyya, muxx aṣil īrān iḥna. yā ḥayātak! iḥna yāna hāḏa lḥijāz

1 *ḏabuṭ ṣōt*, Persian *zabte sout* "tape recorder".
2 *šmāl*, a particle characteristic of the Shaṭṭ al-'Arab area, as in *šmālak* "What is wrong with you?"
3 Persian *sarbāz* "soldier".
4 *wukḏa* < *w-kuḏḏa*.
5 *aḥibban*, suffix *-an*, see p.83.

ilsabbāna wṭaradna, 'ārakna wyiena wil'irāg 'ārakna-wiyyā.(1) wyiena minnā rḥēl lihnā. yiena hnā bilgubān ba'ad mā-lna bgaḏiyat gubān. ga'adna hnā. sabi' miyat sina iḥna hnā. hassa šādigān arba' miyat sina hassa tagrīban iḥna sikanna bšādigān. wa illā hāḏi l'umūr hāḏi bilgubān, bilihmieli, bili'māra. hāḏa killa 'idna 'arik wiyya lxawārij wili'rāg wilḥijāz. 'arik wiyya tturkiyya. iḥna mā niḥmilhum - uhma. yiena hnā sirna b'īrān īrāni lḥamdillā rufa' 'aliena ššāh bṭahrān wiḥna hnā. ḥammal il'irāg iya limḥammara. čānat ilimḥammara ba'ad ṣārat mard.(2) iya ḏāk lilimḥammara wiḥna ča'ab wara ča'ab, wugfaw jiddāmhum. 'ārak u radd il'irāg. yaw minnā yaw minnā. iḥna sarbāz īrān. u gabul mā čān halwasāyil wlā halġudra walā hamma... gufāna ham min gufāna wba'ad mā 'idna kill gufa. iḥna lo inkitalna nišrid ila hāy ilbaxtyāriyya. lo fitaḥna nwaddīhum min halbāb minihnā. iḥna gabul maḥḥad ... / hāḏa xurramsahr, guṣba, bahmanšīr, fieliyya, kārūn, šādigān ḥadd mā bandar maḥšūr hāḏa killa taḥat ḥimāyat ča'ab. ča'ab farmandāriyya(3) xuzistān čān bhaššādigān. biet nāṣir āl ka'biyya, āl nāṣir hāḏōli za'amā gabīlat ka'ab. hāy ḥatta milūk ilbāwiya min ilahwāz iyyūn lihnā. nāyib minna yrūḥ min šādigān yirūḥ lilahwāz ḥākim. lākin hāy māliyātna nwaddi lil īrān. šex ča'ab illiḏi sāyid ywaddi lḥukūmat īrān māliyāt. hassa iḥna ššawwēna mā sawwēna ilā sibāġan 'ala fad wuṣla, iḥna nās īrāniyya whāḏa llisān ba'ad maḥalli 'idna. bamrīka aku haššikil bangaltara haššikil ubkill mukān. uhāḏa ššaṭṭ hāḏa čān ihnā. činna bhāḏa lguṣba wxurramsahr ubahmanšīr iḥna bīha ča'biyya. ammā hāḏa sātirna šādigān min ġazw ilxawārij. maṯalan iyyūn min itturkiyya, 'arāg fulān iyyūn. hāy jazīrat šādigān. hāḏa bāṭlāġ(4) killa min bahmanšīr ilā bandaršāpūr ilā min itrūḥ minnā numra arba'a lmāliḥ ilā lahwāz ilā ḥidūd lahwāz, hāḏa bāṭlāġ ilā an tiji rdūd ilā bahmanšīr. hāy ijjazīra. hāy šādigān. sawwēna kūt, ilā hassa mowjūd farid āṯār minna mowjūd na'am hāḏa yimkin 'alēha ṯalāṯīn xayyāl yiṣiffūn dōm, 'alyōm biflūs. sawwēna hāḏa ilman? ilyaw hijmaw 'alēna mnidduwal ilxawārij, kitannāhum. u mā ḥagg iyḏurtūn. 'ād iḥna ndāfi' sarbāz ihnā b'īrān. ilmuluk ḥafaḏnā, ṣār iya lpahlawi sallamnā. gabul nāṣir iddīn u fataḥ 'ali šā iššex 'idna hnā yṣīr yinṭi māliyāt ilna killhum. ṣārat ilixtilāf bēnna. xarrab šex xaz'al. sawwa xarāb bēnātna ixtilafna ḥna wizza'amā mālīnna. ṣār xarāb. šex xaz'al ḥaṭṭ iddowla, willā hāḏa lmuluk mulukna wihna ndāfi' 'anna wmaḥḥad ydāfi' 'anna wmā čān haṭṭawāyif hāḏa.

1 *sabbāna* for *sabbna*, see p.39.
2 *mard* Persian *mard* "man".
3 *farmandāriyya* Persian *farmandāri* "governorship".
4 Persian *bāṭlāq* "marsh".

TEXT 15 (KA'B) TRANSLATION

A Yes, it [the water] comes from Jarrāḥi.(1) All of it is now by machines and powerhouses. Each person also takes his share approximately of the water at his own machine and they are all farming. All of it is mechanised farming. No, now there aren't any, there are no dams. Yes, because there is very little water. This river which comes from Jarrāḥi uninterruptedly coming from over there, there are on both sides of it water pumps...

B By God, the government gave us these machines, but there is no use from them for agriculture or anyting except moral indebtedness and propaganda. There is no work from them nor is any work possible... A tape recorder? You mean he is recording us. Well, we will say everything about it. If I was to be upset by a tape recorder... By your life! But we will return to the subject. When General X sees me coming in the distance, if he sees any of the shaikhs coming he stands up to greet us from a long way off. From two kilometres distance he stands up for the shaikhs. But as for the other one, he has no breeding! No, let him record it! No, record it! Are you afraid? Why are you afraid? By God, I have said the same to X and others. As for the higher officials, they are honourable men. All of them are human beings.

A Don't bore us [with this talk]! No, it is not a matter of that. He has come to study the language. The main point is the language, the dialect; and as a part of this he asked about the standard of living...

B We are quite satisfied with our government. No, we are content and stand behind our government absolutely like soldiers; but as for that person, the father of the children, the good man,(2) no!

C This is something which one of my colleagues wrote, about the [arabic] language in Libya... I have brought it as an example...

B Why have you brought all this about the Arab states to bother us with? What do we know of these matters?! Yes, this is what is meant by the proverb:

"What use is education in science and writing
when the learner will die on completion of his work?"

What do we know about these matters?

C Naturally there is a difference between nationality and language.

B Yes. This language is a local thing, but otherwise we are of Iranian nationality. This is our language, our own language. And the language of al-Ḥuwaiza is different

1 Jarrāḥi, to the east of Shādigān.
2 Sarcastically.

from ours. The language of the Bāwiya is different from ours. Now, for example, Khurramshahr and the Muḥaisin have their own absolutely different dialect. The Khanāfira are different from us. The 'Asākira are completely different. It's like that! About the dialect, so he should stay with us a while and stay with you a while and he would learn a lot. He might even learn something from the Khanāfira and from those others, the Barhān.(1) Then by God at the time of hunting the wild birds he would shout: "Ho, shoot at it and it falls to earth over there and run and get it!" This is our language.

A No. That is obvious. Leave the matter! [He asks about] in general the good and the bad.

B If he goes with them to the desert to enjoy himself, then we would hear an outcry from them.(2) This is the point. Now in Iran now, this is our language... But those others, the Lurs,(3) do not know the [Persian] language. Once I was with the late head shaikh in Tehran. With him was an Emir from Borūjerd one day in the days of the Bakhtiāri influence. He knew where they lived. And there I found out about them. He [the Lur] said: "I like these [arab] clothes and this *mizwiya* [the cloak worn by the arabs]," and I was watching [and understood what he intended] and speaking. I wanted to speak the Lur language with those people who were coming in to the house. He did not know [Persian]. He was a Lur. Now he did not know the Persian language as well as the fact that he did not know Arabic. Now it is like this with us and the same everywhere else. But we are Iranian citizens, the core and basis of Iran. By your life! The people of Hijaz(4) came to us, those who insulted us and wished to drive us out. We fought them and came away. We fought also with the peple of Iraq and came on a long migration to here. We came here to al-Qubān.(5)

1 'Asākira and Āl bu Ghubaish with the Āl Nāṣir form the Dirīs section of the Ka'b. The other sections such as the Khanāfira and Barhān are regarded as *ṭawāyif* "ascinded tribes". See LORIMER (1908) p.960.
2 i.e. the Iranian security service.
3 The Lur tribes of Fars and northern Khuzistan, the northern tribal neighbours of the Arabs.
4 The people of Hijaz, here perhaps intending the Arabian peninsula in general. The name Najd is not well known in Khuzistan. Here reference is made to the tradition of the early cause of the migration of the Ka'b from the Arabian peninsula.
5 Qubān, the first settlement of the Ka'b in Khuzistan, abandoned in 1747; situated at the head of the Khaur Mūsa.

We are not concerned however with the matter of al-Qubān. We settled here. For seven hundred years we have been here. Now it is four hundred years we have been here. Now it is four hundred years that we have been at Shādigān. But otherwise these other matters were at al-Qubān, at Humaili, at al-'Amāra. All this time we were at war with the foreigners (1) and with Iraq and the Hijaz, at war with Turkey.(2) We paid no heed to any of them. We came here and settled in Iran, praise be to God. The Shah in Tehran relieved us of our problems and we stayed here. Iraq invaded al-Muḥammara. Muḥammara had become a force to be reckoned with. They came to Muḥammara and we were Ka'b behind Ka'b [in rows] standing before them. Iraq came, fought and went back. They came [enemies] from here. They came from there. We were the soldiers of Iran. Formerly there were not the transport facilities and power [of today] and also... our only defence was ourselves and after that we had no defence. If we were defeated we would have to flee all the way back to the Bakhtiāri. If we won we would send them [the enemy] out from this doorway here. Formerly we, there was no one... / All of this Khorramshahr, Quṣba, Bahmanshīr, Failiyya, Kārūn, Shādigān as far as Bandar Maḥshūr, all this was under the tutelage of the Ka'b. Ka'b were the governors of Khuzistan at Shādigān. Bait Nāṣir of the Āl Ka'biyya; those, the Āl Nāṣir, were the leaders of the Ka'b tribe. Even the kings of the Bāwiya from Ahwaz used to come here to us and a deputy would go from us here in Shādigān to Ahwaz as a governor. But we used to send our taxes to Iran. The shaikh of the Ka'b who was in ascendance would send taxes to the Iranian government. Now whatever we have done or not done previously in one word, we are now part of the Iranian state and this is our local language. In America it is the same, in England the same and everywhere. And this river(3) was here, and we were here. We were here at al-Quṣba and Khorramshahr and Bahmanshīr, we were here the Ka'b realm. But this Shādigān was our shield from the attacks of the foreigners. For instance they came from Turkey, Iraq or whatever, this was the island of Shādigān. All this was a marsh from Bahmanshīr to Bandar Shāpūr up till where you

1 Probably here the war of the Ka'b with the Portuguese is referred to, in the 17th century.

2 The Ka'b also repelled a number of Anglo-Turkish attempts to invade Khuzistan in the 1760s. LORIMER (1908) II, 2, p.1627-41.

3 Perhaps "canal" is a better translation. In Khuzistan many of the rivers are wholly or partly man-made and therefore stand as a witness of the possession of the people settled there.

go from here to the salty [well] number four to Ahwaz, to the borders of Ahwaz. This was a marsh until you came back to Bahmanshīr. This was the island. This was Shādigān. We built a fort, a historical monument from us existing still. Yes! On this thirty horsemen could parade continuously, daily receiving regular pay. What did we make this for? For whoever of the foreign states came and attacked us, so that we could beat them off. And they did not even have the right to make a sound. Then we were defending the country here as soldiers in Iran. We protected the kingdom until the Pahlavi regime came, then we delivered it safe to them. Before Nāṣir al-Dīn and Fatḥ 'Ali Shāh,(1) all of them [the people of Khuzistan] would give taxes to us. Then there came the difficulties between us. Shaikh Khaz'al made problems, made things difficult between us. We quarreled with our leaders. Things went wrong. Shaikh Khaz'al formed a state, but otherwise this realm was ours and we used to defend it and no one defended us, and these [other] tribes (2) were not here.

1 The Shahs of the Qājār regime.

2 Referring to the Muḥaisin league which was formed more recently.

TEXT 16

MḤIRZI: PALM CULTIVATION ON THE KĀRŪN

This text was recorded for me by Sālim Fāḍhili of the Muṭūr section of the Muḥaisin of Khuzistan. Mḥirzi is the centre of the Muṭūr and is situated on the left bank of the Kārūn just above Khorramshahr. The dialect is typical of the Shaṭṭ al-'Arab region and similar types were recorded for Basra and 'Abbādān Island, also for both banks of the Shaṭṭ al-'Arab at Sība, Abu l-Khasīb, Fao and Quṣba. This type of dialect was regarded in the area as being typical of the ḥaḍhar or settled population and distinguishable from bādiya speech. It is characterised by heavy phonological and morphological reduction of the type outlined in Chapter 3, in particular also by universality of the occurrence of */i/* rather than */a/* in open syllables in verbal forms, in contrast to the bādiya type which retains */a/* in some phonological environments, i.e. */xiḏa/* vs */xaḏa/* "he took", */kila/* vs */kala/* "he ate".

TEXT 16

innaxla yzir'ūnha ysammūnha farax naxal. tāli hannōba yzir'ūnha ṭṭawwil 'abāra(l) m'addil čam sina lamman mā dgūm tiḥmal, ysammūnha tiḥmal. hassa huwwa nnaxal anwā'. 'indak naxal birḥi, xuḏrāwi, sa'amrān, firsi u gunṭār u ba'dan anwā' wagsām mā adri bīhin ana. amman akṯar liyzir'ūnha hnāka ijjamā'a huwa sa'amrān min jihat hāy issa'amrān, awwalan yṣaddirūn min 'inda wāyid lilxārij. hannōba hatta yištaġlūn bīhin bčirdāġ wiyṣaffūna wiyfaššigūna. tāli nōba yṣaddirūna wilbāji ḏāka ybī'ūna, ḥatta ya'ni kill yōm awādim yištirūna yāklūna, bass ḏāka lakṯar māla yṣaddirūna lilxārij. hannōba naxal aku illi yiḥmal u tāli ḏāka

1 See also Ka'b text, p. 178.

ilfaḥal. ilfaḥal kill gā' itšūf bīha miya mītien naxla, bīha faḥal wāḥid, ḏikar. hāḏa ygūm, 'ugub ma innaxal ygūm yṭalli', yxallūna yṭalli', tāli nōba wāḥid iyyi ylaggiḥ, ysammūna laggāḥči.(1) rayyāl īh! hāḏa yḥuṭṭ ilfarwand(2) māla yiṣ'ad 'alilfaḥal, yguṣṣla čam ṭal'a. tāli hannōba iyyībhin yġassimhin 'ala ġisma, ġisma. hannōba yiṣ'ad innaxal wiḥda wiḥda wiygūm ylaggiḥ. hāḏa ylaggiḥ šlōn? iṭṭal'a mafšūga hiyya šwayya yḥuṭṭa bwaṣṭathin. wiḥda min hāḏi lyābha mnilfaḥal, ġisma, willi māhi ṭāl'a yifšigha ihwa(3) bīda. innōba yḏull ḥatta mjiht(4) ilhawa kūn yṣīr ḥārr. winnaxal mā yiṭla' wilhawa bārid. kūn iyṣīr ḥārr. hannōba 'ugub mā yiṭla' hāḏa, awwal mā yiṭla' iṭṭal'a nsammīha / šwayya tiṭla' itṣīr xaḏar wizġār / hāḏi nsammī ḥabābōk. mā ysammīha tamur, awwal ma yiṭla', ba'ad ma ylaggiḥha yiṭalli' išwayya yḏull heč čam mudda ṣṣīr ḥabābōk. killiš izġār u murr šwayya. šikla xaḏar. tāli hannōba yikbar lamman ma yṣīr čimri. čimri ham šikl ilḥabābōk amman šwayya akbar. hannōba iččimri šwayya tāli yṣīr yṣaffur iyṣīr aṣfar ysammūnha hambūs. min ba'ad hāy iddaraja tāli killa hāḏi lxaḏar iččimri yiswi yṣīr aṣfar lamman ma yṣīr aṣfar ysammūnha xḷāḷ hannōba hāḏi laṣfar nuṣṣa nuṣṣ ilixḷāḷ mā ṣṣīr tamur, halli ysammūna ruṭab ygūm yraṭṭib hāḏa nuṣṣ ixḷāḷ u nuṣṣ tamur. hannōba lamman ma yṣīr killiš/killa tamur ba'ad ygūmūn/iyyi hāḏa ḏḏumāni wāḥid ḏammān yiḏmun ilgā'. tāli hannōba ygūmūn yguṣṣūna yguṣṣūna hāḏa ttamur killa. bilwāḥid ysammūna 'iṯig. ittamur killa a'ni. ittamur ihwa mčallib wiḥda mniṯṯānya ysammūna šarmūx. hāḏa l'iṯig māla mčallib ibfarid ši ysammūnha 'isga. liyčallib il'iṯig binnaxla hāḏa 'isga. hannōba nnaxla, min ba'ad ma tiṭla', bīha sa'fa. hāy issa'fa miṯl irrīša mālt iṭṭēr amman šwayya akbar u bīha xūṣ farid wiḥda xūṣa. hāḏa ssa'af māla, innaxla yā ma tikbar, 'alilḥadir māla miṯil issa'af yṣīr yēbas. ygūm wāḥid ygūm yguṣṣa mšān ḥuṭab. gabil lā agūl 'alissa'fa ngūl minjiht innaxla ilha / mā hwa bass wāḥid yistifīd imnilmaḥṣūl mālha. yimkin tistifīd min kill 'ilij binnaxla. kill jizi' māl innaxla ila jimī' istifādāt. wāḥid yigdar yistifīd min 'inda. maṯalan ittamur ba'ad ma dguṣṣ ittamur ywaddūna liččardāġ yfaššigūna, yṭul'ūn ilfuṣma, ttamra ysiddūnha ywaddūnha lilxārij mā adri šiysawwūn bīha hannōba ilfuṣma wil'inig huwa lli mčallib bittamra, ččallib ittamra biššarmūx, hāḏa l'inig wilfuṣam lawādim yištirūna yiṭṭūna lilḥayawānāt

1 -*či* the Turkish occupational suffix common in the whole area.

2 *farwand*, probably Persian (*ka*)*marband* "belt".

3 *ihwa*, the Shaṭṭ al-'Arab form of the pronoun, also *ihya*, *ihma*, *ihna*.

4 *min jihat* "because" in the Shaṭṭ al-'Arab area.

yāklanna, lilhawāyiš. ba'ad awādim yiṭuḥnūna, mā adri šiysawwūn bī, mā adri šinhou ilḥāṣil. hāy innōba ittamur hamma tigdar, gabul lā yfišgūna w hāya, yḥuṭṭūna bfarid mukān ysammūna mdibsa. tāli iḏā šwayya yiḥtarr ygūm yiṭla' min 'inda dibis. tāli hannōba issa'fa min tēbas iyguṣṣūnha čam ġisma. kill ġisma iṣṣīr ṭaraf. hāḏa lṭaraf liyidrūn yista' milūna mšān nār mšān xubiz lo yṭubxūn lo killši. ilxūṣ yguṣṣūna ygidrūn yšawwūn min 'inda, yṣuffūn bī balla lo zbīl lo sufra lo mhaṯṯa.(1) hannōba issa'fa bkuburha ygidrūn, gabul lā tēbas yguṣṣūnha bass yxallūn brāsha šwayyat xūṣ. hāḏa ysammūnha niṣšāša, yniššūn bīha bazzūna dyāya killši ttiyi. hannōba llimčallib issa'fa binnaxla ihya kurba. issa'fa ḏḏull min ba'ad sina lo akṯar min tēbas wāḥid yiṭla' yrūḥ ykarrub b'akfa yguṣṣ ilkurba. ilkurba hamma mšān ḥuṭab yṭubxūn bīha wminhalḥači. hannōba bien innaxla wilkurba aku līfa. hāy illīfa wāḥid min isti'mālātha ysawwūna miṯil imxadda ysammūnha iskāra. ēh mšān ilbustān. ṭamāṭa wxyār mniyzir'ūn ḥatta ykuḏḏūn ilmāy, min hāḏa lmašrūb iḏḏāk ilmašrūb. hāy iskāra. yiena innōba lil'isga hāḏi limčalliba l'iṯig binnaxla il'isga ygidrūn ykin'ūnha bilmāy wiyguṣṣūnha yšalxūnha 'ala wuṣla wuṣla ysawwūn min 'idha ṭubag lo guffa šwayya ilā ččiffa hēči yṣīr xōš sabstityūt liṣṣīniyya. hāḏa ṭubag. ilguffa šwayya azġar. innōba ilyiḏ'a hāy iḏā mā trīdha lo ṣṣīr čibīra wāyid iṭṭayyiḥha, ham bīha isti'māl.

TEXT 16 (MḤIRZI) TRANSLATION

They plant the palm tree and it is called a palm sapling. So they plant it and it takes about on average a number of years before it begins to bear fruit, they say it bears fruit. Now the palm is of many kinds: you have the Birḥi, the Khuḍhrāwi, Sa'amrān, Firsi and Gunṭār and also many other types which I do not know about. But the type which the people there plant mostly is the Sa'amrān because firstly they export much of it abroad. Firstly they work on them in a hut, cleaning them and opening them. Then they export them and the rest they sell [in the area], every day people come and buy them and eat them. But most of it they export abroad. Now there is the type of palm which bears fruit and then there is also the male palm. In every plot of land in which you see a hundred or two hundred palms, there is one male palm. Now when the palm begins to bring out buds, they let it bring out buds, then someone comes to pollinate them. He is called a *laggāḥchi*. A man, yes! He puts on his climbing belt and climbs up the palm. He cuts off a number of buds. Then he brings them and

1 Also *mhaffa*.

divides them up into parts. Then he climbs up the palm trees one by one and begins to pollinate them. How does he do this? The [female] bud is split open. He puts a little of it in the middle of it, that which he has brought from the male tree, a piece of it. And those which have not sprouted, he splits open by hand. Then it stays like that until the weather becomes warm, since the palm will not sprout if the weather is cold. Now when it begins to sprout, the bud as we call it / at first it sprouts a little and is green and small / this we call the *ḥabābōk*. We do not yet call it a date [*tamur*]. When it sprouts first, after it has been pollinated, it sprouts a little and stays like that for a while and is called *ḥabābōk*. Very small and slightly bitter and green in appearance. Next it grows until it becomes the *chimri*. This *chimri* is also like the *ḥabābōk* but rather larger. Next the *chimri* begins to turn yellow. It becomes yellow and then they call it the *hambūsh*. After this stage all of this green thing ripens and becomes yellow. When it is all yellow it is called *khlāl*. Now this yellow thing, when half of it, half of the *khlāl* has become *tamur* [i.e. brown in colour], this is what is called *ruṭab*, when it becomes moist [*yraṭṭib*]. This is half *khlāl* and half date [*tamur*]. Now when it has all become like a date, then they bring an assessor. This man assesses the plantation. Then they begin to cut it down. They cut down all of the dates. Each bunch is called an *'ithig*. I mean the date bunch altogether. Each stalk with dates on it is called *sharmūkh*, which joins the dates to each other. Then the *'ithig* [the bunch of stalks] is joined to something called the *'isga*. The thing that joins the *'ithig* to the palm trunk is called *'isga*. Now when the palm grows, it has on it fronds. This frond is like the feathers of a bird, but larger and it consists of individual leaves called *khūṣ*, in the singular *khūṣa*. Now the fronds, as the palm tree grows, the lower fronds begin to dry up. Then they can be cut off for firewood. Before I tell you about the palm fronds, let me say that as regards the palm tree, it is not that one can only make use of its fruit. One can use every member of the palm tree. Each part of the palm has many uses, and one can use it. For instance, as regards the date itself, after they have cut it down and taken it to the working shelter and have opened up the dates, then they take out the date pips. Now the dates are closed up again and sent abroad or whatever happens to them, but the pips and the *'inig*, the stalk joining the date to the *sharmūkh*, these are bought by people who give them as feed to their animals. And some people also grind them up for something, but I do not know what the result of this is. Or else, before they split open the dates they can put it into a place called a *mdibsa* [vat]. Here it ferments and date syrup is produced.

Now to return to the fronds, as they dry up, they cut them up into pieces. Each piece is called a *ṭaraf*. This *ṭaraf*, those who know about it, use it for firewood for baking or cooking or anything else. The palm fronds they cut and can weave them into mats or baskets or cloths [for eating off] or fans. Now the fronds, depending on their size, they can cut them off before they dry up and cut off all the leaves except those at the very tip. This is called a *nishshāsha* [switch] and can be used for shooing off cats or chickens or anything which comes near. Now the thing which joins the frond to the palm tree is the *kurba* [frond base]. The higher fronds stay on the palm. Then after a year or more when they have dried up someone goes up and prunes them off with a machete [*'akfa*]. He cuts off the frond base. These also are used for firewood and such uses. Now between the frond base and the palm trunk is the *līfa* [a fibrous substance]. One of the uses of this is that they make from it something like a cushion, called *skāra*. Yes, for the garden. When they plant tomatoes or cucumber they use it to block the water in one channel and lead it to the next, they use this *skāra*. Now we come to the *'isga*, the thing which joins the stalk bunch to the palm trunk. This they can soak in water and cut it and plait it together piece by piece and thenthey can make from this trays or bowls. If you bend it slightly like this it becomes a good substitute for a china tray, that is a *ṭubag* [tray]. The *guffa* [bowl] is slightly smaller. Now the trunk, if you do not want it, or if it gets too big, you can cut it down, and it also has uses.

Bibliography

ABBOUD, P.F. (1964), "The Syntax of Najdi Arabic, PhD Thesis, Austin, Texas.

ABBOUD, P.F. (1979), The verb in northern Najdi Arabic, "Bulletin of the School of Oriental and African Studies, XLII, 3, pp.467-499.

al-'AZZĀWI, A. (1956), "'Ashāir al-'Irāq", vol.I-IV, Baghdad.

BADAWI, M.M. (1965), "An Intonational Study of Riyadhi Arabic", PhD Thesis, London.

al-BADHDHĀL, Murshid ibn Sa'd (1975), "Dīwān", Kuwait.

BAILEY, C. (1974), Bedouin star-law in Sinai and the Negev, "Bulletin of the School of Oriental and African Studies, XXXVII, 3, pp.580-596.

BĀKALLA, M.H. (1975), "Bibliography of Arabic Linguistics", London.

BĀKALLA, M.H. (1979), "The Morphological and Phonological Component of the Arabic Verb", Beirut and London.

BARTH, F. (1961), "Nomads of South-West Persia", Oslo.

BARTH, F. (1964), Ethnic processes on the Pathan-Baluchi border, "Indo-Iranica mélanges présentés a Georg Morgen-stierne à l'occasion de son soixante-dixième anniversaire", Wiesbaden.

BELL, G. (1940), "The Arab War", London.

BERGSTRÄSSER, G. (1915), "Sprachatlas von Syrien und Paläs-tina", Leipzig.

BLANC, H. (1964), "Communal Dialects in Baghdad", Cambridge, Mass.

BLANC, H. (1970), The Arabic dialect of the Negev bedouins, "Proc. Israel Academy of Sciences and Humanities", iv, 7.

BLÜME, H. (1976), "Saudi Arabien, Natur, Geschichte, Mensch und Wirtschaft", Tübingen.

BLUNT, A. (1874), "Bedouins Tribes of the Euphrates", London.

de BODE, C.A. (1845), "Travels in Luristan and Arabistan", London.

BYNON, T. (1977), "Historical Linguistics", Cambridge.

CANTINEAU, J. (1936), Études sur quelques parlers de nomades arabes d'Orient, "Annales de l'Institut d'Études Orientales d'Alger", II, 1-118.
CANTINEAU, J. (1937), Études sur quelques parlers de nomades arabes d'Orient, "Annales de l'Institut d'Études Orientales d'Alger", III, 119-237.
CHATTY, Dawn (1978), "The current situation of the bedouin in Syria, Jordan and Saudi Arabia and their prospects for the future", paper presented at the Conference of the Commission on Nomadic peoples of the International Union of Anthropological and Ethnological Sciences, London.
CLARITY, B.E., Stowasser, K. and Wolfe, R.G. (ed.) (1964), "A Dictionary of Iraqi Arabic", Washington, DC.
CHRISTIAN, A.J. (1918), "A Report on the Tribes of Fars", Shiraz.
COLE, Donald P. (1975), "Nomads of the Nomads: The Āl Murrah Bedouin of the Empty Quarter", Chicago.
CZAPKIEWICZ, A. (1975), "The Verb in Modern Arabic Dialects as an Exponent of the Development Processes Occurring in Them", Warsaw.
al-DAWWĀY, Sālim ibn Tuwaim (1976), "Dīwān", Kuwait.
DENZ, A. (1971), Die verbalsyntax der neuarabischen dialektes von Kwayriš (Irak), "Abhandlungen für die künde des morgenländes", Wiesbaden.
DICKSON, H.R.P. (1949), "The Arab of the Desert", London.
DICKSON, H.R.P. (1956), "Kuwait and Her Neighbours", London.
DIEM, W. (1973), "Skizzen Jemenitischer Dialekte", Beirut, Wiesbaden.
DOUGHTY, Charles M. (1924), "Travels in Arabia Deserta", vol.II, London.
DOUGHTY, Charles M. (1964), "Travels in Arabia Deserta", vol.I (reprint), London.
EDZARD, D.O. (1967), Zum vokabular der Ma'dān Araber in südlichen Iraq, in G. Weissner (ed.), "Festschrift für Wilhelm Eilers", Wiesbaden, pp.305-17.
ERWIN, W.M. (1963), "Short Reference Grammar of Iraqi Arabic", Washington, DC.
FERNEA, C. (1970), "Shaykh and Effendi, Changing Patterns of Authority Among the El Shabana of Southern Iraq", Cambridge, Mass.
FIELD, H. (1939), "Contributions to the Anthropology of Iran", Chicago.
FIELD, H. (1949), "Anthropology of Iraq", I, 2, Chicago.
FISCHER, W. (1959), "Die Demonstrativen Bildungen der Neuarabischen Dialekte", The Hague.
GLUBB, J.B. (1960), "War in the Desert", London.
GLUBB, J.B. (1978), "Arabian Adventures", London.
GRANT, C.P. (1937), "The Syrian Desert, Caravans, Travel, Exploration", London.
GUMPERZ, J.J. (1962), Types of linguistic community, "Anthropological Linguistics", IV, 1, pp.28-40.

HANSMAN, J. (1967), Charax and the Karkheh,"Iranica Antiqua", VII, 27.
al-ḤAQĪL, Ḥamad ibn Ibrāhīm (1980), "Kanz al-Ansāb", Riyadh.
il-ḤĀZMI, A.M. (1975), "A Critical and Comparative Study of the Spoken Arabic of the Ḥarb Tribe in Saudi Arabia", PhD Thesis, Leeds.
HESS, J.J. (1938), "Von den Beduinen des Innerer Arabiens", Zürich/Leipzig.
HITTI, Ph.K. (1960), "History of the Arabs", London.
HOGARTH, D. (1904), "The Penetration of Arabia", London.
HOLES, C. (1980), Phonological variation in Baḥārna Arabic. The (j) and (y) allophones of (j), "Zeitschrift für Arabische Linguistik", IV, pp.72-89.
HYMAN, L.M. (1975), "Phonology", New York.
INGHAM, B. (1971), Some characteristics of Meccan speech, "Bulletin of the School of Oriental and African Studies", XXXIV, 2, pp.273-97.
INGHAM, B. (1973), Urban and rural Arabic in Khūzistān, "Bulletin of the School of Oriental and African Studies", XXXVI, 3, pp.533-53.
INGHAM, B. (1974), "The Phonology and Morphology of the Verbal Piece in an Arabic Dialect of Khūzistān", PhD Thesis, London.
INGHAM, B. (1976), Regional and social factors in the dialect geography of southern Iraq and Khūzistān,"Bulletin of the School of Oriental and African Studies", XXXIX, 1, pp.62-82.
INGHAM, B. (1979), Notes on the dialect of the Muṭair in Eastern Arabia, "Zeitschrift für Arabische Linguistik", II, pp.23-35.
INGHAM, B. (1980a),Najdi Arabic text, in O. Jastrow, "Handbuch der Arabische Dialectologie", Wiesbaden, pp.130-9.
INGHAM, B. (1980b),Languages of the Persian Gulf, in "The Persian Gulf States: A General Survey", Baltimore, Md., pp.314-333.
IVIĆ, P. (1962), On the structure of dialect differentiation, "Word", XVIII, pp.33-53.
IVIĆ, P. (1964), Structure and typology of dialect differentiation, "9th Intl. Congress of Linguists."
JASTROW, O. (1980), "Handbuch der Arabische Dialectologie", Wiesbaden.
JOHNSTONE, T.M. (1961), Some characteristics of the Dōsiri dialect of Arabic as spoken in Kuwait, "Bulletin of the School of Oriental and African Studies", XXIV, pp.249-297.
JOHNSTONE, T.M. (1963), The affrication of "kāf" and "qāf" in the Arabic dialects of the Arabian Peninsula, "Journal of Semitic Studies", viii, 2, pp.210-26.
JOHNSTONE, T.M. (1964), Further studies on the Dōsiri dialect of Arabic as spoken in Kuwait, "Bulletin of the School of Oriental and African Studies", XXXVII, pp.77-113.

JOHNSTONE, T.M. (1965), The sound change of j>y in the Arabic dialects of peninsular Arabia, "Bulletin of the School of Oriental and African Studies", XXXVIII, II, pp.233-41.
JOHNSTONE, T.M. (1967a), Aspects of syllabication in the spoken Arabic of 'Anaiza, "Bulletin of the School of Oriental and African Studies, XL, pp.1-16.
JOHNSTONE, T.M. (1967b), "Eastern Arabian Dialect Studies", London.
KATAKURA, M. (1977), "Bedouin Village", Tokyo.
KASRAVI, A. (1934), "Tārīkhe Pānsad Sāleye Khūzestān", Tehran.
KURATH, H. (1972), "Studies in Area Linguistics", Bloomington, Indiana.
LABOV, W. (1966), Hypercorrection by the lower middle class as a factor in linguistic change, in W. Bright (ed.), "Sociolinguistics", The Hague, pp.84-113.
LABOV, W. (1972), "Sociolinguistic Patterns", Philadelphia.
LAMBTON, A.K.S. (1953), "Landlord and Peasant in Persia", London.
de LANDBERG, C. (1919), "Langue des Bédouins 'Anazeh", Leide.
de LANDBERG, C. (1940), "Glossaire de la Langue des Bédouins 'Anazeh", Uppsala, Leipzig.
LAWRENCE, T.E. (1935), "The Seven Pillars of Wisdom", London.
LAYARD, H. (1846), Description of the province of Khuzistan, "Journal of the Royal Geographical Society", XVI, 1.
LEHN, W. (1967), Vowel contrasts in Najdi Arabic, in Don Graham Stuart (ed.), "Linguistic Studies in Memory of Richard Slade Harrel", Washington, pp.123-131.
LORIMER, D.L.R. (n.d.), "Notebook on the Arabic of Ahwaz", (unpublished manuscript).
LORIMER, J.G. (1908-15), "Gazetteer of the Persian Gulf, Oman and Central Arabia", Calcutta.
al-MĀNI', J. (1971), "Masīrah ila qabāil al- Ahwāz", Basra.
MARÇAIS, P. (1948), Articulation de l'emphase, "Annales de l'Institut des Études Orientals", VII, Algiers, p.5-28.
MARX, E. (1967), "Bedouin of the Negev", Manchester.
MARX, E. (1978), "Economic Change among Pastoral Nomads in the Middle East", paper presented at the Conference of the Commission on Nomadic Peoples of the International Union of Anthropological and Ethnological Sciences, London.
MEEKER, M.E. (1979), "Literature and Violence in North Arabia", Cambridge.
MEISSNER, B. (1903), Neuarabische Geschichten aus dem Iraq, "Beiträge zur Assyriologie und Semitischen Sprachwissenschaft", V, 1, pp.1-148.
MELAMID, A. (1970), Kharg Island, "The Geographical Review", LX, 3, pp.438-9.
MONTAGNE, R. (1935), Contes poétiques bédouins (réceuillies chez les Šammar de Ǵéziré), "Bulletin des Études Orientales", V, pp.33-119.

MONTAGNE, R. (1935-40), Le Ghazou de Šāye' Alemsāḥ (conte en dialecte des Šemmar du Neǧd, sous-tribu des Rmāl), "Melanges Maspéro", iii, Cairo, pp.411-16.
MOSCATI, et al. (1969), "A Comparative Grammar of the Semitic Languages", Wiesbaden.
MUKHLIṢ, Fāyiq Amīn (1964), "Studies in the Comparison of the Cycles of the Bani Hilāl Romance", PhD Thesis, London.
MUSIL, A. (1927), "The Middle Euphrates", New York.
MUSIL, A. (1928a), "The Manners and Customs of the Rwala Bedouins", New York.
MUSIL, A. (1928b), "Northern Neǧd", New York.
NIEBUHR, C. (1772), "Beschreibung von Arabien", Kopenhagen.
OPPENHEIM, M.v. (1939), "Die Beduinen", vol.i, Leipzig.
OPPENHEIM, M.v. (1943), "Die Beduinen", vol.ii, Leipzig.
OPPENHEIM, M.v. (1952), "Die Beduinen", vol.iii, Wiesbaden, (ed. W. Cashel).
PALGRAVE, W.G. (1865), "Narrative of a Year's Journey through Central and Eastern Arabia (1862-3)", London and Cambridge, 2 vols.
PALMER, F.R. (1965), "A Linguistic Study of the English Verb", London.
PERRY, J.R. (1971), The Banu Ka'b: an amphibious brigand state in Khuzistan, in J. Aubin (ed.), "Le Monde Iranien et l'Islam", I, Genève, Paris, pp.131-52.
PHILBY, H.St.J. (1922), "The Heart of Arabia", London, I&II.
PHILBY, H.St.J. (1955), "Sa'udi Arabia", London.
PROCHAZKA, Th. (1977), Architectural terminology of the Saudi-Arabian south-west, "Arabian Studies", IV, pp.118-29.
PROCHAZKA, Th. (198?) The Shi'i dialects of Baḥrain and their relationship to the Eastern Arabian dialects of Muḥarreq and the Omani dialect of Al-Ristāq, "Zeitschrift für Arabische Linguistik", to appear.
QAFISHEH, H.A. (1976), "A Basic Course in Gulf Arabic", Tucson, Arizona.
RASWAN, C.R. (1930), Migration lines of north Arabian bedouin tribes, "The Geographical Review", July.
RASWAN, C.R. (1935), "The Black Tents of Arabia", London.
SALIM, S.M. (1962), "Marsh Dwellers of the Euphrates Delta", London.
SĀMMARRĀI, I. (1968), "al-Tawzī' al-Lughawi fi l-'Irāq", Baghdad.
SA'RĀN, M.H.A. (1951), "A Critical Study of the Observations of the Arab Grammarians", PhD Thesis, London.
al-SĀSI, Omar (1972), "Sprichtwörter und Andere Volkskündliche Texte aus Mekka", Mekka.
SCHREIBER, G. (1971), "Der Arabische Dialekt von Mekka", Freiburg in Breisgau.
SIENY, M. (1972), "The Syntax of Urban Hijazi Arabic", PhD Thesis, Ann Arbor, Michigan.
SĪRAT, 'Abd al-Sattār (1961), Nakhostin tahqiqe, Arabiye 'Āmiyāne dar havāliye Balkh, "Majalleye Adab Kābul", I.

SOCIN, A. (1900-01), "Diwan aus Centralarabien", Leipzig.
STANKIEWITZ, W. (1957), On discreteness and continuity in structural dialectology, "Word", XIII.
STOCQUELER, J.H. (1832), "Fifteen Months' Pilgrimage Through Untrodden Tracts of Khuzistan and Persia", London.
al-SUDAIRI, Muḥammad ibn Aḥmad (1968), "Abṭāl min al-ṣaḥrā", Beirut.
al-SUDAIRI, Muḥammad ibn Aḥmad (1974), "al-Dam'a al-ḥamrā", Jidda.
al-TĀJIR, M. (1979), "A Critical and Comparative Study of the Baharna Dialect of Arabic as Spoken in Present-Day Bahrain", PhD Thesis, Leeds.
THESIGER, W. (1964), "The Marsh Arabs", London.
TRAGER, G.L. and Smith Jr., H.L. (1951), "An Outline of English Structure", Studies in Linguistics, Occasional Papers 3, Norman, Okla.
TRUDGILL, P. (1978), "Sociolinguistic Patterns in British English", London.
TRUDGILL, P. and FOXCROFT (1978), On the sociolinguistics of vocalic mergers: transfer and approximation in East Anglia, in Trudgill (ed.) "Sociolinguistic Patterns in British English", Edward Arnold, London.
TSERETELI, G.V. (1956), "Arabske Dialektuy Srednei Azii", Tiflis.
al-'UBAYYID, A.R.A.K. (1971), "Qabīlat al-'Awāzim", Beirut.
WAKELIN, M.F. (1972), "The English Dialects", London.
WEINREICH, U. (1954), Is a structural dialectology possible?, "Word", X, pp.300-340.
WEINREICH, U. (1970), "Languages in Contact", The Hague.
WEISSBACH, F.H. (1930), "Beiträge zur Künde des Irak-Arabischen", Leipzig.
WESTPHAL-HELLBUSCH and Westphal, H. (1962), "Die Ma'dan, Kultur und Geschichte der Marschen Bewöhner", Berlin.
WETZSTEIN, I.G. (1868), Sprachliches aus den Zeltlagern der Syrischen Wüste, "Zeitschrift der Deutschen Morganländische Gesellschaft", XXII, pp.69-164.
WILSON, A. (1941), "S.W. Persia, a Political Officer's Diary 1907-14", Oxford.
WILSON, A.T. (1911), "Précis of the Relations of the British Government with the Tribes and Shaikhs of Arabistan", Bushire.
WIRTH, E. (1962), "Agrargeographie des Irak", Hamburg.
YASSIN, M.A.F. (1977), Bipolar terms of address in Kuwaiti Arabic, "Bulletin of the School of Oriental and African Studies", XL, 2.

Index

This index is designed to supplement the contents page and lists references to names of persons, localities and tribes occurring in the text. It also lists linguistic topics not included in the contents.

-ā (pl. suffix), 132
'Abaćli ibn Fāliḥ, 133
'Abbādān, 22, 173, 185
'Abda, 70, 86, 131
Abu al-Khaṣīb, 19, 185
'Abūda, 25
active, 41-53
Afghanistan, 3
'agāl, 23, 24, 66
-ah (3rd m.s. suffix), 120
-ah (fem. suffix), 67, 71, 139
Ahl Gibly, 12
Ahl al-Shimāl, 12, 60-62, 65, 67-69, 73, 77, 80, 82, 85-87, 89, 92-93, 136, 142-6
Ahwaz, 22, 66, 68, 80, 82, 147, 167, 169, 183, 184
Aja, 9
al-Ajfar, 131
'Ajmān (more accurately 'Ujmān), 12, 15, 31, 65, 88-9, 96, 98, 103-6, 125
'Ajmi (see 'Ajmān)
Ajwad, 65
'Alya, 111, 129, 154-8
-am (suffix), 76, 120
'Amāra, 17, 19, 22, 66, 80, 84, 92, 93, 162-6, 176, 183
'Amārāt, 11, 30, 48, 68, 74
'Amr, Bani, 77, 106
-an (suffix, in Classical), 53, 55, 56
-an (suffix, = -ni), 68, 71, 74, 139
-an (suffix, = ana), 68, 83, 151, 178
'Anaiza, 45
analogical change, 63, 74-6
anaptyctic vowels, 56-62, 143
anhār (sing.: nahr), 19
'Aniza, 9, 11, 14, 16, 30, 46, 48, 56, 61, 63, 66, 68-9, 72-4, 76, 79, 80, 83, 86-8, 91-101, 102, 116-19, 144
'Arai'ir, Āl, ibn- (more accurately 'Urai'ir), 65, 142-6
al-'Āriḍh, 15, 22, 23, 73, 106
'Arma plateau, 65
Asad, Bani, 25
'Asākira, 182
'Aṣīr (dialect), 45
Aslam, 139
-at (suffix), 70, 132
'Awāja, 48, 55, 61, 69, 88-9, 91, 94

'Awāzim, 12, 31,59, 60-1, 73, 76-7, 88-9, 91-6, 98, 99, 101, 120-30
-āy (f.pl. suffix), 69, 70, 71, 75-6
Azīrij, 19

bādiya, 15, 20, 33, 51-2, 72, 80, 97, 170, 185
al-Bag'a, 131
Baghdad, 17, 38, 51, 80
Ba'gūba, 17, 147
Baḥārna, 23-5, 31
Bahrain, 19, 24-5, 31, 34, 38-9, 51, 96
Bakhtiari, 182
Bandar Maḥshūr, 183
Bandar Shāpūr, 183
Barhān, 182
Basra, 12, 17, 22, 25, 27, 38, 72, 147, 185
Baṭḥa, 21, 26, 35
Bāṭin, 30
Bāwiya, 173, 182, 183
Bāzaid (see Zaid, Abu)
"bedouin" speech characteristics, 31, 61, 69
Birkat Bghadād, 19
-bl- (particle), 131
border dialects, 27
Borujerd, 182
Bu'aij (more accurately Bu'aiy), 136
Budūr, 8, 21, 49, 69, 77, 80, 82-7, 92, 167
Buraida, 16
burgu', 88
Butaira, 80
Buṭūn, 21

causative verb type, 39-40, 53, 109
chaffiyya, 23
Chawādir, 147
Chibāyish, 19, 80
cisterns, water, 72
Classical Arabic, 42-3, 53-4, 56
communication structure, 29
complexity, linguistic, 63
conservatism, linguistic, 35
consonant clusters, 56, 59-62
"core" dialects, 26-9

-d̲a, d̲i (demonstrative pronoun), 92-3, 104, 113
d(i) (verbal prefix), 151
Damīr al-'Āyid, 84
Dammām, 22
Darb Zubaida, 63, 72
Dasht Mīshān, 175, 176
Dawāsir, 12, 14-16, 58, 88-9, 92-3, 96, 98-100, 103, 109
Dhabīḥa and Manīḥa, 144
Ḍhafīr, 8, 11-13, 16, 20-2, 30, 48, 52, 56, 59, 61, 63, 65-9, 73-4, 76, 79, 81, 84, 87-9, 91-100, 101, 131, 142
Ḍhahrān, 22, 84
dhow, 19
dialect area, 27, 28, 77
dīra (tribal area), 9, 12, 63, 73, 100, 110, 114, 138
Dīwāniyya, 80
Dōsiri (see Dawāsir)
dress, 24, 66
duwāb, 20

-ē- (infix), 39
ē~ī contrast, 80, 168, 170, 175
Eastern Region, 15
'ēb (negative particle), 173, 175
-eih (form of fem. suffix), 69, 75-6
emigration (from Najd), 11, 13, 15
Euphrates, 9, 10, 17, 19, 20-3, 26, 30, 35, 63, 65-6, 72, 74, 80, 83, 142, 144
Euphrates bedouin, 20-2, 52, 56, 62, 65, 67-9, 73-4, 77, 79, 80, 82, 84, 88, 92-3, 95-6, 99, 101, 139

fad/farid, 56
Fad'ān, 144
faiḍhāt, 8
Failaka (or Failiča), 29, 89
Failiyya, 183
family tree (Stammbaum) theory, 30
Fao, 19, 83, 185
fellāḥ, 16
fringe dialects, 65, 66
fronting of kāf and qāf, 95-6, 112
Fuhūd, 19, 80

Gachsārān, 170-2
gaṣīda, 2, 135, 139
Gāyid, ibn, 141
Gḥaṭān (see also Qaḥṭān), 109-11
Gḥaṭān, Ḥasāt, 111
Ghizya (see Jash'am)
Ghubaish, Āl bu, 178
ghutra, 23, 66
glottal stop, xv
grazing, 9, 13-15
Gulf dialects, 49, 50, 52, 77, 82, 88, 95-6, 98, 100
Gurna, 80

ḥaḍhar, 52, 185
ḥadra, 10
Ḥafar al-Bāṭin, 8, 9, 12, 102
Hail, 16, 45, 65, 69, 72, 88, 131
Haj road, 72
Ḥajara, 63
Hājiri, 90, 93
Hakar, 21
Ḥalfāya, 19
ḥamḍh (ḥamaḍhāt), 21, 109
Ḥarb, 8, 59, 60, 66-7, 70, 73, 76-7, 83, 88-9, 91-6, 98-9, 101, 102, 107, 112-15
al-Hasa, 15, 19, 22, 24-5, 31, 34-5, 38, 49, 65, 72, 98, 105, 144
Haur al-Ḥammār, 9, 20, 35
Haur al-Ḥuwaiza, 20, 35, 176, 177
al-Ḥauṭa, 35
ḥauz, 19
Ḥauz 'Abd al-'Azīz al-Rāshid, 19
Hebrew, 75
-hi for -ha, 148
Ḥiblān, 88
Hijaz, Hijazi, 44, 66, 72-4, 77, 88-9, 92, 95, 102, 182, 183
Hilāl, Bani (literature), 11, 111, 129, 139-41, 147, 162
Ḥilla, 17, 26-7, 49, 139
Ḥimyar, 140
Ḥuchaim, Bani, 30
Hufūf, 22
Ḥumaid, 8, 20-1, 49-50, 59-60, 62, 65, 82, 83, 85, 87, 89, 136, 142
Ḥumaid, ibn, 11, 90, 109-11
Ḥuwaiṭāt, 133
Ḥuwaiza, 80, 173, 175, 181

i/a contrast (in open syllables), 47, 142, 167, 185
idiosyncratic type, 63
-ih for -ah (fem. suffix), 69, 136, 148
impersonal verbs, 47
-in (suffix, tanwīn, nunation), 34-5, 53-6, 112, 118, 121, 143
internal passive, 33, 39, 41, 81-2, 132, 152, 174
internal vowel morphology (of the verb), 33, 39-43
interrogative sentences, 79
intransitive verb type, 39-41, 53
Iran, 34, 176, 177, 183, 184
Iraq, 20, 22, 24, 176, 182, 183
'Īsa, Āl, 20
isogloss, 26-7, 77-9, 87

j>y sound change, 26, 30-1, 142, 143, 162, 177
Jabal Shammar, 9, 15, 16, 22, 23, 63, 72-4, 88

Jabal Ṭuwaiq, 72
Jahra, 9
Jarba, 65, 72, 74
Jarrāḥi, 17, 22, 181
Jash'am, 20, 142-6
al-Jauf, 66
Jawāsim (or Źawāsim), 20
Jazīra, 63, 72
Jūkha, 110

-k and -ć (suffixes), 31, 74, 96-8, 120
Ka'b, 19, 23-4, 172, 178-84, 185
-kam, -ham (suffixes), 68-9, 71, 74-6, 167
Karbala, 19, 20
Karkha, 176
Kārūn, 17, 22, 92, 172, 183, 185
Kathīr, Āl, 65
Kawāwila (gypsies), 49-52, 81, 86-7, 90, 100, 147-61, 166, 171
Khafāya, 19
Khafājiyya (more accurately Khafāyiyya), 173, 175
Khaibar, 14
Khālid, Bani, 8, 15, 49-50, 65-8, 73, 79, 87-8, 92, 95, 142, 144
Khalīfa, Āl, 24
Khamīsiyya, 9
Khamseh, 17
Khanāfira, 182
Khaur Bahmanshīr, 19, 183, 184
Khaur Mūsa, 182
Khaz'al, Shaikh, 176, 177, 178, 184
Khazraj and Chināna, 176, 177
Khorramshahr, 19, 22, 80, 177, 182, 185
Khruṣa, 86
khuffiyyāt, 8
Khuzistan, 17, 20, 22-4, 34-5, 38-9, 51, 80, 88, 90, 92-3, 167, 168, 170, 175, 178, 182, 183, 184
Koiné, 2
Kurds, 17, 172
Kūt, 17, 19, 26, 35, 66, 68
Kūt Sayyid 'Anāya, 81, 83, 167-9
Kuwait, 15, 19, 23-5, 30-1, 38, 49-50, 61, 65, 72-3, 84, 86, 93-4, 100, 116, 120, 130, 144
Kwida, 21

la- (prefix), 149, 153
Lām, Bani, 14
lexical distinctions, 77, 86-7, 91, 100-1
Līna, 63
linguistic change, 63
liquid consonants, 57
Lurs, 170, 182

ma' or mi' (meaning "in"), 85, 93, 131
Maarib dam, 13
Madāin Ṣāliḥ, 116
Madina, 30, 73, 112, 114
majhūr, 58
Manāḍhra, 76
marshdwellers (see also Mi'dan), 136
marshland, 79
Mas'ūd, Shammar, 139-41, 102
Mawāli, 87
Māy'a, 19
Mecca, 14, 72-3
Mecca, dialect of, 35, 37-8
merger (phonological), 36-7, 63
Mesopotamia(n), 17, 40, 44, 59, 77, 97-8, 83
Mḥirzi, 185-9
Mi'dān (also Mi'aidi), 11, 19-20, 30, 61, 80, 83, 173, 175, 177
Midhnab, 40, 45-6, 79, 142
Mintifij (see Muntafiq)
mobilisation, 34
morphological distinctions, 79
Mubārak al-Hīm, 125
Muḥaisin, 19, 177, 178, 182, 185

Muḥammad, Āl bu, 19, 118
Muḥammara (Khorramshahr), 183
Muntafiq (see also Euphrates bedouin), 30, 65, 142, 144
Muraikh, battle of, 125
Murra, Āl, 12, 15
musābila, 10
Musayyab, 17
Muṭair, 8, 12-6, 30-1, 56, 60-1, 65-6, 69, 73-4, 76-7, 81-2, 88-90, 92-9, 101, 107-11, 167
Muṭūr, 178, 185
Muwāhib, 116

Nafūd, 9, 15, 22, 63, 73, 131
Najaf, 10, 11, 19, 26, 30, 63, 72, 80
Najd, 16, 17, 37-8, 40, 83
Najd, Western, 30, 73
Najdi/bedouin identity, 45, 54
Najrān, 15, 103
-nan (suffix), 68, 71, 74
narrative imperative, 132, 143, 164
Nāṣir, Āl, 182, 183
Nāṣiriyya, 8, 11, 17, 19, 20-2, 30, 69, 80, 136, 142, 167
negative construction with bi-, 94, 113
Negev bedouin, 80, 82, 87, 92-3, 98, 107, 148
neogrammarians, 26
nomads, 7-11, 13
non-territorial distribution, 77

Old Arabic, 39-40
Oman, 88
Ottomans (see also Turks), 24

passive (see internal passive)
Persian (race), 34, 172
Persian (vocabulary), 99, 167, 168, 170, 174, 178, 179, 180, 186
phonological distinctions, 77-9
poetry, 49, 61
population movement, 11, 12, 13-17, 73, 77
Portuguese, 183

Qaḥṭān (see also Għaṭān), 14, 15
Qarāmiṭa, 24
Qash'am (see Jash'am)
Qaṣīm, 14-15, 22-3, 40-1, 56, 65, 67-9, 72-3, 77, 81-2, 84, 88-9, 92-9, 101
Qaṭar, 24
Qaṭari, 58, 93
Qaṭīf, 22
Qubān, 182, 183
Quṣba, 183, 185
Quṣmān, 65

Rashāyida, 12, 31, 61, 73, 76-7, 88-9, 92, 95-9, 120
Rashīd, house of, 131
Rashīd, Ibn, 10, 16-17, 65
Rauḍhatain, 8, 107
reductional change, 33-62, 95
redundant feature, 33-4
relic area, 65
Riyadh, 77, 89, 92-6, 98-100, 109
riyāḍh, 8, 113
routes, 72
Rub' al-Khāli, 15, 22
Rufai', 8, 20-1, 49, 50, 59, 62, 65, 80, 82-7, 89, 93, 136-8, 142
Ruwala, 59, 66, 69, 74, 76, 82

-š (negative suffix), 30
Sā'da, 136
Ṣafwān, 16
Saif, Āl, 15
Sājir al-Rfidi, 46
Salām, 19
Ṣakhar, Bani, 66-7, 73
Ṣāliḥ, Āl bu, 8, 19, 20
Sālim, Bani, 77

Salma, 9
Samāwa, 11, 21, 30, 63, 80, 144
Ṣannā', 10
Sardiyya, 35, 66, 73
Sa'ūd, house of, 12, 17
Ṣāyiḥ, 136
Ṣayyāḥ, Bait, 173
Sba'a, 30, 46, 48, 52, 59, 69, 74, 76, 79, 81-3, 88-91, 93, 97, 99, 116
Shādigān (Fallāḥiyya), 19, 80, 178, 181, 183, 184
Shammar, 8, 10-12, 16, 21, 30, 45-6, 52, 55-6, 58, 60-3, 65-6, 69-70, 72-4, 76, 80-1, 84, 86, 88-99, 101, 131-5, 136, 139-41, 142, 144
Shaṭra, 19
Shaṭṭ al-'Arab, 17, 19, 22-5, 34, 39-40, 42, 51, 72, 80, 92, 100, 149, 178, 185, 186
Shaṭṭ al-Gharrāf, 9
Shawāya (see Shāwiya)
Shāwiya, 21, 30, 142
shepherd tribes (see also Shāwiya), 21, 30, 52, 62
shewa, 58
Shi'a (also Shi'ite), 21-2, 24-5, 30, 35, 37-9, 51, 96, 136
Shibića, 12
Shilgān, 12, 131, 133-5
shmāgh, 23
Shu'aibāt (Shu'aibāy), 8, 131
Shuṭaiṭ, 172
Shūyān (see Shāwiya)
Sība, 19, 185
Sibila, 16
simplification (of syllabic structure), 44
Sinjāra, 8, 12, 133
slave population, 34-5
Ṣmida, 16, 21
sociosymbolic, 54
sound shifts (phonology), xv
standard dialect, 34
stress, 58, 60
Ṣubāḥ, Āl, 24, 130
Subai', 15, 105, 106
Sudair, 15-16, 45-6, 54-6, 61, 70, 77, 79, 82, 84-5, 89, 92, 94-9, 101, 103, 150
Sudair, Āl, 15, 22
Sūdān, 136
Ṣufairi, 8, 12
Ṣugūr, 69, 88-90, 93
Sunni, 25, 30
Sūq al-Gharrāf, 19, 20
Sūq al-Shuyūkh, 80
Sūsangard (Khafāyiyya), 173, 175, 176
syllable structure, 34, 44, 58
syntactic distinctions, 79
Syria, 44, 72-4, 116
Syria, Lebanon, Palestine, Jordan (dialects of), 66
Syrian desert, 13, 33-5, 48, 61, 63, 65-6, 68, 72-4, 76, 80-1, 83, 93, 96

Taima, 63
ṭa'ṭi'ōh, 24
al-Ṭayyār, Kan'ān, 11
Thāni, Āl, 24
Tigris, 17, 22, 26, 35, 65, 80
transitional dialects, 28-9
transitivity system, 33, 39-53
Tūmān, 11
al-Ṭumār, 19
Turks, Turkey, Turkish, 17, 105, 170, 183, 186
Ṭuruf, Bani, 167, 170, 173-7
Ṭuwāl al-Ḍhafīr, 9
Ṭuwāl Mutair, 9

ū~ō contrast, 117
-u(h) (3rd per. suffix), 31, 66-7, 71, 74-6, 98, 139
Umm al-'Aish, 8, 142
'Umūr, Slūṭ, Sirḥān, 66-8, 73, 76, 83, 87
'Utaiba, 12, 14-15, 58, 70, 72, 76, 79, 88-9, 96-8, 109-11

'Uwairiḍh, Ḥarrat, 116
'Uzair, 19

verbal measures, 40, 42, 82,
  103-4
vocalic transition, 58-9
vowel shortening, 103-4, 112

Wādi al-Risha, 136, 109-10
Wādi Turmus, 8, 77, 131
Washm, 22
wave theory, 30
Wild 'Ali, 74, 93
Wild Sulaimān, 74, 88

Yaman, 1, 13, 72
yō for yā, 143

-ž for j, 30, 112, 162, 175,
  177
Zaid, Abu (also Bāzaid), 111,
  129, 153-4, 157-61
Zaitān, 172
Zanāti (Khalīfa), 111
Zayyād, 21, 79, 80, 83
zone of communication, 22
Zubair, 9, 11, 19, 27, 30,
  38, 72, 82-4, 87, 89,
  92-4
Zuhairiyya, 82, 167, 169

Glossary of technical terms

حالة المفعولية	accusative
المبني للمعلوم (الفعل)	active
المخاطب	addressee
الظرفي	adverbial
الاثبات	affirmative
الانفجاري الاحتكاكي (الصوت)	affrication
الصائت الزائد (للتخلص من التقاء الساكنين)	anaptyctic
المماثلة/الادغام	assimilation (phonological)
التجانس	assimilation (non-linguistic)
نظام الحالات الاعرابية (في النحو)	case system
الجَعل/التسبيب	causative
الانشطار/الانشقاق	cleavage
متدرّج/سلّمي	clinal
العنقود الصوتي (النهائي)	cluster (final)
المشتركات اللفظية	cognate
المعقد/المركب	complex
تصريف الافعال	conjugation
المحافظ	conservative
الصامت	consonant
منطقة المركز/منطقة مركزية	core area
صفات مميزة	defining characteristic
وظيفة الإشارة (إلى وقت ومكان وقوع الحدث)	deictic function

اسم الإشارة	demonstrative
الفونولوجيا الاشتقاقية	derivational phonology
منطقة اللهجة	dialect area
الصائت المركب	diphthong
المخالفة/التخالف	dissimilation
التكافؤ التوزيعي	distributional equivalent
المفعول الدمية (ضمير المفعول غير العائد إلى شيء معين)	dummy object
الجزء (الوظيفي)/زوال	eclipse (functional)
يحذف	elide
الاستنطاق	elicitation
الإسقاط/الحذف	elision
الانكليف (منطقة جغرافية تابعة لغوياً وليس سياسياً لبلد ما)	enclave
الانضوائي	enclitic
البيئة/السياق	environment
فعل الوجد/الكينونة	existential verb
نظرية شجرة العائلة اللغوية (في علم اللغة التاريخي)	Family tree theory
الفعل الناقص	Finally weak verbs
أصناف الصيغة	form classes
لهجات طرفية (ليس لها كل صفات المجموعة	fringe dialects
التقديم (تحرك الصوائت من موقع خلفي إلى موقع أمامي)	fronting
الانصهار	fusion
التضعيف	gemination
الجنس	gender
الصائت الانزلاقي	gliding vowel
الحلقي	gutteral
الفعل الاجوف	Hollow verb
الحذلقة	hypercorrection
الانفرادي	idiosyncratic
النكرة	indefinite

indefinite marker	علامة التنكير
instability	عدم الثبات
instrumental preposition	حرف الجر الآلي (الدال على الوسيلة)
interrogative	الاستفهامي
interrogative complex	المركب الاستفهامي
interlocutor	المتكلم
internal (to the stem)	الداخلي (داخل الجذع)
internal passive	صيغة المجهول الداخلية (التي تعتمد على تغير الحركات داخل الكلمة)
internal vowelling	حركات داخلية (داخل جذع الكلمة)
intransitive	اللازم (الفعل)
inventory	مجموع الوحدات (اللغوية)
isogloss	الايسوگلوس (الخط الفاصل لِلّهجات)
juncture	الوقفة
jurative	الصيغة القَسِميّة (الدالة على القسم أو الحلف)
levelling	التنظيم (على أساس القياس)/التبسيط
lexeme	المفردة
lexical derivation	الاشتقاق المعجمي (اشتقاق المفردات)
lexical usage	الاستعمال المعجمي
linguistic change	التغير اللغوي
liquid	حروف الذلاقة
locative preposition	حرف الجر المكاني
marking	التأشير (وجود أو وضع علامة للدلالة على معنى)
Measures of the verb	أوزان الفعل
merger	الدمج/الاندماج
morpheme	المورفيم/الوحدة الصرفية
multivalency	متعدد الدلالة (أو القيمة أو الوظيفة)
negative particle	أداة النفي
non-conditioning environment	السياق الحر (غير المشروط)
non-obligatory	غير الالزامي
non-structural	غير البنيوي

التوزيع اللااقليمي (غير الجغرافي)	non-territorial distribution
ضمير المفعول	object suffix
جدول التصريف	paradigm
الحَدّ/العامل	parameter
اسم الفاعل أو المفعول به	participle
الأداة	particle
المبني للمجهول	passive
المفعول الباطني (الحالة النحوية للمفعول به المتأثر بحدث الفعل في البنية العميقة	patient
حالة الوقف	pausal position
التام (الفعل)	perfective
الهامش	periphery
التكييف الفونولوجي	phonological conditioning
الفونولوجيا (دراسة النظام الصوتي)	phonology
حرف الجر	preposition
الملمح السيادي	prestige marking feature
اللاحقة الضمير	pronoun suffix
الصائت المحض	pure vowel
العنصر المعدّل (كالصفة)	qualifying element
الأصل/الجذر	radical
التحقيق (بالنطق الفعلي)	realisation
الاختزال	reduction
التغير الاختزالي	reductional change
الملمح الحشوي	redundant feature
السليلة	reflex
المطاوَعة	reflexive
المنظّم/الاطّرادي	regularising
إطلاق الصامت	release of a consonant
المنطقة اللغوية المحافظة	relic area
نظام الإبقاء/المحافظة	retaining system
الإبقاء/المحافظة	retention

النحت	sandhi
الانتشار	scatter
دلالي	semantic
الشوا	shewa
اجتماعي لغوي	sociolinguistic
المكوّن الوحيد	sole constituent
الرنّان	sonorant
التحول الصوتي	sound shift
الانشطار	split
غير المطّرِد	sporadic
الجذع	stem
النبر	stress
المنبور	stressed
الفعل السالم/الصحيح	Strong verb
الضغط البنيوي	structural pressure
الزائدة الدالة على الفاعل	subject affix
اللاحقة	suffix
الاشتقاق الظاهر (السطحي)	surface derivation
التقطيع	syllabication
المقطع	syllable
بنية المقطع	syllable structure
النظمي (الخاص بنَظم الكلام)	syntactic
الكتابة الصوتية	transcription
المنطقة الانتقالية	transitional area
المتعدّي	transitive
نظام التعدية	transitivity system
النقل الكتابي	transliteration
عنقود الصوامت الثلاثي	triconsonantal cluster
الفونولوجيا العميقة	underlying phonology
غير المعَلَّم	unmarked
غير المنبور	unstressed

valency	ذو قيمة أو عمل (وظيفي)
variable	متغيّر
verbal inflection	التصريف في الافعال
vocalic transition	الانتقال الصائتي
vocalisation	التصويت (تحويل الصامت إلى صائت أو المهموس إلى مجهور)
voiced plosive	(الصوت) الانفجاري المجهور
voiceless	المهموس (الصوت)
Wave theory (Wellentheorie)	نظرية الموجة (اللغوية)

تقديم

للعرب والمسلمين الأوائل باع طويل في ميدان الدراسات اللغوية أو اللسانية. فقد شهدت القرون الأربعة الأولى من ظهور ديننا الحنيف اهتماماً كبيراً ومتزايداً في هذا المجال درساً وبحثاً وتأليفاً. ولا تزال أسماء كثير من العلماء الأوائل ممن ندين لهم بالسبق والريادة مشهورة ولا تزال أعمالهم موضع الدراسة والبحث في الجامعات الشرقية والغربية. ومن أشهر هؤلاء الاعلام النابغين الخليل بن أحمد الفراهيدي الأزدي، وتلميذه سيبويه، وأبو عثمان المازني، والمبرد، وأبو علي القالي، وابن دريد، والكسائي، والفراء، وثعلب، وابن قتيبة، وابن فارس، وأبو حنيفة الدينوري، وأبو علي الفارسي، وأبو الفتح عثمان بن جني.

مساهمة العرب المسلمين في الدراسات اللهجية

وعلى الرغم من أن الدراسات اللغوية انصبّت أساساً على اللغة الفصحى، فإن هنالك ملاحظات كثيرة جداً وردت في ذكر اللهجات العربية آنذاك. ومن المراجع الأساسية في دراسة اللهجات العربية كتب المعاجم واللغة، وكتب النحو والصرف والقراءات. وكتب تقويم اللسان والفصاحة. ولم يقدر لهذه الدراسات أن تنفصل كعلم مستقل كما حدث لعلوم النحو والصرف والبلاغة وغيرها. على الرغم من توفر إمكانيات الدراسة ووسائلها في ذلك الوقت كالرحلات الميدانية إلى القبائل والاهتمام بالدراسات اللفظية والصوتية والدلالية والبحث فيها، على أسس علمية ثابتة.

ومن الجدير بالملاحظة أن لفظة «لهجة» لم تستخدم في كتب اللغويين الأوائل بنفس الدلالة والتردد. فقد كان المستعمل آنذاك مصطلح «لسان» بمعنى اللغة Language في عصرنا، في حين أن كلمة «لغة» استخدمت في ذلك الوقت غالباً للدلالة على اللهجة Dialect بمفهومها المعاصر. وتعرّف اللهجة بأنها «مجموع الخصائص المشتركة التي تميّز بيئة جغرافية ما عن البيئات الأخرى المجاورة». وقد وصلتنا كتب كثيرة تستخدم لفظة «اللغات» بمعنى اللهجات. ومنها كتاب «اللغات في القرآن: من رواية ابن حسنون المقرىء باسناده إلى ابن عباس» من تحقيق صلاح الدين المنجد (الطبعة الثالثة، بيروت: دار الكتاب الجديد، ١٩٧٨م). وقد صدرت الطبعة الأولى منه عن مطبعة الرسالة في القاهرة عام ١٩٤٦م. ويحتوي هذا الكتاب على مسرد لبعض الالفاظ التي وردت في القرآن الكريم مع اسنادها إلى لهجات القبائل التي تستعملها. ونورد هنا نصاً جاء في صفحتي ٢٠ – ٢١ ويشتمل على الالفاظ الواردة في سورة آل عمران.

سورة آل عمران

«قوله عز وجل: «كدأب آل فرعون» – يعني كأشباه آل فرعون بلغة جرهم.

قوله: «سيّداً وحصوراً» – يعني بالسيّد الحليم بلغة حمير والحصور الذي لا حاجة له في النساء بلغة كنانة.

«كونوا ربّانيين» – يعني علماء. وافقت لغة السريانية. «تَدّخرون» – بلغة كنانة.

«وأخذتم على ذلكم إصري» – يعني عهدي. وافقت لغة النبطية.

«يتلون آيات الله آناء الليل» – يعني ساعات الليل بلغة هذيل. وكذلك في سورة طه «ومِن آناء الليل» – يعني ساعات الليل.

«لا يألونكم خبالاً» – يعني غيّاً بلغة عمان.

«إذ همّت طائفتان منكم أن تفشَلا» – يعني تجبنا بلغة حِمير.

«يأتونكم من فورهم هذا» – يعني من وجوههم بلغة هذيل وقيس عيلان وكنانة.

«ولا تَهِنوا» – يعني تضعوا بلغة قريش. وكذلك في سورة محمد (صلى الله عليه وسلم): «فلا تَهِنوا وتدعوا إلى السلم» – يعني لا تضعفوا أيضاً بلغة كنانة.

«يمسسكم قَرح» – القَرح (الجرح، قَرح) بلغة الحجاز وقرع بلغة تميم.

«رِبّيون كثير» – يقول رجال كثير بلغة حضرموت.»

ونلاحظ هنا الإشارة إلى اللهجات (اللغات) العربية في ذلك الوقت بالإضافة إلى إشارات عابرة عن اللغات (الاستخدام هنا مجازي) غير العربية الفصحى كالنبطية وحمير والسريانية. ويكفي هذا دليلاً على اهتمام الصحابي الجليل عبدالله بن عباس رضي الله عنه والسلف الصالح بتدوين هذه الملاحظات الدقيقة عن لغات ذلك العصر ولهجاتها مما لا يستغني عنه الباحث الحديث الذي يرغب في ربط الحاضر بالماضي، واللهجات المعاصرة باللهجات القديمة، والمجتمعات المعاصرة بالمجتمعات السابقة.

ابن جني ودراسة اللهجات

يعد أبو الفتح عثمان بن جني (ت ٣٩٢هـ) من أوائل العلماء الذين حاولا وضع أسس للدراسات اللهجية التي يمكن تطبيقها ليس على اللغة العربية وحدها وإنما على اللغات الأخرى أيضاً. فقد تناول ابن جني أبحاثاً لهجية مختلفة في كتبه كَسِرّ الصناعة (سر صناعة الاعراب، طبع الجزء الأول منه في مكتبة مصطفى البابي الحلبي بالقاهرة عام ١٣٧٤هـ/١٩٥٤م) وكتاب المنصف شرح ابن جني لكتاب التصريف للمازني (طبع في ثلاثة أجزاء في مكتبة عيسى البابي الحلبي بين ١٩٥٤ - ١٩٦٠م). وأهم كتبه على الإطلاق في دراسة اللهجات هو كتاب الخصائص (طبع الجزء الأول منه في مطابع الهلال بالقاهرة عام ١٩١٣م، وطبع مرة أخرى كاملاً في ثلاثة أجزاء بتحقيق محمد علي النجار في دار الكتب المصرية بالقاهرة بين ١٩٥٢ - ١٩٥٥م، وللكتاب طبعات أخرى مصورة في بيروت). فقد وضع ابن جني بعض المفاهيم والأسس الخاصة باستنطاق «المخبرين اللغويين» (انظر في ذلك سر الصناعة والخصائص)، كما أنه أول من نادى وكرر النداء بأن اللغات (أي اللهجات) كلها حجة ويمكن الاستشهاد بها (انظر الجزء الأول من الخصائص). وعالج ابن جني الاختلافات اللهجية ليس فقط على المستوى الصوتي بل تعداه الى مستويات الصرف والنحو والدلالة، حيث توجد الفروق بين اللهجات العربية. إلا أن هذه الفروق ليست كبيرة لدرجة أنها تحولها الى لغات مستقلة.

وهذه بعض الملاحظات اللهجية التي وردت في بعض مؤلفات ابن جني:

«وقد قلبت تاء افتعل دالاً مع الجيم في بعض اللغات. قالوا: اجدمعوا في اجتمعوا، واجدزّ في اجتزّ.» (سر الصناعة، الجزء الأول ٢٠١)

ويعرض ابن جني لظاهرة الشنشنة (انظر ص ١٢٢ من كتاب لهجات العرب لأحمد تيمور باشا، القاهرة: الهيئة المصرية العامة للكتاب، ١٣٩٣هـ/١٩٧٣م)، فيقول:

«ومن العرب من يبدل كاف المؤنث في الوقف شيناً، حرصاً على البيان لأن الكسرة الدالة على التأنيث فيها تخفي في الوقف. فاحتاطوا للبيان بأن أبدلوها شيناً، فقالوا عليش ومنش ومررت بش (يريد: عليك ومنك ومررت بك) ... ومن كلامهم «إذا أعاياش جاراتش، فأقبلي على ذي بيتش».

(سر الصناعة، صص ٢١٦ - ٢١٧)

ويذكر القلقشندي في كتابه صبح الأعشى أن هذه الظاهرة موجودة في لغة اليمن كما ينسبها أيضاً إلى لسان حمير.

(لهجات العرب لتيمور صص ٧٣، ١٢٢)

فالهمزة في أديَة ليست بدلاً من الياء، إنما هي لغة في الكلمة، بمنزلة يسروع وأسروع. ويَلَملَم وألَملَم.... فهذه كلها لغات. وليس بعضها بدلاً من بعض.»

(سر الصناعة: ٢٤٣)

«عن الأصمعي، قال: ارتفعت قريش في الفصاحة عن عنعنة تميم، وتلتلة بهراء. وكشكشة ربيعة. وكسكسة هوازن، وتضجّع قيس، وعجرفية ضبة. فأما عنعنة تميم، فإن تميماً تقول في موضع (أن): (عَن)... وأما تلتلة بهراء، فإنها تقول تِعلمون وتِفعلون وتِصنعون بكسر أوائل الحروف...

ومعنى قوله كشكشة ربيعة، فإنما يريد قولها مع كاف ضمير المؤنث إنكش ورأيتكِش وأعطيَتكش. تفعل هذا في الوقف. فإذا وَصَلَت أسقطت الشين. وأما كسكسة هوازن فقولهم أيضاً: أعطيَتكِس. ومِنكِس وعَنكِس. وهذا أيضاً في الوقف دون الوصل.»

(سر الصناعة: ٢٣٤ - ٢٣٥)

ويفرق ابن جني بين اللهجة واللثغة (وهي عاهة كلامية). ففي صدد تحليله لقول الشاعر سحيم عبد بني الحسحاس:

فلو كنت ورداً لونـــــــــــه لَعَسِقتَني ... ولكن رَبّي سانني بسواديــــــــــــا

يقول في سر صناعته (ص ٢١٤):

«فإنما قَلَبَ (يريد سحيماً) الشين سيناً لسواده، وضعف عبارته عن الشين، وليس ذلك بلغة. وإنما هو كاللّثغ.»

ولمزيد من الفروق اللهجية القديمة يستحسن الرجوع إلى كتاب الدكتور نهاد الموسى بعنوان «في تاريخ العربية: أبحاث في الصورة التاريخية للنحو العربي» (عَمّان: مطابع المؤسسة الصحفية الأردنية، ١٩٧٦م).

مساهمة بعض العلماء المسلمين في الدرس اللهجي

ويعتبر الفارابي من العلماء الأوائل الذين فرقوا بين لغات المركز ولغات الأطراف في كتابه «ديوان الأدب» من تحقيق الدكتور أحمد مختار عمر ونشره مجمع اللغة العربية بالقاهرة في أربعة مجلدات بين ١٩٧٤ - ١٩٧٩م).

وهناك ملاحظات أخرى دقيقة جيدة وجديرة بالدراسة. من ذلك ما أشار اليه المداني (ت ٣٣٤هـ):

«أما العروض ففيها الفصاحة ما خلا قراها. وكذلك الحجاز فنجد السفلى فإلى الشام وإلى ديار مضر وديار ربيعة ففيها الفصاحة إلا في قراها.»

(صفة جزيرة العرب. القاهرة ١٩٥٣م. ص ١٣٦)

ومن ملاحظات الرحالة المقدسي في القرن الرابع الهجري: —

«لغتهم (يقصد لهجة شمالي العراق) لغة حسنة، أصحّ من لغة الشام لأنهم عرب أحسنها الموصلية.»

(أحسن التقاسيم في معرفة الأقاليم، القاهرة: ١٤٦)

ثم يقول:

«لغاتهم (يقصد لهجات العراق) مختلفة. أصحها الكوفية لقربهم من البادية، وبعدهم عن النبط، ثم هي بعد ذلك حسنة فاسدة بخاصة بغداد. أما البطائح فنبط لا لسان ولا عقل.»

(أحسن التقاسيم: ٢٠٣)

الدراسات اللهجية الحديثة

وننتقل إلى العصر الحديث فنجد أن الدراسات اللهجية العامة أصبحت علماً قائماً بذاته له نظرياته ومدارسه ورجالاته وجمعياته ونشاطاته العالمية المتجددة ومؤتمراته. كما نشأ في ظل هذه الظروف علم اللهجات العربية بالمفهوم المعاصر. وربما كان أول من أسس علم اللهجات العربية في الوطن العربي هو المرحوم الدكتور ابراهيم أنيس من كلية دار العلوم في جامعة القاهرة. فبعد حصوله على الدكتوراه من جامعة لندن عاد إلى مصر كرائد من رواد علم اللسانيات بمفهومه الحديث. وقد ألف أول كتاب علمي منهجي باللغة العربية أسماه «في اللهجات العربية» (صدرت الطبعة الرابعة منه عن مكتبة الانجلو المصرية عام ١٩٧٣م). وقد ظهرت الطبعة الأولى من هذا الكتاب في أوائل الخمسينات على وجه التقريب. وهي أول دراسة تجمع بين معطيات علماء اللغة الأقدمين والدراسات اللسانية الحديثة.

وشارك الغرب مشاركة فعالة طيبة في الدراسات الميدانية للهجات العربية معتمدين في كثير من الاحيان على نظريات علم اللهجات العام ومناهجه العامة في دراسة اللهجات الغربية وغيرها. وظهرت دراسات جيدة في لهجات الوطن العربي المتعددة على اختلاف فيما بينها في الدقة والعمق والشمول والجدّية. ويشارك أبناء العربية أيضاً في البحث اللغوي بعامة والبحث اللهجي على وجه الخصوص. وقد سجلت كثيراً من هذه الدراسات في كتابَيّ: «معجم مصادر الدراسات اللغوية العربية» (لندن: مانسل، ١٩٧٥م) و «اللسانيات العربية: مقدمة وببليوغرافية» (لندن: مانس، ١٩٨٢م).

هذا الكتاب:

والكتاب الذي بين يدي القارىء الآن هو محاولة جدية دقيقة في الدرس اللهجي العربي. ويتناول منطقة واسعة من حيث المساحة أطلق عليها مؤلف الكتاب «شمال شرقي الجزيرة العربية.» ويدرس هنا لهجات هذه المنطقة التي تشمل جزءاً من المناطق الوسطى والشمالية والشرقية من المملكة العربية السعودية والكويت وجنوبي العراق ومنطقة عربستان. وهذه الدراسة عصارة تفكير طويل وثمرة مجهود كبير وبحث ميداني متواصل دام اكثر من عشر سنوات.

والكتاب إضافة جديدة إلى المكتبة العربية. فهو إلى جانب أنه دراسة لغوية في الأساس إلا أنه يمكن اعتباره دراسة اجتماعية وفولكلورية وأنثربولوجية وبيئية للمنطقة التي تحت الدراسة أو ذات العلاقة. إذ تربط هذه الدراسة بين الموضوعات هذه جميعاً. وبطريقة أخرى يمكن القول بأن هذه العوامل المختلفة اعتبرت أحياناً متغيرات لها تأثيرات واضحة على الاتجاه اللغوي والتغيرات اللغوية في المنطقة المدروسة. ويفرق الكتاب بين لهجات الحضر ولهجات البادية كما يبحث في الفروق الدقيقة داخل كل مجموعة لهجية. ويشير الكتاب إلى الهجرات المختلفة في المنطقة وما تركه من تأثيرات واضحة في الساحة اللغوية. كذلك يعالج التطورات اللغوية الطارئة على اللهجات لهذه الأسباب أو لأسباب أخرى. ويستفيد الكتاب في منهجه من عدد من مشاهير أساتذة علم اللغة الاجتماعي من أمثال لابوف وقومبيرز وغيرهما.

ويسلك الكتاب منهج علم اللغة الجغرافي أو الجغرافيا اللغوية في اكتشاف الظواهر اللهجية وتصنيفها ووضعها في مكانها الصحيح على الخارطة اللغوية. فكما يضع عالم الجغرافيا على الخارطة الصمّاء أسماء الأماكن ويحدد عليها التضاريس والمناخ وعدد السكان والمصادر الطبيعية وما إلى ذلك فكذلك يستطيع عالم اللغة أو اللهجات أن يضع المعلومات اللغوية على الخارطة بدقة وتحديد كتوزيع الوحدات الصوتية والصرفية والنحوية والدلالية وما إلى ذلك. ويستطيع عن طريق وضع الخطوط الفاصلة أو الأيسوگلوسات أن يحدد بالضبط أماكن وجود الظاهرة أو تداخلها أو انتشارها كما يمليه عليه الواقع اللغوي لهذه الظاهرة أو تلك. ومجموع هذه الخارطات قد تكوّن أطلساً لغوياً للمنطقة المدروسة. ويشتمل الكتاب الذي بين أيدينا على بعض من هذه الخارطات التي توضح ما قصدناه هنا. والواقع أن وطننا العربي والجزيرة العربية على وجه الخصوص بحاجة ماسة إلى أطلس لهجي أو لغوي عام لأسباب تاريخية وحضارية وثقافية ولغوية وتراثية. إن الاكتشافات اللغوية لها أهميتها في هذا الصدد فهي لا تقل وزناً وأهمية من الناحية العملية عن اكتشاف حقل من الحقول المعدنية أو البترولية أو غيرها. وربما تقفنا الاكتشافات المقبلة على ماضينا وتاريخنا، وتربط حاضرنا بماضينا ومستقبلنا. فالمصادر اللغوية في أبعادها أكثر ثباتاً وأكبر وزناً وأبعد عمقاً وأثمن قدراً من المصادر الطبيعية الأخرى.

وقد ألقى البحث مزيداً من الضوء على لهجات الحضر ولهجات البادية ودرسها على ضوء «نظرية الموجة اللغوية» إلى جانب نظريات أخرى. فبيّن الفروق بينها والتغيرات التي أدت إلى تطور ظواهرها. وصنف اللهجات على أساس نوعها أو تايبولوجيتها. أما

النتائج التي توصل اليها البحث فقد قامت على أساس من الدراسات الميدانية والتسجيلات الصوتية وفحص النصوص المسجلة واستنطاق المخبرين اللغويين والتجارب العملية وما إلى ذلك. وتؤيد بعض نتائج هذا البحث تقسيمات العلماء العرب المسلمين للهجات العربية إلى لهجات الأمصار أو الحضر ولهجات البادية وكذلك الملاحظات عليها. ويعد ابن خلدون (ت ٨٠٨هـ) أول من وضع نظرية لهذا التقسيم على أساس علمي دقيق. ووضح التأثير البيئي والاجتماعي على اللغة. ومن ملاحظاته عن لغة الامصار نقتبس النص التالي (مقدمة ابن خلدون من تحقيق علي عبد الواحد وافي. ج ٤ ص ١٢٧٤): -

«اعلم أن عرف التخاطب في الأمصار وبين الحضر ليست بلغة مضر القديمة ولا بلغة أهل الجيل، بل هي لغة أخرى قائمة بنفسها بعيدة عن لغة مضر وعن لغة هذا الجيل الذي لعهدنا. وهي عن لغة مضر أبعد. أما أنها لغة قائمة بنفسها فهو ظاهر يشهد له ما فيها من التغاير الذي يعد عند صناعة أهل النحو لحناً. وهي مع ذلك باختلاف أهل الأمصار في اصطلاحاتهم. فلغة أهل المشرق مباينة بعض الشيء للغة أهل المغرب. وكذلك أهل الاندلس معهما. وكل منهم متوصل بلغته إلى تأدية مقصوده والإبانة عمّا في نفسه. وهذا معنى اللسان واللغة. وفقدان الإعراب ليس بضائر لهم كما قلناه في لغة العرب لهذا العهد. وأما أنها أبعد عن اللسان الأول من لغة هذا الجيل فلأن البعد عن اللسان إنما هو بمخالطة العجمة. فمن خالط العجم كانت لغته عن ذلك اللسان الأصلي أبعد.»

فابن خلدون هنا لا يعترف بوجود لهجات متعددة فحسب بل إنه يرى أن هناك نظاماً لغوياً مستقلاً لكل لهجة إلا أن اللهجات تشترك فيما بينها في خصائص عامة.

ومن المتغيرات التي تؤدي إلى التغيّر اللغوي أو التطور اللغوي الاختلاط بين الاجناس المختلفة. وعادة ما يحدث هذا في المدن كما يشير إليها هذا الكتاب. وهذا يثبت أيضاً ما ذهب إليه ابن خلدون في حديثه عن لغات الأمصار بقوله (المقدمة، ج ٣، ص ٨٨٩): -

«ثم فسد اللسان العربي بمخالطة الألسنة الأعجمية في بعض أحكامه وتغيّر أواخره وإن كان بقي في الدلالات على أصله. ويسمى لساناً حضرياً في جميع أمصار الاسلام.»

وهكذا فإن الدراسة التي أمام القارىء الآن تطلعه على منطقة لغوية واسعة جغرافياً وبشرياً ولهجياً. وهي تحاول الربط بين هذه اللهجات من جهة وذلك بتحديد خصائصها اللهجية المشتركة مع ربطها باللغة الفصحى. ومن جهة أخرى فالبحث يحدد أيضاً الفروق اللغوية بين نطاق لهجي وآخر، وبين لهجة وأخرى، والفروق الداخلية لأفرع اللهجة الواحدة متى ما وجدت.

والكتاب يضيف لبنة جديدة إلى الدراسات اللهجية العربية. فهو يضيف هنا منطقة لم تدرس دراسة منظمة جيدة بعد. تلك هي منطقة عربستان. فهي من الناحية اللغوية والبشرية تقع ضمن نطاق وإطار الوطن العربي الذي هو جزء من الوطن الاسلامي الكبير. والكتاب يساهم مساهمة كبيرة في ترسيخ الدراسات اللغوية والحضارية والاجتماعية والديموغرافية للمنطقة المدروسة. وهي منطقة هامة تستحق مزيداً من الاهتمام العلمي ومزيداً من البحث عن الجذور في الأعماق.

كلمة عن المؤلف

مؤلف الكتاب هو الدكتور بروس إنغام. وهو خبير لغوي وباحث مدقق في اللغة العربية الفصحى ولهجاتها، وبخاصة لهجات المنطقة المدروسة في هذا الكتاب.

ولد الدكتور إنغام في لندن عام ١٩٤٢م. ودرس اللغة العربية وآدابها وحضارتها في قسم الشرق الأوسط بمعهد الدراسات الشرقية والأفريقية التابع لجامعة لندن، حيث حصل على درجة البكالوريوس عام ١٩٦٤م. وفي عام ١٩٦٧م انتقل إلى قسم اللسانيات والصوتيات في نفس المعهد حيث حصل على الدكتوراه في اللسانيات العربية عام ١٩٧٤م. ولا يزال يعمل في نفس القسم أستاذاً ومشرفاً على رسائل الماجستيراه والدكتوراه. ويتكلم الدكتور إنغام اللغتين العربية والفارسية بطلاقة، بالإضافة إلى عدد من اللغات الأوربية. وله دراسات عديدة ومراجعات للكتب كثيرة في ميدان اللسانيات العربية واللهجات العربية. وله اهتمامات خاصة بلغة الأطفال ومقياس السمع اللغوي مع التركيز على اللغة العربية. وقد أقام الدكتور إنغام في بلدان الشرق الأوسط مدة من الزمن ولا يزال يسافر إليها بانتظام. وقد شارك بأبحاثه في مؤتمرات كثيرة داخل الوطن العربي وخارجه.

وإنني إذ أقدّم هذا الكتاب الثالث في سلسلة مكتبة اللسانيات العربية للقارىء العربي أجد نفسي فخوراً بتقديم واحد من الأعلام اللغويين المحدثين والذين نعقد عليهم آمالاً كبيرة في خدمة قضايا اللغة العربية بخاصة والمجتمع العربي الاسلامي بعامة.

والله نسأل أن يحقق آمالنا الكبيرة ويثبت أقدامنا ويوفقنا لما يحبه ويرضاه. إنه سميع الدعاء.

رئيس التحرير
محمد حسن باكلا

مقدمة المؤلف

يتناول هذا الكتاب شرحاً للهجات العربية المحكية في نطاق Zone يشمل قسماً من شمال المملكة العربية السعودية ودولة الكويت، وقسماً من جنوب العراق ومنطقة عربستان (خوزستان*) في دولة ايران. فقد قام الباحث بجمع المعلومات في رحلات عديدة إلى المنطقة خلال عشر سنوات من ١٩٦٩ الى ١٩٧٨م. ولا ينهج هذا البحث منهجاً لغوياً فحسب بل يقوم أيضاً على مقارنات بين توزيع اللهجات المختلفة أو بالأحرى المناطق اللغوية Dialect Areas وبين البيئات الجغرافية الموجودة. ويقوم البحث كذلك بربط توزيع اللهجات بهجرات القبائل والمجموعات العربية خلال القرون الأربعة الماضية، ويرسم للقارىء خارطة لغوية linguistic Map تبين مواقع اللهجات في المنطقة، ويربط التوزيع اللغوي Linguistic Distribution بعوامل غير لغوية Extra-Linguistic سواء أكانت بشرية أم جغرافية. وينقسم الكتاب إلى الأقسام الأساسية التالية:

١ شرح الجغرافية التضاريسية والبشرية في المنطقة (الفصل الأول).
٢ عرض سريع للأساليب المستخدمة في الدراسات اللهجية (الفصل الثاني).
٣ مقارنة بين اللهجات المحافظة Conservative واللهجات المتجددة Innovating أو غير المحافظة وتوزيعها (الفصل الثالث).
٤ شرح للتغيرات اللغوية التي حدثت في شمالي نجد وأهمية الانعزال الجغرافي في وقوعها (الفصل الرابع).
٥ شرح التوزيع العام لخطوط الايسوگلوس Isogloss في المنطقة (الفصل الخامس).
٦ نصوص من اللهجات المختلفة مع ترجمة لها وبعض الملاحظات عليها (الفصل السادس).

وهنا علينا أن نؤكد مجدداً أن البحث لا يقدم شرحاً كاملاً للّهجات المدروسة هنا أو لأيّ واحدة منها. بل يركّز على نقاط خاصة تبيّن نسب اللهجات وتقاربها بعضها من بعض، ويوضح حالة اللهجات على نطاق أوسع. أما الشرح العام والتفاصيل فهناك دراسات مفصلة سابقة لكثير من اللهجات في الأبحاث العربية والأجنبية الموجودة. وفيما يلي نقدم ملخصاً لكل من الأقسام الرئيسية التي سبق ذكرها:

المنطقة: نجد والمناطق المجاورة لها (الفصل الأول)

ميدان البحث هو منطقة يلاحظ فيها تعامل بين ثلاثة مراكز رئيسية. وهي:

١ المراكز الحضارية الواقعة في أواسط نجد.
٢ المراكز الحضارية الواقعة على شطوط العراق وعربستان.
٣ المراكز الحضارية الواقعة على الخليج العربي. ويهمنا هنا أولاً الكويت.

فلقد استمر هذا التعامل في التجارة العالمية منذ زمن قديم. حيث أن أهالي نجد كانوا يتاجرون مع مدن العراق والكويت للحصول على بضائع وسلع مصنوعة فيها أو مستوردة من الخارج. ويهمنا هنا أيضاً التعامل الناتج عن رحلات القبائل والمجتمعات العربية في المنطقة متجهة بالدرجة الأولى من نجد إلى العراق والخليج، وبالدرجة الثانية من العراق متجهة من شط العرب بالتحديد إلى الجنوب على ساحل البحر وإلى الكويت والأحساء والبحرين. ونقرأ في التاريخ أن اللهجات قد توزعت من قلب الجزيرة العربية خارجة الى المناطق المجاورة. ويلاحظ مثل هذا الاتجاه أيضاً في أيامنا هذه في تنقّل القبائل البدوية بين نجد وبين العراق ومنطقة الخليج في

* على أن عربستان ربما تكون أصوب في تسمية المنطقة. أما استخدام كلمة (خوزستان) أحياناً فلأن بعض الأبحاث الميدانية كانت قد تمت بمساعدة حكومة الشاه الفقيد في أوائل السبعينات. وكانت كلمة (خوزستان) الاصطلاح الدارج آنذاك. كما أنها تقع أيضاً في النصوص المدرجة في آخر هذا الكتاب.

رحلاتهم طالعين في الربيع وراجعين في الصيف. وعندما يقل الكلأ في نجد أحياناً نجدهم يطيلون مكوثهم في العراق والشام ويذهبون شيئاً فشيئاً حتى يتخذوها مواطن لهم. وفي الصيف ينزلون على آبار في سورية أو على شط الفرات وفي الربيع يعودون إلى بادية الشام مستمرين هناك على صلة مع القبائل البدوية التي تقطن صيفاً في نجد. ونرى مثل هذه الحركة في هجرات قبائل عنزة من نواحي خيبر في الحجاز إلى بادية الشام في الشمال، وهجرة قبيلة مطير من حدود الحجاز إلى الكويت وبعدهم بعض طوائف حرب. وأيضاً من جهة أخرى هجرات عجمان من نواحي نجران في جنوب نجد إلى الأحساء والكويت في الشرق. ويلاحظ القارىء أن في وسط هذه الحركة إلى الشرق والشمال توجد نقاط استيطان مستقرة على جبل طويق وفي القصيم وجبل شمر تمثل مراكز لها سكان مستقرون من قديم الزمان ولها دور خاص في الحفاظ على أصول اللغة العربية وصورتها الأصلية. فتقابل الخارطة اللغوية هذه الخارطة البشرية. فإذا تتبعنا اللهجات من قلب الجزيرة العربية نرى أنها تتحول تدريجياً من طبيعتها النجدية إلى طبيعة عراقية. ولكن الخط الرئيسي الفاصل بين اللهجات النجدية واللهجات العراقية يقوم تقريباً على شط الفرات لأن لقبائل الشامّية غرب الفرات لهجة أقرب الى اللهجات النجدية. وإذا عبرنا شط الفرات نرى أيضا تحولاً تدريجياً من نوع يقترب من لهجة البادية إلى نوع عراقي خالص يستخدم على شط العرب وفي قرى دجلة والفرات وفي المدن الكبرى. وعلى هذا الأساس يمكن تقسيم جنوب العراق من حيث الطبيعة واستعمال الأرض الى ثلاثة أقسام، وهي:

١ المركز النهري على شط العرب ودجلة والفرات الذي يمكن أن يزرع به النخيل وأنواع أخرى من الزراعة التي تحتاج إلى الري.
٢ الأهوار وهي منطقة بها بحيرات وشبكة من الشطوط والأنهار تفيض في الشتاء والربيع ويزرع فيها الرز وترعى فيها الجواميس.
٣ البادية وهي منطقة تزرع فيها الحنطة والشعير في أماكن قريبة للأنهار وتربى الإبل والاغنام في غيرها.

ومن الملاحظ أن اللهجات العراقية الخالصة ينطق بها في المنطقة النهرية. أما اللهجات النجدية أو شبه النجدية فإنها تستعمل في البادية. وأما المعدان أو سكان الاهوار فلهم لهجة عراقية في أكثر صفاتها ولكنها تميل إلى لهجة البادية. ويهمنا أيضاً هنا مجموعات أخرى وهم الكواولة (أو النَوَر) وهؤلاء جماعات من أصل غير عربي ولكنهم يستخدمون العربية، والشاوية وهم قبائل عربية يربون الأغنام ويتنقلون بين الفرات وشمال المملكة العربية السعودية والكويت. وهؤلاء لهم مقام متوسط ويتكلمون لهجة عراقية في أكثر خواصها وخصائصها إلا أنها مائلة إلى لهجات نجد. وأما الخليج – ونقصد هنا الكويت والإمارات – فهي أقرب إلى قلب الجزيرة العربية منها إلى العراق من حيث الاتصال والصلات العائلية والتجارية والثقافية. ولذلك تمثل لهجات الخليج قسماً فرعياً من اللهجات النجدية.

وعلى أساس المعطيات اللغوية يمكن توزيع المنطقة إلى كتلتين رئيسيتين من حيث اللغة أو نطاقـين Zones من حيث الاتصال. وهما النطاق النجدي وهو متشعع وممتد من أواسط نجد إلى الخليج شرقاً وإلى حدود الفرات شمالاً، والنطاق العراقي ويتركز على شطوط العراق وعربستان ومنطقة الأهوار.

عرض سريع للأساليب التي تستخدم في الدراسات اللهجية (الفصل الثاني)

منذ أوائل الدراسات اللهجية في أوربا – لدى «النحويين الجدد The Neogrammarians» بألمانيا في القرن التاسع عشر الميلادي – واجه اللغويون مشكلة هامة وهي أنه لا توجد بين اللهجات حدود مضبوطة بل تتداخل لهجة في لهجة أخرى بدرجات غير ملحوظة أو من الصعب ملاحظتها. ولذلك لا يمكن تقسيم منطقة ما إلى مناطق Areas لغوية محددة أو نطاقات لغوية Linguistic Zones إلا إذا أخذنا بعين الاعتبار مبادىء بسيطة جداً للتقسيم لا تستند إلى الواقع القائم. ولكن إذا غيرنا اهتمامنا من اللهجة ذاتها إلى الظواهر اللغوية كلٌ على حدة فإننا نرى أنه توجد هناك حدود واضحة جداً بين ظاهرة وظاهرة ثانية. ولموقع «الخط الفاصل» Isogloss نسق ونظام وترتيب يعتمد على نقاط جغرافية معينة. ولذلك نركز اهتمامنا على الحدود أو الخطوط التي تلاحظ بين ظواهر لغوية معينة. وعلى هذا المبدأ نستطيع أن نؤسس مفهوم النطاق اللغوي Linguistic Zone الذي يمكن تعريفه بأنه «المنطقة التي تحدّها خطوط فاصلة Isoglosses، وهي ملحوظة وواضحة حتى ولو لم يمكن تحديدها بالضبط.»

وعندما ننقل اهتمامنا من «اللهجة» Dialect إلى النطاق اللغوي فاننا نستطيع أن نميز أيضاً بين مركز النطاق Core وطرفه Periphery. ونرى أن مراكز النطاقات Zones هي مراكز استقرار أو مراكز حضارة في المنطقة.
ويتبع هـذا النوع من الدراسة نظرية «الموجة اللغوية» Wave Theory التي ابتكرها اللغوي الألماني شميدت J. Schmidt والتي يرى فيها أن الصفات أو الملامح اللغوية Features تمتد عبر منطقة ما، كالأمواج التي تتسع على سطح ماء الغدير عند قذف حصاة فيه، وتَتَنقّل من قرية إلى قرية أو من مجموعة إلى مجموعة.
وتناقض هذه النظرية نظرية اللغوي الألماني شليخر J. Schleicher الذي كان يرى أن الملامح Features اللغوية تتبع هجرات الشعوب في المنطقة آخذاً هذه الفكرة من هجرات الشعوب الآريّة والسامية وتطور اللغات الآريّة والسامية من انعزال الشعوب أو الجماعات بعضها عن بعض. وأصل الاختلاف بينها أن «نظرية الموجة اللغوية»

ترى تنقّل اللغة مستقلة عن تنقل الشعوب بينما ترى النظرية الثانية التي تسمى بـ «نظرية الانشعاب اللغوي» Family-Tree Theory بأن تنقّل الملامح اللغوية يعتمد على تنقّل الناطقين بها. وإن نظرة سريعة إلى التوزيع اللغويّ في منطقتنا لتبين أن نظرية الموجة اللغوية تنطبق بسهولة في المناطق الحضارية أي مراكز النطاقات اللغوية كما شرحناها. وأما نظرية الانشعاب اللغوي فتنطبق إلى حد كبير على لهجات البادية لأن لهجات القبائل البدوية يمكن ارجاعها بصورة واضحة إلى مواطنهم الأصلية.

مقارنة بين اللهجات المحافظة واللهجات المتجددة وتوزيعها (الفصل الثالث)

وهنا نقوم بمقارنة بين اللهجات التي توجد في قلب الجزيرة العربية أي نجد وبادية الشام واللهجات الموجودة في أطراف المنطقة أي ساحل الخليج والعراق وعربستان. وتقوم المقارنة على الفروق اللغوية بين لهجات محافظة ولهجات متجددة من حيث نظام الأصوات Phonology ونظام صيغ الفعل والاسم. فاللهجات المركزية تحافظ على جزء كبير من النظام الذي كان في اللغة الفصحى بينما ألغت لهجات الأطراف كثيراً من الوحدات الصوتية Phonemes القديمة كما ألغت أيضاً بعض الصيغ الصرفية Morphological Patterns التي كانت تستعمل في الأفعال. وقد لوحظ مثل هذه الفروق أيضاً في اللهجات الانجليزية حيث نرى أن اللهجات الريفية لها طابع محافظ بينما لهجات المدن لها طابع متجدد. وهنا يلزم أن نؤكد ان الكلمتين «محافظ» و«متجدد» تتعلقان بالنظام الصوتي والنظام الصرفي فقط وليس لها علاقة بالمفاهيم التي يعبّر عنها الناطق باللغة. فاللغة المحافظة واللغة المتجددة تستطيعان التعبير عن نفس المعاني والمفاهيم ولكن اللغة المتجددة تنقلها بنظام أخف أو أبسط أو مختزل reductional. فقد لوحظ أن التجدد في اللغة ينتج غالباً عن اختلاط الشعوب والاتصال على مستويات عديدة. ويمكن أن يحصل هذا في امتزاج شعب مع شعب أجنبي كما هو حاصل في المناطق الساحلية أو في المراكز التجارية أو حتى في أماكن تجمعات عناصر من مناطق مختلفة في البلد الواحد كما هو الأمر في العاصمة أو في المدن الكبيرة. وأما المحافظة اللغوية فتوجد غالباً في مناطق صارت لها صفة الاستقرار والثبات الاجتماعي الراسخ، ولم تتأثر بعوامل خارجية على كثير من المستويات.

وفي هذا الفصل نعالج التغيرات الصوتية Phonogogical Changes التالية:

١ الاندماج Merger بين أصوات التاء والثاء، وبين الدال والذال في مدن الحجاز.
٢ الاندماج بين الثاء والفاء، والدال والذال في الأحساء والبحرين.
٣ الاندماج بين الياء والجيم في منطقة الخليج وجنوب العراق وغيرها من المناطق.

ومن حيث الصرف نعالج في المقام الاول زوال التنوين في الاسم وزوال العلامات التي تميز بين المؤنث والمذكر في صيغ الفعل أي أن الصيغ «فَعَلنَ وفَعَلتنّ ويفعلنَ وتَفعلنَ» غير مستعملة أو مهجورة في لهجات الأطراف. وننتقل من هذا إلى بحث صيغ الفعل المتعلقة بالحالات المتعدّية وغير المتعدّية وبالوجهة Aspect في الفعل. فكان في الفصحى أربع صيغ لها علاقة بعمل الفاعل في الفعل وهي «فَعَلَ» تجيء عادة بجذور Stems تعبر عن عمل متعدّ Transitive مثل قَتَلَ وكَتَبَ وحَفَرَ، و«فَعِلَ أو فَعُلَ» تجيء عادة بجذور تعبّر عن عمل غير متعد Intransitive مثل عَطِشَ وحلِمَ وحَلَمَ وتَعِبَ و«فُعِلَ» وهي صيغة المبني للمجهول Passive فقد اشتقت من «فَعَلَ» مثل قُتِلَ وكُتِبَ، و«أفعَلَ» وهي صيغة الجَعل أو التسبيب Causative مثل اركَبَ وأنزَلَ وأصعَدَ. وفي لهجات المركز بقي هذا النظام في صورته الأصلية مع وجود فوارق بسيطة في الصيغ حيث نرى نظاماً يشمل الصيغ «فَعَلَ» و«فِعِل» و«فعِل» و«أفعل». وأما لهجات الأطراف Peripheries فقد قامت بتخفيف أو اختزال Reduction هذا النظام في اللهجات العراقية التي تمثل نوعاً متطرفاً. فلم تبق في هذه اللهجة إلا صيغة «فَعَلَ» حيث قامت صيغة «انفعَلَ» بعمل «فعِلَ»، وقامت «فَعَّلَ» بعمل «أفعل». وهنا نرى أنه لم يَنمَح عمل أي صيغة ما عدا صيغة «فَعِلَ» فقد سقطت كلية. أما صيغة «أفعَلَ» فقد نابت عنها صيغ أخرى. والنقطة التي تهمنا هنا أن هذا التغير Change يمثل تبسيطاً Simplification لغوياً من حيث الأصوات والمقاطع Syllables والصرف Morphology. لأن النظام الجديد يستعمل حروفاً زائدة كالنون في «انفعل» وتضعيف الحروف Doubling الموجودة كتشديد عين «فَعّلَ» ولا يبقى للحركات دور. بينما في النظام القديم أي نظام اللغة الفصحى ولهجات المركز يبقى للحركات دور هام فهي التي تحمل المعنى.

وعلى هذا يمكن تصنيف لهجات المنطقة إلى أربعة أصناف من حيث درجة التبسيط في أوزان الفعل.

عرض للتغيرات اللغوية التي حدثت في شمالي نجد وأهمية الانعزال الجغرافي في وقوعها (الفصل الرابع)

في هذا القسم نعالج نوعية اللهجات في القسم الشمالي من نجد أي جبل شمّر والقصيم ولهجات قبائل بدوية في بادية الشام لهم صلة بشمال نجد. وتمتد بعض الملامح اللغوية التي ندرسها في هذا القسم إلى لهجات الفرات والعَمارة التي قد شرحناها في القسم السابق بأنها غير مبسطة Non-Reductional أي لا تشتمل على إلغاء صيغة قائمة أو إدماج صيغة في صيغة أخرى بل تحافظ على النظام الموجود حتى ولو كان هناك تغير في ملامح الصيغة. إلى جانب ذلك فإن بعض التغيرات قد تؤدي إلى استحداث نظام أكثر تعقيداً من النظام السابق. ونعالج هنا الظواهر التالية:

١ إبدال تاء التأنيث اللاحقة إلى ياء في «ـَت» و «ـَة» و «ـات».

٢ إبدال ضمة بفتحة في اللواحق «ـتم» و «ـكم» و «ـهم» وفي الضمير «أنتم».

٣ استبدال الضمائر اللواحق Pronoun Suffixes «ـَن» و «ـه» و «ـه» بـ «ـني» و «ـه» و «ـها» على التوالي.

فنرى أن هذه الظواهر توجد في منطقة مركزها بادية الشام وجبل شمر. وهي بيئة الحياة البدوية والقبائل الرحّل التي يبقى سكانها منعزلين إلى حدّ ما عن البيئات الزراعية التي تحيط بها والتي هي اكثر منها كثافة من حيث عدد السكان. ففي الشمال يقع الهلال الخصيب وفي الجنوب أواسط نجد والأحساء التي تلاحَظ فيها مجموعات من المدن والقرى. وتقع هذه البيئات الزراعية على طرق التجارة القديمة، وتترابط فيما بينها بصلات عائلية وتجارية. فهي بهذا تشكل شبكة اجتماعية تتسع فيها التغيرات اللغوية التي قد أدت الى تقارب لغوي فيما بينها. وأما القسم الشمالي من نجد فهو خال من القرى والمدن نسبياً لذلك فإنه لا تربطها مثل هذه الصلات بالمناطق المجاورة. فاذا نظرنا إلى جغرافية جنوب العراق وعربستان فإننا نرى أن البادية تمتد من شمالي الأهوار في منطقة شط الغرّاف إلى كوت العمارة حتى تصل الى الحويزة والاهواز في عربستان. وبصورة عامة فان القبائل العربية الساكنة عبر شط الفرات لا يزالون على حالتهم البدوية حتى في منطقة الجزيرة وفي شمال عربستان وتربطهم صلات قوية ببادية الشام.

شرح للنطاقات اللغوية الرئيسية التي تلاحظ في المنطقة (الفصل الخامس)

في هذا الفصل نبحث بعض الظواهر اللغوية Linguistic Phenomena التي لا تدخل في باب الفصلين السابقين (الثالث والرابع). وهنا نرجع لمفهوم الخط اللغوي الفاصل Isogloss كما ذكر في الفصل الثاني. ويعرّف عادة بأنه «الخط الذي يقسم بين منطقة توجد فيها صيغة أو كلمة ومنطقة أخرى توجد فيها صيغة أو كلمة أخرى لنفس المعنى. فمثلاً الخط الفاصل الذي يقسم بين كلمة «إقط» وكلمة «وقَل» في نجد، أو بين كلمة «رَوبة» وكلمة «لَبَن» بالعراق. فالظواهر التي نعالجها هي على المستويات الصوتية والصرفية والمفرداتية (المعجمية) Lexical. فتكشف الظواهر التي درسناها ما يسمى بالتوزيع الطبيعي Natural Distribution. أي أن الخطوط الفاصلة لا تقسم المنطقة إلى مناطق فرعية مضبوطة. وتمر الخطوط الفاصلة في جهات مختلفة ولكن يلاحظ فيها أثر امتداد اللغة العربية من قلب الجزيرة العربية إلى الخارج. ويلاحظ فيها أيضاً مناطق اتصال Communication Areas هامة. والخطوط الرئيسية هي كما يلي:

١ الخط الفاصل الذي يقسم المنطقة النهرية أي العراق وعربستان من باقي المنطقة.

٢ الخط الفاصل بين قسم شمالي وقسم جنوبي يمر من الكويت بين القصيم وحائل وينتهي في الحجاز.

٣ الخط الفاصل الذي يقطع المركز أي قلب الجزيرة العربية عن الأطراف.

ولهجات البدو في بادية الشام منعزلة عن الهلال الخصيب وساحل الخليج. ويهمنا هنا أيضاً التمييز بين لهجات الحضر ولهجات البدو. فعلى الرغم من أنها نشأت من مواطن مشتركة إلا أن القبائل البدوية تحافظ على الصلات العائلية مما يؤدي إلى المحافظة على وحدة اللغة حتى ولو كانت طوائف هذه القبائل منتشرة على مسافات واسعة جداً.

نصوص من اللهجات المختلفة مع الترجمة والملاحظات (الفصل السادس)

جمعنا في هذا الفصل نصوصاً مسجّلة من أماكن مختلفة في المنطقة. ونقدم هنا خاصة نصوصاً تفيدنا من حيث معرفة اللهجة وفي الوقت نفسه من حيث معرفة تاريخ البيئة وثقافتها وطبيعة الحياة فيها. وقد يلاحظ القارىء أن النصوص تعود إلى المناطق الريفية والحياة الريفية أكثر من الحياة المدنية. ولهذا سبب واضح هو أن لهجات الريف تحافظ على طبيعتها أكثر من لهجات المدن التي تقع تحت تأثيرات خارجية كثيرة. وفي هذه النقطة تكمن ماهيـة البحث. وهو بحث تقليدي Traditional Dialectology في لهجات المناطق الريفية. وتقوم الخارطة اللغوية التي نرسمها على خارطة المواصلات «التقليدية» التي وجدت قبل وصول وسائل النقل والاتصالات الحديثة. وأما لهجات المدن فتتغير بسرعة أكثر ويناسبها منهج آخر من البحث اللغوي يتطلب عقد مقابلات شخصية Interviews وعمليات استجواب واستفتاءات Questionnaires مفصلة عن مواضيع اجتماعية نستوضح منها اتجاهات التحول والتغير اللغوي. ومايهمّنا في البحث في لهجات الريف بدرجة أكبر هو جمع معلومات عن الكلمات والصيغ التي نفترض أن تكون على حالة ثابتة نسبياً مستندين في هذه المعلومات على نصوص تعالج الحياة التقليدية. وقد رتّبت هذه النصوص على أساس جغرافي يبدأ من قلب الجزيرة العربية وينتهي في الأطراف. ولذلك فإن النصوص تبدأ من الجنوب الغربي وتنتهي في الشمال الشرقي. وهي كما يلي:

اللهجات النجدية

١ سالفة ثامر بن سعيدان السبيعي رواها محمد الشامري في إذاعة الكويت. وتمثل لهجة منطقة نجران.
٢ سالفة تركي بن حميد رواها حامد المطيري. وتمثل لهجة أواسط نجد.
٣ حوار خيالي بين رجلين رواها حمزة المزيني. وتمثل لهجة حدود نجد والحجاز.
٤ حوار بين طالبين عنزيين في جامعة الكويت. وتمثل لهجة بادية الشام.
٥ حديث مع الشاعر العازمي سالم بن تويم في الكويت. وتمثل لهجة أواسط نجد.
٦ سالفة غزو الشلقان على الحويطات. وتمثل لهجة شمالي نجد. وقد سجلت في القصيم.
٧ قصيدتان وتعابير Expressions سجلت عند قبيلة الرفيع على قرب من الناصرية في جنوب العراق.
٨ قصيدة من تغريبة بني هلال رواها السيد أحمد العلاوي من قبيلة المسعود على قرب من كربلاء. تمثل لهجة تجمع بين ملامح لهجة شمالي نجد وجنوب العراق.
٩ سالفة ابن قشعم وابن عريعر سجلت لدى بدو من الفرات مقيمين عند بئر الروضتين على قرب من الكويت.

اللهجات العراقية

١٠ سالفة من تغريبة بني هلال سجلت عند كواولة بيت طاؤوس في ملاّ ثاني على مقربة من الأهواز.
١١ سالفة المقداد الكندي وجابر الضحاك رواها واحد من آل أبو محمد من العمارة وسجلت في البصرة.
١٢ حديث مع شاب من كوت سيد عناية على مقربة من الأهواز.
١٣ حديث مع سيد من سادات كاش ساران على حدود عربستان الشمالية.
١٤ حديث مع شيوخ من بني طرف وهي قبيلة في شمال عربستان وسجّل في المحمّرة.
١٥ حديث مع الشيخ محيي آل ناصر من بني كعب وهو يتحدث عن تاريخ بني كعب في عربستان.
١٦ حديث مع سالم الفاضلي من المطور وهم من قبائل نهر القارون وشط العرب في عربستان.

والله الموفق في الحل والترحال.

بروس انغام

بسم الله الرحمن الرحيم

تأليف
الدكتور بروس انغام
أستاذ اللسانيات العربية
جامعة لندن

دراسات في
لهجات شمال شرقي
الجزيرة العربية

الكتاب الثالث

مؤسسة كيغان بول العالميّة
لندن - هنلي - بوستن
١٤٠٢هـ/١٩٨٢م

مكتبة اللسانيّات العربية

سلسلة كتب عالمية في الدراسات اللغوية العربية

رئيس التحرير
د. محمد حسن باكَلاّ
جامعة الرياض – المملكة العربيّة السعوديّة

هيئة التحرير الاستشاريّة

البروفيسور يوسف الخليفة أبو بكر (جامعة الخرطوم)، البروفيسور آرنه امبروس (جامعة فيينا – النمسا)، البروفيسور بروس انغام (جامعة لندن)، البروفيسور السعيد محمد بدوي (الجامعة الأمريكية في القاهرة)، البروفيسور بوغو سلاف زغوريسكي (جامعة وارسو)، البروفيسور أحمد محمد الضبيب (جامعة الرياض)، البروفيسور محمد حسن عبدالعزيز (جامعة نيروبي – كينيا)، البروفيسور بيتر فؤاد عبّود (جامعة تكساس الولايات المتحدة الأمريكية)، البروفيسور صالح جواد الطعمة (جامعة انديانا – الولايات المتحدة الأمريكية)، البروفيسور مارتن فورستنر (جامعة جو هانس غوتنبرغ – المانيا الغربية)، البروفيسور تشارلس فيرستيغ (الجامعة الكاثوليكية في نيجميغن – هولندا)، البروفيسور مايكل كارتر (جامعة سيدني – استراليا)، البروفيسور رجا توفيق نصر (الكلية الجامعية في بيروت)، البروفيسور أوتو ياسترو (جامعة ارلانغن – نورنبرغ في المانيا الغربية).

دراسات في
لهجات شمال شرقي
الجزيرة العربية

مكتبة اللسانيات العربية

الحمد لله وحده ، والصلاة والسلام على من لا نبي بعده . أما بعد : فإن هنالك أسباباً عدة دعت إلى إنشاء هذه السلسلة من الكتب في حقل اللسانيات والصوتيات العربية .

أولاً : إن هذا الحقل يمر بتطور سريع في إطار الدراسات اللغوية المعاصرة . كما أن كثيراً من الجامعات العربية والغربية قد بدأت تدخل علم اللسانيات وعلم الصوتيات وبعض العلوم اللغوية الحديثة ضمن مواد التدريس بها . بالإضافة الى الإهتمام المتزايد في الدوائر اللغوية العالمية بهذا الميدان .

ثانياً : ومع ازدياد الاهتمام بالدراسات اللسانية والصوتية العربية بدأت تصل هذه الدراسات إلى مرحلة متقدمة في النضوج ليست مستفيدة من معطيات علم اللسانيات العام والعلوم الأخرى النسبية فحسب . بل وأيضاً من معطيات الدراسات اللغوية العربية القديمة .

ثالثاً : بدأت تظهر في حقل اللسانيات العربية فروع ونظريات مختلفة تشمل الصوتيات والفونولوجيا والنحو والدلالة ، وعلم اللغة النفسي ، وعلم اللغة الاجتماعي ، وعلم اللهجات العربية ، وصناعة المعاجم . ودراسة المفردات . وتدريس العربية أو تعلمها كلغة أولى أو ثانية أو أجنبية ، وعلم الاتصال ، وعلم الإشارات اللغوي . ودراسة المصطلحات ، والترجمة ، والترجمة الآلية ، وعلم اللغة الإحصائي ، وعلم اللغة الرياضي ، وتاريخ العلوم اللغوية العربية ، وما إلى ذلك .

يضاف إلى هذا كله أن الاقبال على اللغة العربية دراسة وتدريساً وبحثاً يزداد يوماً بعد يوم على الصعيدين المحلي والدولي . ولما لم يكن هناك منبر يرتفع منه نداء لغة الضاد وتعلو منه أصوات الباحثين والمتخصصين فيها لذا وجدت مكتبة «اللسانيات العربية» لتسد هذا الفراغ الكبير والفجوة العميقة وتدفع بالبحث اللغوي العربي قدماً إلى الأمام خدمة للغة القرآن الكريم والتراث العربي الأصيل ، وسيراً بالبحث اللساني العربي للحاق بركب اللسانيات العامة المتقدم . وإثراءً للدراسات اللغوية واللسانية العربية .

وتحرص هذه السلسلة العالميّة على تقديم الجديد من البحث اللغوي وإعطاء الفرصة للبحاثين من العرب وغيرهم للمشاركة في بناء صرح اللسانيات العربية حتى تستعيد الدراسات اللغوية مجدها الماضي العريق .

ولأن هذه السلسلة تعد الأولى من نوعها في الدراسات اللسانية العربية المتخصصة . فإننا نهيب بكل باحث متخصص في مجال اللسانيات العربية بمختلف فروعها النظرية منها والتطبيقية أن يشارك بجهوده وأفكاره وأبحاثه وألا ينجل بتقديم أجود ما لديه من عطاء في سبيل دعم أهداف هذه السلسلة وتطوير مجالاتها الواسعة . والباب مفتوح أمام جميع الأقلام العربية والشرقية والغربية التي تخدم هذه الأهداف الخيّرة .

ونسأل الله العلي القدير أن يحقق لهذه السلسلة ما تصبو اليه من نجاح وتقدم . قال سبحانه وتعالى :
«وقل اعملوا فسيرى الله عملكم» . صدق الله العظيم . والله الموفق لما فيه الخير والصواب لصالح أمتنا العربية الإسلامية المجيدة ولغتها العريقة الأصيلة . إنه سميع مجيب .

رئيس التحرير
محمد حسن باكلا